Challenges and Opportunities for Science Education

Edited by Elizabeth Whitelegg,
Jeff Thomas and Susan Tresman
at The Open University

Published in association with
The Open University

P·C·P
Paul Chapman
Publishing Ltd

The Open
University

Paul Chapman Publishing Ltd
144 Liverpool Road
London
N1 1LA

British Library Cataloguing in Publication Data

Challenges and Opportunities for Science Education
I. Whitelegg, E.
507

ISBN 1 85396 244 9

Typeset by Inforum, Rowlands Castle, Hants
Printed and bound by Athenaeum Press Ltd., Newcastle-upon-Tyne

A B C D E F G H 9 8 7 6 5 4 3

Contents

Acknowledgements

We thank those listed below for their permission to use the following copyright material:

1.1 Black, P. (1992) The purposes of science education, from Hull, R. (ed.) *ASE Science Teachers' Handbook (Secondary)*, Simon & Schuster.

1.2 Ogawa, M. (1989) Beyond the tacit framework of 'science' and 'science education' among science educators, *International Journal of Science Education*, Vol. 11, no. 3, pp. 247–50.

2.1 Tresman, S. and Edwards, D. Reflecting on practice: some illustrations.

2.2 Mackinnon, A. M. (1987) Detecting reflection-in-action among preservice elementary science teachers, *Teaching and Teacher Education*, Vol. 3, no. 2, pp. 135–45.

2.3 Baird, J. R., Fensham, P. J., Gunstone, R. F. and White, R. T. (1991) The importance of reflection in improving science teaching and learning, *Journal of Research in Science Teaching*, Vol. 28, no. 2, pp. 163–82. © 1991 by the National Association for Research in Science Teaching.

2.4 Handal, G. and Lauvås, P. (1987) The 'practical theory' of teachers, from *Promoting Reflective Teaching: Supervision in Action*, Society for Research in Higher Education and The Open University Press, pp. 9–29.

3.1 Fensham, P., Reflections on science for all, adapted from Fensham, P. (1985) Science for all: a reflective essay, *Journal of Curriculum Studies*, Vol. 17, no. 4, pp. 415–35.

3.2 Harlen, W. (1989) Education for equal opportunities in a scientifically literate society, *International Journal of Science Education*, Vol. 11, no. 2, pp. 125–34.

3.3 Dennick, R. (1992) Analysing multicultural and antiracist science education, *School Science Review*, Vol. 73, no. 264, pp. 79–88. Reprinted by permission of the author.

3.4 Solomon, J. Science teaching in areas of social deprivation, unpublished.

3.5 Purnell, R. Teaching science to children with special educational needs, unpublished.

3.6 Blin-Stoyle, R. Science education through school, college and university, *School Science Review*, June 1993.

3.7 Scanlon, E., Edwards, D. and Whitelegg, E. Science for all: a case study of the science foundation course at The Open University, unpublished.

4.1 La Follette, M. C. The end of progress: promises and expectations, from La Follette, M. C. *Making Science our Own: Public Images of Science 1910–1955*, University of Chicago Press, pp. 158–73.

4.2 Jenkins, E. (1990) Scientific literacy and school science education, *School Science Review*, Vol. 71, no. 256, pp. 43–51.

4.3 Millar, R. and Wynne, B. Public understanding of science: from contents to processes, *International Journal of Science Education*, Vol. 10, no. 4, pp. 388–98.

4.4 Chapman, B. The overselling of science education in the eighties, *School Science Review*, Vol. 72, no. 260, pp. 47–63, March 1991.

4.5 Baez, A. (1980) Curiosity, creativity, competence and compassion – guidelines for science education in the year 2000, from *World Trends in Science Education*, McFadden, C. (ed.), Atlantic Institute of Education, Halifax, Nova Scotia.

Contributors' details

Paul Black is Professor of Science Education at King's College, London.

Masakata Ogawa is Associate Professor in Science Education in the Faculty of Education at Ibaraki University in Japan.

Susan Tresman is an Academic Liaison Adviser in the Centre for Science Education at The Open University, Milton Keynes.

Dee Edwards is a Lecturer in Science Education at The Open University.

Allan MacKinnon is an Assistant Professor in the Faculty of Education at Simon Fraser University, Burnaby, British Columbia, Canada.

John Baird is a Senior Lecturer in the Department of Curriculum, Teaching and Learning, Institute of Education, University of Melbourne, Australia.

Peter Fensham is Professor of Science Education at Monash University, Australia.

Richard Gunstone is an Associate Professor in the Faculty of Education at Monash University, Australia.

Richard White is Professor of Psychology in Education at Monash University, Australia.

Gunnar Handal is a Professor of Higher Education in the Institute for Educational Research, University of Oslo, Norway.

Per Lauvås is a Senior Lecturer in Higher Education at the Institute for Educational Research, Blindern University, Oslo, Norway.

Wynne Harlen is the Director of the Scottish Council for Research in Education.

Reg Dennick is a Lecturer in Science Education at Nottingham University.

Joan Solomon is a Research Fellow at Oxford University's Department of Educational Studies.

Roy Purnell is a Principal Lecturer and Head of Science at Gwent College of Higher Education.

Roger Blin-Stoyle is Emeritus Professor of Physics at Sussex University.

Eileen Scanlon is a Senior Lecturer in Educational Technology at The Open University.

Elizabeth Whitelegg is an Academic Liaison Adviser in the Centre for Science Education at The Open University.

Jeff Thomas is a Senior Lecturer at the Centre for Science Education at The Open University.

Marcel LaFollette is Associate Research Professor of Science and Technology Policy, George Washington University, Washington DC, USA.

Edgar Jenkins is a Reader in Science Education at the University of Leeds.

Robin Millar is a Senior Lecturer in Science Education at the University of York.

Brian Wynne is the Director of the Centre for Science Studies and Science Policy in the School of Independent Studies, at the University of Lancaster.

Bryan Chapman is a Senior Lecturer in Physics at the University of Leeds.

Albert Baez was a Professor of Physics at several universities in the USA and elsewhere.

Preface

This collection of readings has been chosen to complement The Open University's course in science education which is part of a Master's degree. This book is the second of two volumes and together they provide students with in-depth examination of current issues and concerns in science education across the full educational spectrum of primary, secondary and tertiary education.

Volume 1 includes perspectives on teaching and learning science and assessment in science, Volume 2 is concerned with scientific literacy and reflection on the practice of science teaching. After Part 1 of this volume has set the scene, Part 2 introduces students to a variety of models of reflection on professional practice, where it can be seen that insights into the idiosyncratic and reflective nature of scientific investigation constitute a major advance towards scientific literacy. This theme of scientific literacy is examined further in the following part on 'science for all' where a case for a broader approach to schooling is presented, one that encourages and motivates students to engage with a science curriculum that is appropriate for them and will result in an adult population that is scientifically literate.

Finally, in Part 3, the images and understanding of science that are held by adults in the general population are considered and the need for a scientifically literate population is debated.

As the two Readers form only part of the course (which also consists of a written study guide discussing the issues raised in the Reader articles) they cannot claim to offer a comprehensive account of perspectives on science education. Whilst some of the material in this Reader is quite new, having been commissioned by the editors for use in ES821 *Science Education*, other items have been adapted and edited from previously published papers. As a consequence, students of ES821 may notice that the references do not conform to the course style. The selection of articles has been designed to highlight specific problems and to develop students' critical understanding. Opinions expressed within the articles are therefore not necessarily those of the course writers nor of the University. However, the editors believe that the selection focuses on major issues in the field and will be useful to anyone with an interest in science education.

The editors would like to thank the ES821 course team for their help in the selection of material.

Elizabeth Whitelegg

PART 1: Setting the Scene

1.1

The purposes of science education

Paul Black

WHY DISCUSS PURPOSES? AN INTRODUCTION

It is not inevitable that science be given the high priority that it now enjoys in the school curriculum, or even that it be a subject at all. A case could be made out, for example, that medicine, or politics should be essential components. Thus one priority in a discussion of purposes is to justify the place of science in schools. Why, for example, should science be required in both primary and secondary stages, rather than, as for languages, at secondary only? And does it have to be a separate subject, when other aspects of education are deemed worthy only of cross-disciplinary or extracurricular attention, notably personal and social education and environmental education?

The orientation and practice of science education have to be consistent with the justifications given for its place in the curriculum. So a second function of any discussion of purposes is to set out the aims which science education should deliver and in the light of which it should be evaluated.

There could be a cynical response to the inevitably general and idealistic tone of this article. We are living in National Curriculum country (DES 1991) and whilst a trip to an imaginary island could provide entertainment and relaxation, it might also generate frustration on return. One justification here is that there is a wide range of classroom interpretations of the curriculum and it is in the classroom that each teacher's personal hopes strongly influence their children's experience.

A second justification is that the motivations behind a formal curriculum document need to be understood by anyone who has to put it into practice. Many of the issues discussed in this article receive no explicit mention in the National Curriculum order, yet teachers' views about these issues must influence their practice. This point leads on to a more general justification – curriculum thinking is a product of its time and is open to change. We all need to be prepared to contribute to change in the future, and not just to be victims of its tides (ASE 1992).

From Hull, R. (ed.) (1992) *ASE Science Teachers' Handbook (Secondary)*, Simon & Schuster.

This last issue is taken up in the next two sections of this article, which survey the historical context, and then review the factors that might influence change. Following these preparatory discussions, the subsequent sections deal with the main aims of science education for all, and the needs of future specialists. These lead to an outline of a proposal for the main elements of science learning which could implement the purposes. The problem of the place of science in the whole school curriculum is then considered and the article concludes with discussion of some implications.

Little has been said here of the concept of 'scientific literacy' (Champagne and Lovitts 1989, Atkin and Helms 1992). It could be said that the phrase stands for no more than the science needed by all. However, the use of the metaphor of 'literacy' might be a way of giving a particular emphasis, giving priority to narrowly instrumental needs. In short, the phrase either adds nothing to the arguments here, or is used to introduce, by implication, a bias of priorities. Therefore, it does not seem to be helpful.

HOW DID WE GET HERE? THE HISTORICAL CONTEXT

The nineteenth century beginnings of science education in schools have been described in David Layton's book *Science for the People* (Layton 1973). Conflict arose between two groups holding opposed views about the purposes of the new development. One proposed a science that would focus on everyday practices and artefacts. The second wanted to focus on academic science so that school science would help to recruit future scientists. The second view prevailed then and has done so ever since, although that original tension continues to bedevil school science to this day.

Whilst such influence dominated in the first part of this century, there also emerged educational reformers, notably Armstrong, who had a vision of a change which would give pupils a more authentic engagement with the practice of scientific enquiry (Jenkins 1979). However, the style of science teaching remained largely formal, based on teaching of definitions and derivations, and on experiments which illustrated foregone conclusions, with some discussions of applications added at the end.

This tradition was transformed in the 1950s and 1960s by a worldwide movement for reform, driven by and originating from two main foci. One was in the United States, where fears of technological inferiority sparked off by a Russian lead in space flight served to generate support for curriculum reform. The other was in Britain; here, it was the dissatisfaction of science teachers themselves which led them to press for reform. However, the outcome, in the Nuffield Foundation's science teaching project, was supported and influenced strongly by university scientists.

The assumption in the USA movements was that better school curricula would lead to better prepared students for science and engineering. In consequence, the courses were 'top-down' in their construction, showing originality in devising quite new routes to the understanding of fundamental concepts.

The agenda of these was chosen to represent current science in an authentic way, an aspect in which existing courses notably failed. This new strength was also a weakness, for the courses were ambitiously abstract and paid little attention to everyday consequences. A later physics project, *Project Physics,* differed from the others in giving more emphasis to the history of the development of ideas and to showing how they developed within the societies – and technologies – of their times. Subsequent evaluations showed that on the whole these courses, and the many international applications and imitations which they fostered, did not achieve their aims (Tamir et al 1979).

The Nuffield courses were more successful in holding those originally committed. The first courses were designed for the most able and were thereby biased to academic science, again giving priority to clearer emphasis on modern concepts rather than to any broader perspectives on science. They were characterized however by more emphasis on changes in teaching method. A second generation of Nuffield courses struggled with a different problem, the provision of courses firstly for those placed in streams or schools designed for the less able, later for the mixed ability groups of the secondary comprehensive school.

The implementation of comprehensive schooling led to new challenges, as it became increasingly clear that quite new arrangements for science teaching would be needed. Growing dissatisfaction, with courses that were too specialized, and with the need for pupils to opt out of one or more of the separate science subjects, culminated in the 1980s in a move for broad and balanced science, supported by the ASE, the DES and, notably, by the Secondary Science Curriculum Review (ASE 1981, SSCR 1987).

These changes were motivated by a desire to realize the purpose of making science education accessible and meaningful to all pupils. However, this needed more than a change in the arrangement of courses. Three further aspects were given a powerful impetus in the 1980s. One emerged from research studies reporting both that pupils' enthusiasm for science declined from a high point of enthusiasm at age 11 to a low level by the end of schooling, and that only a small minority attained any satisfactory grasp of even the most elementary concepts by age 16 (Driver et al 1985, Osborne and Freyberg 1985).

The second trend started from the new emphasis given to the processes and skills of science, particularly through the work of the APU science monitoring (Black 1990). This led to more complex views of the essential links between the learning of concepts and of skills. These developments also led to a new emphasis on pupils' own science investigations, culminating in the emergence of Attainment Target One of the National Curriculum.

The third trend started with the growing concern with environmental issues and with the moral responsibilities of scientists, which led some to promote the study in school science of its technological and social implications (Lewis 1980, Solomon 1983, Holman 1986, Hunt 1988). Others argued for a more human approach which would discuss scientists as persons developing their contributions in particular historical contexts. A third group criticized science teaching for failing to give explicit attention to the methods of science, and yet presenting, by implication, quite false veiws about them (Hodson 1985, Lucas 1990). These strands have converged in arguments that a broader, more humanistic, definition of school science is now needed (Matthews 1990, 1992).

The position is no less stable in the area of primary science (Black 1985). The early predominance of the 'nature table' approach was first replaced by attempts to set up a broader agenda of interesting topics for basic knowledge. This was further replaced by an emphasis on process skills, with reduction or even exclusion of specific topic knowledge. This has been replaced again, notably in the National Curriculum, by a model which emphasizes investigative skills, together with a mixture of basic topics ('know that' statements) and elementary concepts ('understand that').

The sum of these trends has been a definition of the science curriculum for the present decade which is different in several fundamental respects even from that of the early 1980s. Indeed, there have been fundamental changes in every one of the last few decades.

STOP THE WORLD WE WANT TO GET OFF! THE FUTURE FOR CHANGE

It might be comforting to imagine that future decades will be marked by greater stability. However, it seems unlikely that the forces which have driven the changes of past decades will disappear. The first of these is the influence of changes in science and technology themselves. Areas such as genetic engineering, the AIDS epidemic and the burgeoning environmental crises, let alone others that are yet to emerge, must surely affect priorities in science education.

The second drive for change will come from changes within education itself. In the last ten years, research in education has become notably more relevant to pedagogy than at any previous time, and this process is hardly likely to stop. At the same time, developments in information technology have yet to achieve anything like the impact which is currently foreseeable. For example, when vast resources, in knowledge bases and training systems, are available to anyone at the touch of a button, what then will be the point of much of the work that now takes up time in classrooms?

The third drive will come from changes in society, leading to changes in expectations for schools. The National Curriculum itself is not an accident arising from the 1987 general election, but rather the culmination of longer term political and social trends. There is no sign that public and political interest in education has since declined, and no evidence at all that the definition of a National Curriculum will be followed by suspension of debate about curriculum purposes or practices.

Finally, there is the less evident but most potent catalyst, changes in pupils themselves. Radical changes in influences outside the school, notably in family life and in the media, may well be producing profound changes in the needs of the pupils. A recent authoritative review of the condition of children in the USA (Hamburg 1992) talks of a generation in crisis, because of the disastrous stresses for those growing up in poverty in inner cities, and the neglect of parenting in all classes. As society starts to suffer the consequences of such changes, it may look to schools to provide a redeeming framework for many children – a task which far transcends their traditional role.

Given all this, it is up to teachers and schools to develop to the full their understanding of, and so their commitment to, their purposes for education. They might thereby be better able to hold on to their own interpretations of change, so that they can filter or distil the pressures in the interests of their pupils, rather than be disoriented and de-skilled by them. They might also be better prepared to influence public debate about re-definitions of their purposes and priorities.

However, the influence of teachers is bound to be limited. Others professionally involved in science education, whether as academic researchers, as inspectors, as trainers or as administrators, will all exert pressure. The growing emphasis on the need to expand the numbers in tertiary education will give that sector more influence. More uncertain will be the strength of public, notably political pressure. Business, industry, and environmentalists may play enhanced roles, whilst it seems that political control over the curriculum, far from leading to stability, is leading to more questioning of school practices and to weakness in the face of the temptations to exert one's powers to 'improve' as soon as difficulties are publicized.

Thus, the determination of purposes and priorities for the science curriculum has to take place in an essentially political struggle between competing traditions, perspectives and interests. In this respect, it does not differ from other significant social issues. However, the point deserves emphasis here, both because current trends and proposals have to be examined in this light, and because formulation of policies and practices in the future have to be made in this context. However, whilst schools are not in full control of specification, they have very strong control over implementation, so that their own priorities, and their views of the priorities of others, are of outstanding importance.

SCIENCE FOR ALL?

The starting point must be to consider the purposes of a curriculum which might be the only experience of serious learning about science that pupils have in their lives. Given the large and growing relevance of science in the private, social and political spheres, the optimum planning of this experience must be of the utmost importance.

None of the main purposes can be achieved unless certain subsidiary purposes are met. The first of these is *accessibility*. Pupils must understand and feel confidence with the science they are studying. This purpose may present very difficult dilemmas, for it is clear that in experience to date, it has not been achieved.

Likewise, the main purposes cannot be achieved unless pupils can see the *relevance* of what they are trying to learn and can find stimulus and *enjoyment* in it. Very few pupils can persevere with work which, being difficult and apparently irrelevant, brings little immediate reward.

To turn to the main purposes, the first is that pupils should be given *a basis for understanding and for coping with their lives*. Science has a lot to say about problems in people's personal lives, notably in health, including nutrition, drug abuse, the AIDS epidemic and in broader issues, such as those concerned with sexuality. Here, as for most applications of science in personal and social life, impersonal knowledge and understanding have to develop in conjunction with appreciation of issues of moral and social value. This purpose embraces the need to look after oneself, and to help protect oneself and others from the flow of incomplete and misleading information which seems to be an inevitable feature of a democratic society.

The need to become capable of taking part in positive initiatives to improve life for all follows naturally. Indeed, the social dimension expands this agenda to such an extent that a further purpose, that of *understanding the applications and effects of science in society*, is worth formulating. The considerations here also need to be related to issues of value and morality, and also raise the question of whether such issues should be tackled only, or even mainly, in the science classroom. Almost any of the main examples, for instance pollution or global warming, could well be tackled from a variety of non-science perspectives. This point is taken up further below.

The two aspects of the purpose discussed so far involve learning *from* science, by using its results as a starting point, rather than *about* science, by studying how those results are achieved. Learning about science constitutes the second main purpose. It involves learning about *the concepts and the methods which are combined in scientific enquiry*. Pursuit of this purpose in isolation can give too much emphasis to purely instrumental reasons for learning science. One function of schools, however, is to be the guardians and transmitters of a society's culture. Science is one of mankind's greatest achievements, and without some knowledge of its history, some appreciation of the personal genius of famous scientists in determining the course of science, and some insight into the particular way in which science searches for truth, a pupil will have little *insight into what science, seen as a human activity, is really like*. For example, a pupil struggling with the ideas that air fills the space around her, and that it has weight and that it even exerts a very large pressure, might understand her own confusions and the nature of science better if she were told about how some of the greatest intellects grappled with the same difficulties in previous centuries. Historical examples can also make clear that imagination and creativity are essential to the development of science, and that it proceeds through obstacles of misunderstanding, and controversy, rather than by smooth deductions and experimental 'proofs'.

Such purposes should be so pursued, that the experience of science that school learning gives will be *authentic*. This need affects the style of the work undertaken, the range of issues covered and the image of science that is conveyed.

Science education cannot be planned as an isolated experience, contributing only to its own particular purposes. Thus a third main purpose is that *it must contribute to the general personal and intellectual development of the pupils*. Such contribution tends to be considered automatically in primary education, but to fall away at secondary level where the practice of subjects working in isolation is too prevalent.

There are many possibilities here. One is that a pupil should gain experience in science of the *logic of explanation* using assumptions, models, evidence and argument to reach conclusions. Such experience can build up pupils' confidence in their power to construct explanations. A different emphasis appears in the possibility of pursuing practical investigations. These can contribute to building up practical capability, since such investigations call for powers of initiative, of making decisions, of overcoming obstacles. They can also provide outstanding opportunities for learning to work in small groups. For both of these aspects, it is essential that emphasis be given to helping pupils to reflect on what they have done so that they become more aware of the way in which science works (White and Gunstone 1989). Here, the pursuit of the goal of authentic understanding of the nature of scientific enquiry contributes powerfully to pupils' general development. Such contribution can be enhanced if pupils can relate the way in which they work in science to the ways in which they work in other disciplines.

This agenda cannot be complete without attention to the fact that a common curriculum should provide pupils with *a basis for making choices, together with positive motivation* to consider seriously a further commitment to science. This, the fourth main purpose, is discussed in the next section.

YOUR COUNTRY NEEDS YOU! PROVIDING FUTURE SPECIALISTS

Given the spectrum of purposes set out above, it can be asked whether a curriculum which gave its main priority to the selection and preparation of future scientists ought to be very different. The needs of understanding science, with its implications for developing powers of explanation and of practical capability, are of direct significance for future specialists. It can hardly be argued that a broader view of science as a human activity is not needed by those in whose hands the future development of science will lie. Indeed, it can be argued that the neglect of this aspect at all levels of study, particularly in specialized tertiary education, has been an intellectual weakness and a practical impoverishment of the scientific community. The need for the experience of science to be authentic would seem to be a top priority in providing pupils with a basis for choice. It might be argued that a far narrower range of subjects, studied in greater depth, and giving less attention to the broad range of everyday applications, might be appropriate. This raises the prospect that future specialists would be less well served than their peers in using science to cope with their personal and social needs.

However, it is also necessary to consider the need to attract pupils to specialize in science as well as the need to prepare them if they are attracted. The number attracted has always been too small and, for science and engineering, has always included far too few girls. This means that the images and experiences of science presented to school pupils have to be changed. Studies of the links between adolescent personality development and choice of science (Head 1986) indicate that the closed and algorithmic view of science that courses usually present tend to repel those extrovert pupils, particularly boys, who wish to challenge authority and question values. For girls, the impersonal view of science presented by a narrow concentration on 'basics' is a severe obstacle. Thus, emphasis on a narrow preparation can limit recruitment. It might have the further disadvantage that those who are attracted are being misled, because the reality of professional practice will be quite different from their experience of 'preparation'.

The conclusion from these arguments is that future specialists cannot do without any of the work that all pupils require. However, their needs argue for the provision of more in-depth work in at least a sample of areas of science, so that any pupils who wish can explore their commitment and test out their ability to take science further. This particular part of the argument has no relevance for primary science. However, in so far as primary science generates enthusiasm, an appreciation of science as the work of people, and a growth in capability and in understanding, it is laying essential foundations for all of the purposes discussed as well as providing the first inspiration for future scientists.

Evidence that students in tertiary education suffer from the same misconceptions about science fundamentals as their secondary peers, and that transfer of learning to new contexts is notoriously difficult to achieve, casts doubt on the notion that school study can at present provide a 'firm grounding'. A counter-argument, that a spiral curriculum in which a broader range of aims is addressed at each stage may be more effective, is at least plausible. Thus, for example, an interplay between principles, applications, and 'hands-on' investigation should characterize both sides of the secondary–tertiary interface, just as it should the primary–secondary interface, for it would be absurd to propose that primary pupils should learn only concepts, leaving project investigations to build on this 'preparation' at secondary level.

The arguments may be different if the aim is to provide pupils with preparation that is more directly vocational. Arguments about the needs of different vocational groups are often in mutual conflict, so that it emerges that the range of needs can only be met by distilling out what they have in common. Thus the argument reduces to one about basic knowledge and skills. The metaphor of 'basic skills' has many attractions. There are dangers here also. The implied assumption, that these skills are the same across different contexts, needs careful examination; this assumption may be evident in the case of reading instrument scales but it is very doubtful if (say) problem-solving is assumed to be the same skill in many different occupations. It is also notorious that pupils are usually unwilling or unable to apply a skill, learnt in one context, to a problem in a quite different context.

Finally, it should be noted that some parts of higher education are also calling into question the view that specialist education should proceed by the learning of required components at early stages and should only tackle the 'synthesis-in-application' of these at advanced stages. There is, for example, a move in engineering schools in the USA to emphasize the integrative and holistic activity of tackling real problems right from the start of freshman courses (Bordogna 1989), whilst science degree courses in this country now incorporate substantial components of project work where thirty years ago they would have assumed that such work had to wait until the postgraduate stage.

A MODEL FOR PURPOSES – ESSENTIAL COMPONENTS OF A LEARNING PROGRAMME

A brief discussion is offered here about components essential to any learning programme designed to achieve these purposes, partly because this will help to bring out some of the implications of the aims presented.

A first essential is that students should come to understand science and to understand how science is made, by being engaged in doing it. This involves three main aspects. One is that they have to learn about its main concepts, seen as abstract yet powerful agents for predicting and controlling natural phenomena. This in itself is a formidable requirement. The difficulties pupils of all ages have in grasping and accepting many science concepts have been well documented. It seems clear that to overcome this problem requires that more classroom time be spent on any one idea, so the range of concepts to be covered will have to be reduced (Scott et al 1992).

The second aspect is that pupils should be able to use the main skills which go to make up the scientific method. Such skills as observation, measurement, making generalizations, inventing hypotheses, devising fair tests, designing experiments, and analysing data and interpreting results should all be included. A full exploration of many of these has been made in the work of the science teams of the APU (Black 1990, Strang 1990, Strang et al 1991).

However, neither the concepts nor the skills can be properly understood in isolation from one another. It is not possible, for example, to propose hypotheses except in the light of some preconceived model of the system under consideration. Conversely, understanding of the ways in which concepts have developed can only be conveyed through activity which uses these skills. This leads to the third aspect – which is that pupils should have personal experience of working with the interaction of concepts and skills in planning, designing, carrying out and interpreting their own experiments. Only through such activity can pupils develop an authentic understanding of what is involved in doing science. It is important that at least some of these should involve the application, and subsequent modification, of scientific ideas to test explanations. Science involves far more than systematic comparison of materials or products, and whilst consumer tests may have some value in teaching some skills, some published materials so emphasize this approach that they give a misleading image of science.

It is not implied that every new idea must be developed through students' own personal investigation. However, their own personal experience of investigating some ideas and phenomena should help pupils in understanding the way in which others have come to new ideas through scientific investigation.

Whilst it should be clear that the careful pursuit of these three aspects in an interconnected way must be the main vehicle for achieving some of the main purposes, other activities will be needed to complete the agenda. Students should come to know about science as a human activity, by studying how its achievements have emerged in particular historical contexts and have depended on beliefs, technology, social systems and above all the human personalities of those involved. Reflection on their own investigations should help pupils to develop understanding of the ways in which evidence, experimentation, hypotheses, models and mathematics are combined in the development of science.

The above requirements demand that more time be spent on some science topics, because there is evidence that unless this is done we shall continue to leave pupils with serious misunderstandings, not only about particular scientific ideas, but also about what the whole activity of science is about. However, this need conflicts with the purposes of giving pupils a basis to cope with everyday needs, for this requires that they know about the many results of scientific work which are important to them in their lives. It seems neither possible nor necessary that all of this large number could be studied in the depth suggested in the tripartite interaction of concepts, skills and processes discussed above. Whilst a few must be studied in this way, others could be studied more superficially, with emphasis on those features which must be known about in order to lead a healthy and responsible adult life.

The need to know about the many applications of science, and about the ways in which, through its contribution to technology, science has had a profound effect on our society, is indisputable. However, it is difficult to specify what level of understanding of a scientific idea is needed to be able to make use of it in daily life (Layton 1991): electricians know far less about circuit theory than physicists, but they are better at fixing a new ring main. At a more general level, the extent to which science has been the driving force of modern technology is often exaggerated, there being many technological changes in which the contrivance technology of craftsmen and entrepreneurs has been the main driving force (Gardner 1992). Finally, since technological change is a complex human activity in which many areas of thought and action play a part, it may be misleading to present it to pupils in the restricted context of the science classroom (Black and Harrison 1985). This point will be taken further in the next section.

All of this discussion has treated science as a single entity. The conceptual basis of science has a structure in which the separate components of biology, chemistry, physics and earth sciences are identifiable, albeit overlapping, components. Furthermore, these different areas of science differ significantly both in philosophy and in their styles of work so, for example, biologists overlap with social scientists in the way that physicists do not, and biologists have to do experiments with many of the variables uncontrolled, the design of which would be unthinkable for a physicist (Black 1986).

Opinions differ about the implications of these features. Several varieties of combined, co-ordinated, or integrated science are used. Almost all agree that to teach three or four sciences separately and without close co-ordination is unacceptable and that up to age 16 all the main areas should be encountered by all. It is also the case that, in almost all courses, whatever their ideology, there is a mixture of separate discipline topics and topics which clearly cross the boundaries. These features contribute to an overall purpose of understanding the nature of science, which has within itself elements both of unity and of diversity.

ACROSS THE CURRICULUM?

If a broad definition of technology is adopted, then it has a place of its own in the curriculum which does not derive from science. In this view, one problem about implementing technology in the curriculum is to ensure that, in their learning and involvement in technology, pupils summon up and bring into use contributions from many school subjects, of which science is one. Science teachers should try to make their contribution to technology, both to serve other parts of the curriculum, and give their own pupils a mature appreciation of the role of science in technology.

There is a broader set of possibilities to which similar considerations apply. Science is an arena in which the purposes of other important parts of the curriculum can be realized, e.g. uses of descriptive and imaginative language, or application of mathematical modelling, or development of moral education in relation to the choices presented by science. Conversely, it can be enriched by work in other subjects. Examples are overlaps between earth sciences and geography, and overlaps with history; the latter would be important if the scope of science study were to be broadened to make it more human (Watts 1991).

Such opportunities are taken up in primary schools, although it needs careful planning if topic work is to bring out the interconnections. There are more serious difficulties at secondary level. Where school subject departments work as separate empires, the pupils are left to make the interrelationships which their teachers have failed to make for them; most cannot do so and keep their learning of subjects in separate compartments. This grave weakness can be overcome if schools give priority to planning the curriculum as a whole. This requires that overarching themes be formulated and agreed, from which the roles of separate subjects can be assigned and the possibilities of inter-subject work explored.

Sadly, the National Curriculum, with its almost exclusive concentration on separate subjects and avoidance of general curriculum principles or aims, gives too little encouragement to such important work.

MAKING IT HAPPEN

The realization of purposes in classroom work is notoriously difficult. Of course, where discussion of them is treated as academic indulgence without any vision of accepting the struggles needed to make any important changes, there can be little point in discussing purposes at all. If the possibility that they are to make a serious difference is accepted, then one approach would be to carry out an audit of present activities to judge which are being served and where gaps occur. This would then lead to difficult decisions as to whether the purposes can be more fully met by a set of small adjustments, or whether quite radical changes are needed, at least in part.

A helpful part of any such planning is to derive from the broad aims some secondary aims which necessarily follow from them; for such aims, being closer to practice, can help cross the bridge between high-minded purposes and day-to-day work. Some of the discussion in the two previous sections can be read as contributions to such a strategy. Within such a strategy, the issues of progression, implying the matching of the purposes to the development of pupils with age, would also need consideration. This has not been attempted here, apart from a few references to the differences between primary and secondary stages. It is not proposed that any of these purposes should be uniquely reserved for one phase only – they all apply at most ages, albeit in different ways.

Realization of new purposes can imply more than shuffling of lesson plans so that new topics are introduced or the old ones realigned. For example, if moral issues are to be taken up, discussions which cannot lead to the right answer have to be managed; if pupils are to learn from taking responsibility for their own experiments, the role of their teacher will be quite different from the role needed to guide routine practical exercises (Black et al 1992). Such role changes are the most difficult obstacles in the path of any large shift in the purposes of a curriculum.

Finally, success might also require that pupils be aware of the underlying plan and perhaps build up their own portfolio of ideas about science and about the point of studying it (Claxton 1990). Central to any debate about purposes is the need to achieve reconciliation between what is needed by all, what is wanted by all and what is feasible for all. What is wanted by all is an oft neglected aspect.

What is feasible for all is the great uncertainty. Wherever new purposes, or a radically different balance between purposes, are explored, implementation changes the view, not only of what is feasible, but of what is really desirable (Roberts, 1988). Commitment to a new vision of purposes is a moral adventure – a voyage in which the purposes themselves are explored as well as the uncharted tracks that lead to them.

REFERENCES

References are given in the sections above where they are relevant to particular points and a list of these is given below. However, for more general discussions of purpose, a few of those listed are particularly valuable – these are identified by asterisks.

*ASE (1981) *Education through science*. Policy statement, ASE, Hatfield.
*ASE (1992) *Change in our future: a challenge for science education*, ASE, Hatfield.
Atkin, J. M. and Helms, J. (1992) Private communication, Stanford University, California.
Black, P. J. (1985) Why hasn't it worked? In Hodgson, B. and Scanlon, E. (eds.), *Approaching Primary Science*, pp. 61–64, Harper & Row, London.
Black, P. J. (1986) Integrated or co-ordinated science? (Presidential address given to Association for Science Education at University of York on 4 January 1986), *School Science Review*, Vol. 67, no. 241, pp. 669–681.
Black, P. J. (1990) APU science: the past and the future, *School Science Review*, Vol. 72, no. 258, pp. 13–28.
Black, P. and Harrison, G. (1985) *In Place of Confusion*, Nuffield/Chelsea Curriculum Trust, London.
Black, P. J., Fairbrother, R., Jones, A., Simon, S. and Watson, R. (1992) *Open work in science: a review of practice*, King's Research Paper, CES, King's College, London.
Bordogna, J. (1989) Entering the 90's: a national vision for engineering education, *Engineers' Education*, Vol. 79, no. 7.
Champagne, A. and Lovitts, B. (1989) Scientific literacy: a concept in search of a definition. In Champagne, A., Lovitts, B. and Calinger, B. (eds.), *This Year in School Science 1989: Scientific Literacy*. Papers from the 1989 AAAS forum for school science, AAAS, Washington DC, USA.
Claxton, G. (1990) Science lessens?, *Studies in Science Education*, Vol. 18, pp. 165–171.
DES (1991) *Science in the National Curriculum 1991*, HMSO, London.
Driver, R., Guesne, E. and Tiberghien, A. (eds.) (1985) *Children's Ideas in Science*, Open University Press, Milton Keynes.
*Fensham, P. J. (ed.) (1988) *Development and Dilemmas in Science Education*, Falmer, Lewes.
*Fensham, P. J. (1992) Science and technology. In *Handbook of Research on Curriculum*, pp. 789–829, Macmillan, New York.
Gardner, P. L. (1992) The application of science to technology, *Research in Science Education*, Vol. 22, pp. 140–148.
Hamburg, D. A. (1992) *Today's Children: Creating a Future for a Generation at Risk*, Times Books – Random House, New York.
Head, J. (1986) *The Personal Response to Science*, Cambridge University Press.

Hodson, D. (1985) Philosophy of science, science and science education, *Studies in Science Education*, Vol. 12, pp. 25–57.

Holman, J. (1986) *Science and Technology in Society: General Guide for Teachers*, ASE, Hatfield.

Hunt, A. (1988) SATIS approach to STS, *International Journal of Science Education*, Vol. 10, pp. 409–420.

Jenkins, E. (1979) *From Armstrong to Nuffield*, Murray, London.

Layton, D. (1973) *Science for the People*, Allen and Unwin, London.

Layton, D. (1991) Science education and praxis: the relationship of school science to practical action, *Studies in Science Education*, Vol. 19, pp. 43–78.

Lewis, J. (1980) *Science in Society: Readers and Teachers Guide,* Heinemann, London.

Lucas, A. M. (1990) Processes of science and processes of learning, *Studies in Science Education*, Vol. 18 pp. 172–177.

Matthews, M. R. (1990) History, philosophy and science teaching: a rapprochement, *Studies in Science Education*, Vol. 18, pp. 25–51.

Matthews, M. R. (1992) History, philosophy and science teaching: the present rapprochement, *Science and Education*, Vol. 1, pp. 11–47.

Osborne, R. and Freyberg, P. (1985) *Learning in Science: the Implications of Children's Science*, Heinemann, Auckland, NZ.

Roberts, D. A. (1988) What counts as science education? In Fensham, P. J. (ed.) *Development and Dilemmas in Science Education*, pp. 27–54, Falmer, Lewes.

*Rutherford, F. J. and Ahlgren, A. (1989) *Science for All Americans*, Oxford University Press, Oxford.

Scott, P. H., Asoko, H. M. and Driver, R. (1992) Teaching for conceptual change: a review of strategies. In Duit, R. *et al.* (eds.) *Research in Physics Learning: Theoretical Issues and Empirical Studies*, IPN – Institute for Science Education, Kiel.

Solomon, J. (1983) *SISCON in Schools – Readers and Teachers Guide,* Blackwell, Oxford.

*SSCR (1987) *Better Science: Making it Happen*, ASE/Heinemann, London.

Strang, J. (1990) *Measurement in school science*. Assessment Matters No. 2, Schools Examinations and Assessment Council, London.

Strang, J., Daniels, S. and Bell, J. (1991) *Planning and carrying out investigations*. Assessment Matters No. 6, Schools Examinations and Assessment Council, London.

Tamir, P. *et al.* (1979) *Curriculum implementation and its relationship to curriculum development in science*, Israel Science Teaching Centre, Jerusalem.

Watts, M. (ed.) (1991) *Science in the National Curriculum*, Cassell, London.

White, R. and Gunstone, R. (1989) Meta-learning and conceptual change, *International Journal of Science Education*, Vol. 11, no. 5, pp. 577–586.

Beyond the tacit framework of 'science' and 'science education' among science educators

Masakata Ogawa

In an established discipline there exists a common and tacit understanding of the terms used among researchers. In the discipline of 'science education' most of the terms we use as science educators can be understood, and their meanings agreed upon. Recently, however, I have become aware of a significant problem relating to this issue.

The problem concerns the meanings of 'science' and 'science education'. I feel that these two terms, which are, of course, most important ones in the discipline of science education, can have different meanings and that such meanings can give a broader perspective on the discipline. In this paper, I present my views on this problem in order to share a common understanding of its nature and to invite comments from colleagues elsewhere.

WHAT IS SCIENCE?

What is science? This may be a simplistic question for most science educators. For them, science is science. That's all and that is sufficient. Hence there are few discussions on this question among science educators. Nonetheless, the question is of great concern to me. Let me give an example to show how indifferent science educators can be to it. Professor Yager, in 1983, triggered off a stimulating debate on the issue 'Science education as a discipline' (Yager 1983). Since then, many investigators have contributed to this debate, for example Watson (1983), Westmeyer (1983), Wandersee (1983), and Good *et al.* (1985). The main controversy at the heart of the debate is summarized by the phrase 'Science education: education *in* or *about* science?' (Barrentine 1986). Looking at this issue from the viewpoint of a non-Western person, I cannot help feeling that both sides in the debate still share a tacit and common presupposition on the question 'What is science?' Science as interpreted by them is undoubtedly the science born and developed in modern Western society. When considering what the discipline 'science education' should be,

From the *International Journal of Science Education*, (1989) Vol. 11, no. 3, pp. 247–50.

they never seem to extend their consideration to the 'science' part of this discipline to deal with the question of what it should be.

My position on 'science' is quite different from theirs. I prefer Elkana's understanding of 'science'. He argues that 'every culture has its science' (Elkana 1971, p. 1437), and gives the following definition of science: 'By science, I mean a rational (i.e., purposeful, good, directed) explanation of the physical world surrounding man.' Western science is the most dominant one in the world. But it is only *one* form of science among the sciences in the world. Although a clear definition of what may be called 'indigenous science' is still uncrystallized in my own mind, I believe that every culture has its own science, has something like its own way of thinking and/or its own world view (Ogawa 1986b). Also, an indigenous science itself may be such that even people living in the particular culture do not recognize its existence; hence, it may be transferred from generation to generation merely by invisible or hidden curricula in non-formal settings. Western science is, of course, distributed across almost all cultures of the world, albeit to different extents in terms of its effects. Therefore, it may be appropriate to claim that 'every culture has two sciences'. For this reason, I would argue that the term 'science' as it relates to the discipline of science education, should not simply be taken to mean 'Western science', at least not in a non-Western society.

WHAT IS THE SCHOOL SUBJECT CALLED 'SCIENCE'?

Another problem concerns the meaning of the term 'science' when we refer to it as a school subject. In the discipline of science education, the school subject 'science' is tacitly understood as the one in which the knowledges, concepts and processes of Western science alone are taught. But we should not think that components other than those of Western science (for example, those of indigenous science) should be excluded from the school subject 'science'. As an example, I should like to refer to the Japanese elementary science education programme (called 'Rika'), in which, I believe, another component than that of Western science is actually involved.

The overall objectives of Japanese elementary science education are described in the Course of Study (Ministry of Education, Science and Culture 1983) as follows:

> Developing the ability and aptitude to make inquiries about nature through observations and experiments as well as enhancing the children's understanding of natural things and phenomena, thereby nurturing a rich desire to love nature.
>
> (Author's translation)

'To love nature' is not directly related to the components of Western science. Rather, it is closely related to the Japanese traditional (or indigenous) culture (Okamoto and Mori 1976, Ogawa 1986a). Nurturing a desire to love nature has been usually involved in the overall objectives of elementary school science education ever since elementary school science was established in Japan in 1891. But some Japanese science educators, as well as most Japanese elementary teachers, seem completely unaware of this heterogeneity. They believe that 'inquiries about nature through observations and experiments' ultimately lead children to 'a rich desire to love nature'. It is interesting that this type of elementary science is positively accepted by society, by elementary teachers and by parents, as well as by children. In contrast, most pupils do not like secondary science. The secondary science education programme in Japan is quite similar to that in Western societies. This should enable readers to understand that Japanese elementary school science is 'Japanized'. Therefore elementary school science cannot strictly be said to be 'elementary science' in the Western sense. This example suggests the possibility of 'science', at least in a non-Western society, being a school subject that is different from that taught in the West.

WHAT IS 'SCIENCE EDUCATION'?

The view expressed above inevitably leads me to re-examine the concept of 'science education'. I would argue that both sciences (Western science and indigenous science) should receive equal weighting, at least in the early stages of examination of science education in a non-Western society (Ogawa 1986b, Ogunniyi 1988). I also take the position that Western science and indigenous science should be taught as the same school subject, because children are never free from their own indigenous science. It is only in this way that the interrelations between two sciences can be properly treated. Furthermore, the separation of two sciences into two independent school subjects would confuse the children.

I do not deny the dominance, the power and the significance of Western science in our modern civilization. However, this dominance raises important questions. I am concerned that most non-Westerners face the prospect of losing their identity during the modernization process. Here, I must come back to the question of what the objectives of 'science' as a school subject should be. I think that every culture has its own expectations of this school subject, just as it has its own science. In view of this, I want to argue that we cannot simply associate a set of general or universal goals with this kind of subject. I feel that the goals of science as a school subject need to be examined and defined by each particular society and that they have to be tailored by that society to fit its own needs.

What can we do to achieve this? As a first task, we should identify what our own indigenous science is, as well as understand what Western science involves. In this context, we have investigated in recent years how we recognize and interpret 'nature' in the Japanese cultural context (Ogawa and Hayashi 1988, Ogawa and Matsumoto 1988). Our work is similar in its approach to that of Ogunniyi for the African cultural setting (Ogunniyi 1987). In relation to other cultural settings, investigation of this kind is still needed, but it should be done from the viewpoint of science education and not from that of anthropology.

In this context, I usually have the urge to address two sets of questions to Western science educators. The first one is this: Do they (i.e., Western science educators) think it possible that some kind of 'indigenous science' (other than Western science) exists even in a Western culture? (I feel it possible that even Westerners have such a kind of 'indigenous science'!) If so, what kind of contributions does this 'indigenous science' make to Western cultural identity? What kind of relation exists between the two sciences? Does the 'indigenous science' really have to be replaced by Western science?

The other set of questions is this: How, in their view, should the 'indigenous science' of some minority or ethnic groups be dealt with in science education programmes for these groups? Should their 'indigenous science' simply be replaced by Western science?

In these days, I sometimes feel as if I am out of tune with the discipline of science education as it is seen by my colleagues, because my view is so different from theirs. But I am still convinced that my view presents a broader perspective on our discipline of 'science education'.

ACKNOWLEDGEMENT

I wish to express my gratitude to Dr Alfred DeVito for the helpful advice received from him during the preparation of this manuscript.

REFERENCES

Barrentine, C. O. (1986) Science education: education *in*, or *about* science? *Science Education*, Vol. 70, pp. 497–499.

Elkana, Y. (1971) The problem of knowledge. *Stadium Generale*, Vol. 24, pp. 1426–1439.

Good, R., Herron, J. D., Lawson, A. E. and Renner, J. W. (1985) The domain of science education. *Science Education*, Vol. 69, pp. 139–141.

Ministry of Education, Science and Culture (Government of Japan) (1983) *Course of Study for Elementary Schools in Japan*. Notification No. 155 of Ministry of Education, Science and Culture. In Japanese.

Ogawa, M. (1986a) A preliminary study on a key concept 'Nature' involved in science education. *Bulletin of the Faculty of Education Ibaraki University (Educational Sciences)*, No. 35, pp. 1–8. In Japanese with English abstract.

Ogawa, M. (1986b) Toward a new rationale of science education in a non-western society. *European Journal of Science Education*, Vol. 8, pp. 113–119.

Ogawa, M. and Hayashi, M. (1988) Studies on the methods for extracting traditional views of nature in the context of science education. I Extracting images of 'Nature' in the consciousness by word association method. *Bulletin of the Faculty of Education Ibaraki University (Educational Sciences)*, No. 37, pp. 41–50. In Japanese with English abstract.

Ogawa, M. and Matsumoto, H. (1988) Studies on the methods for extracting traditional views of nature in the context of science education. II Extracting images of 'Nature' in the subconsciousness. *Bulletin of the Faculty of Education Ibaraki University (Educational Sciences)*, No. 37, pp. 51–60. In Japanese with English abstract.

Ogunniyi, M. B. (1987) Conceptions of traditional cosmological ideas among literate and nonliterate Nigerians. *Journal of Research in Science Teaching*, Vol. 24, pp. 107–117.

Ogunniyi, M. B. (1988) Adapting western science to traditional African culture. *International Journal of Science Education*, Vol. 10, pp. 1–9.

Okamoto, M. and Mori, K. (1976) The influence of Japanese traditional view of nature on science education: a study on enactment of 'The Principal Point of Science Study'. *Kagakushi Kenkyu (Journal of History of Science Japan)*, Series II, Vol. 15, no. 118, pp. 98–101. In Japanese.

Wandersee, J. H. (1983) Suppose a world without science educators. *Journal of Research in Science Teaching*, Vol. 20, pp. 711–712.

Watson, F. G. (1983), Science education: a discipline? *Journal of Research in Science Teaching*, Vol. 20, pp. 263–264.

Westmeyer, P. (1983) The nature of disciplines. *Journal of Research in Science Teaching*, Vol. 20, pp. 265–270.

Yager, R. E. (1983) Editorial: defining science education as a discipline. *Journal of Research in Science Teaching*, Vol. 20, pp. 261–262.

PART 2: Reflecting on Practice

Introduction

Susan Tresman

'Reflecting on Practice' opens with a wide range of contributions from practitioners working in a broad spectrum of occupations in the field of science education. These include the Head of Interpretation and Education at the Science Museum in London, a course leader of a programme of science training for primary teachers, a member of the Northumberland Supported Self-Study Unit and the project director of a curriculum initiative, backed by the Association for Science Education. We asked them to reflect on a challenging aspect of their practice where through the act of reflection they gained insight which motivated them to make changes.

In this part of the book you will also be introduced to a range of models which analyse how practitioners in the field of science education reflect on their professional practice. Since these models are based on the practice of science teaching or experiences encountered during teacher training, they provide strategies for reflection on practice to help the reader develop modes of reflection suited to his or her own professional practice.

The first of these models is contained in Allan Mackinnon's article, 'Detecting reflection-in-action among preservice elementary science teachers'. Here the author separates the process of reflection into three phases. The three phases can be used to view a problematic situation within one's professional practice, examine it from alternative perspectives and to make changes to the practice as a result of new personal insights gained.

In the article which follows, entitled 'The importance of reflection in improving science teaching and learning', John Baird, Peter Fensham, Richard Gunstone and Richard White evaluate the extent to which a model of collaborative reflection can enhance the teaching and learning of science in the classroom.

In doing so, they concentrate on establishing what it is to be a teacher of science and a learner of science. They explore the mechanisms that underlie these two areas of practice, especially the processes by which individuals can change with experience, how best to facilitate this change and how the effects of change can be gauged.

The existence of a personal 'practical theory' as the strongest determining factor in the execution of one's professional practice underlies the fourth article in this part.

The authors Gunnar Handal and Per Lauvås examine the opportunities and implications of employing a form of shared reflection on practice, thereby making it susceptible to change where appropriate.

2.1

Reflecting on practice: some illustrations

Susan Tresman and Dee Edwards

INTRODUCTION

In Donald Schön's book *The Reflective Practitioner* he offered an approach to the exploration of practice that was based on the close examination of what a range of practitioners actually *do*. His study involved the work of architects, psychotherapists, engineers and town planners; all of these are professions that involve a balance, of practical application and of relevant theory. Science education and science teaching, too, involve such a balance and it was, therefore, natural that science educators and trainers should recognize that a reflective approach would encourage teachers to become better practitioners.

In some of the extracts that follow, the authors asked colleagues who work in science education but outside the conventional classroom milieu to reflect on their practice, so that we could learn from their experience. Their contributions have been augmented by previously published material in the field of adult education.

WHAT IS IT ABOUT?

In a special issue of *Adult Learning* in January 1992 the editors Linda Lewis and LuAnne Dowling wrote:

> On a daily basis each of us, to one degree or another, looks back on how things went and reviews actions taken. We puzzle over nuances that have made today's presentation better than a previous one, marvel how well we did 'on our feet' or realize in hindsight what else we might have done to resolve a situation. Reflection is one of the ways we make meaning and sense of our own performance. And while we may not label ourselves as such, in this we become researchers of our own practice.
>
> Sometimes we observe ourselves 'in action'; other times we conduct a 'post-mortem audit'. Through reflection we bring our actions to consciousness, reinterpret a situation in the light of the consequences of our behaviour, identify performance gaps, and conceptualize ways for improving our practice in the future.

In our roles as educators, administrators, practitioners and professionals, reflective practice is one of the most beneficial activities we can undertake. The notion of engaging in critical reflection in order to draw meaning from past actions becomes the basis for modifying future outcomes. In *Theory into Practice: Increasing Professional Effectiveness* (1974) Argyris and Schön have suggested that learning is governed by the extent to which we examine our assumptions, bring them to consciousness and challenge them. Ultimately, it is through such a process that the potential for changing and improving performance is created.

(Lewis and Dowling, 1992, p. 7)

They went on to say that we all have the potential to be continuous learners and that 'as professionals we have a responsibility to look beyond or behind the routine implementation of knowledge. We must continually review our daily activities with a commitment to improving our practice' (Lewis and Dowling, 1992, p. 7).

WHY DO IT?

The next contribution is made by Patricia Soper, a professional writing instructor and consultant at Syracuse University in New York. In this article published in *Adult Learning* in 1992 we see Soper detailing her own transformation from reluctant participant in the process of 'enforced' reflection, to enthusiastic advocate of the practice among her colleagues.

Resistance, re-examination and resolution: the three R's of my reflective practice

'Five to six hours' I exploded. Storming into a colleague's office, I flung the offending memo on her desk. She greeted me with a blank stare. Obviously, she had not read the memo. I pointed at the third paragraph. 'It says that "the reflective portion of your portfolio might take as much as five to six hours to prepare"', I railed. 'Just who has five to six hours at the end of the school year to "reflect" on anything?' This whole notion was absurd.

All year we had been prodded into weekly sessions of 'reflective practice' during small group meetings where we were encouraged to reflect on classroom experience as a way of enhancing teaching. As stimulating as some of the sessions were, most of us were not really enamoured of these mandated sharing sessions. I fantasized about rounding up existing copies of *The Reflective Practitioner*, by Donald A. Schön (1983), as bonfire fuel. I had had my fill of reflective *anything* and to have yet another reflective task added to my over-full schedule was too much!

I was not alone in my resistance to the mandated reflective practice: other colleagues complained about such a 'waste of time'. Indeed, some opted to take early retirement as a way to avoid this intrusion into their teaching practice. A few moved to other schools where all they had to do was 'just teach English'.

However, I did write my reflective statement, putting in the extra hours for its completion. I love to teach, so if writing a reflective statement was a mandated part of the teaching, then I would churn out those reflections until retirement. There were other reasons, however, for yielding to the mandate. Many colleagues, with whom I had worked for years, were subscribing whole-heartedly to reflective practice. Also, I had a good deal of respect for the intellectual leadership of the program director. Surely, a person of her capabilities would not force something into the program without weighing the possible consequences. She obviously had some vision that I didn't have.

That assignment occurred almost five years ago. Now, I find myself at the opposite pole as I give reflection a premier place in my own course design. I hear my own distant voice as students complain that reflective statements are a 'waste of time'. Many of my nursing students, married and working, have returned to school after several years. Juggling schedules for school, home, children, and the workplace leaves little time 'to sit around and think about stuff'. Because I was myself so resistant to reflection and to writing about it, I appreciate their impatience. But at the same time, I hope my teaching practices demonstrate what Schön (1983) refers to throughout his work as 'reflection-in-action'.

Contemporary lifestyles are complicated, so that our time is dictated by the demands before us. As educators we're forced to react to demands and have little to devote to thoughtful responses to learning. The result is intellectual clutter as we try to cram more into hectic schedules. As teachers we are responsible for creating space in our classrooms, space in our heads to walk around an idea and look at it from various perspectives. Such walking around is what reflective practice is all about for both teacher and the learning adult.

Reflective practice takes as many forms as those who engage in it. For me, reflective practice is not the experimentation or re-framing suggested by Schön; instead it is a varied seeing – seeing in a new way. This scrutiny leads to questioning every aspect of my teaching. Did this work? Why? Why not? And if it did work, how? Will it work in another context? Were there any surprises? I literally schedule a minimum of fifteen minutes at the end of each day to reflect, sometimes in writing. True, there are days when I am extremely weary, but the reflection compensates for the fatigue. My day is reviewed and evaluated; my mind is revitalized to take on the next challenge.

So what about the resistance to reflection? To reflective practice? To writing about that reflection? Where did it go? As our group continued to consider reflection, often joking about 'reflecting on reflecting, on reflecting', the original resistance dissipated, leaving an awareness of the educator's imperative to remain open to the possibilities afforded by any reasonable, new approach to the profession. We began to shape our space for reflection, to allow room for walking around, re-examining ideas in light of classroom experience. Reflection became more than an add-on: it became a way of life in the Writing Program. We were reflecting, and in turn, we were expecting students to do the same. Students reflected on their own writing, their expectations, and their progress towards participation in specific academic discourse communities, making reflection an integral part of their intellectual development.

On my journey to acceptance, I re-examined my first, frustrated year-end reflective statement, eventually reshaping it as a conference presentation that was later published and awarded special recognition within my own discipline. Not every re-examination of reflective practice is published or recognized, but the processes provide a special kind of enhancement for life beyond the classroom.

For example, finding time to reflect on the stresses associated with my recent divorce was a challenge, but I did find time because not to do so would have forced the continuation of those stresses. And partly, because of fruitful experience with putting reflection to paper, I wrote down my conflicts and confusions. The result, *A Diary of Divorce*, may never be published, but the reflection has allowed me to see in a new way as I walk around the experience.

I frequently have my freshman students again as upperclassmen. My 're-peaters' who were themselves resistant to reflective practice often admit that it has altered understanding, perceptions, and even career choices.

I guess I have come to share the program director's larger vision. Certainly, I cannot imagine functioning without the benefits of reflective practice. Because reflective practice has worked so well for me, for my students, and for my family, I want to share it, and I want people to know that resistance to reflection is okay, but they must fairly re-examine the notion towards a resolution, a resolution to engage consciously in and reap the rewards of reflective practice.

(Soper, 1992, p. 28)

REFLECTION AND SUPPORTED SELF-STUDY

Robert Peers is Co-ordinator for Teacher Support at the Northumberland Supported Self-Study Unit (Morpeth, Northumbria, UK). We are able to 'look through the window' at Peers reflecting on his experience of using a style of tutoring based on the belief that post-16 students learn more effectively by reflecting on *their* own experiences.

Reflecting on reflections
Reflecting on experience is the way we adults learn.
Build on what the learner already knows.
Make sure your students' foundations for learning are theirs, not yours.

As a member of Northumberland's supported self-study team, I've heard myself saying such things many times when running post-16 professional development courses. As a part-time teacher in two local high schools, I've been interested to see how far my own teaching has been affected by such ideals. In other words, I have found myself reflecting on my own experience of using a style of teaching that is itself based on the idea that students learn best by reflecting on their own experience.

In practice, Northumberland's philosophy of learning through supported self-study is based on encouraging more effective use of students' independent learning time. It bears many similarities to the 'plan–do–review' approach used in primary schools. As such, the contact time commonly exprienced by many post-16 students requires a shift of emphasis. In a group tutorial, joint planning by students and teacher sets up opportunities for learning in the students' own time. This demands that students develop

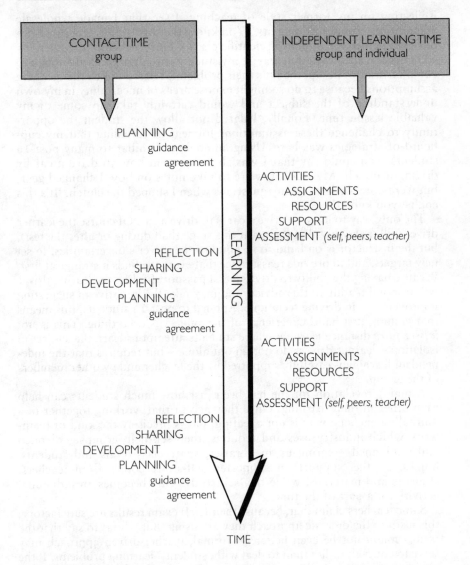

CONTACT TIME
group

INDEPENDENT LEARNING TIME
group and individual

PLANNING
guidance
agreement

ACTIVITIES
ASSIGNMENTS
RESOURCES
SUPPORT
ASSESSMENT *(self, peers, teacher)*

REFLECTION
SHARING
DEVELOPMENT
PLANNING
guidance
agreement

LEARNING

ACTIVITIES
ASSIGNMENTS
RESOURCES
SUPPORT
ASSESSMENT *(self, peers, teacher)*

REFLECTION
SHARING
DEVELOPMENT
PLANNING
guidance
agreement

TIME

Figure I One way through the learning cycle

appropriate learning skills. The first part of the following tutorial has a review function. Using a jointly produced agenda, this allows students to build on learning initiated in their own time, as well as to develop their learning skills.

We represent this model in a diagram (Figure 1) which expresses learning as a continuous, evolutionary process. This model is itself an adaptation of one proposed by Philip Waterhouse (Waterhouse, 1990).

My work over the last four years has given me a valuable opportunity to analyse my own methods in the light of watching other teachers at work.

Reflecting on my former style of teaching, I see that I made wholesale assumptions about my students. (You know the sort of thing: because no-one ever helped me to plan a scientific essay – I just picked it up – then my students can also learn that way; if my students aren't organized enough to complete that write-up, then it's their problem.) I dared not challenge these assumptions because to do so might expose areas of uncertainty in my own understanding of the subject and would certainly take up some of my valuable lesson time. Equally, I dared not allow the student the opportunity to challenge these assumptions for fear of revealing that my cupboard of strategies was bare. Using an analogy familiar to many post-16 students, you could say that I was showing them how to drive a car by driving it myself. My students were to take notes on how I changed gear, but were not to ask too many questions when I slipped the clutch. 'It's this engine you know!'

The only way to learn to drive a car is to drive a car. Of course the learner driver will make mistakes (better at this stage than during or after the test), but the instructor is on hand to respond to the driver's uncertainties, to set new targets, and to provide reassurance that everyone finds it strange at first. Because having the ability to drive gives a passport for life, the learner driver will respond readily to this advice, and may take the initiative in suggesting improvements in driving technique. Applied to post-16 students, this means that gaining first-hand experience of the subject is everything. This is not *laissez faire* distance learning where students attempt to learn the subject in isolation – learner drivers do not go out alone – but requires that the independent learning is carefully supported by the teacher and by other members of the group.

A major revelation for me has been just how much students can help each other in their learning. Once they accept that working together in a mutually beneficial way is not cheating, but is precisely the kind of teamwork which industry uses and requires, then self-help groups – planned and unplanned – spring up in libraries, spare classrooms and students' homes. So the 'support' in supported self-study comes from teachers, students and materials, while the 'self-study' only becomes an individual activity for a part of the time.

Some teachers claim that, because their (*sic*!) exam results are satisfactory, this justifies the didactic approach they are using. But who is to say that the results might not be even better? A formal, teacher-driven approach may serve to conceal, rather than to deal with, students' learning problems. If the analogy of the driving lesson fails to convince, I offer the following line of reasoning which my recent teaching experience has highlighted.

Exams require students to communicate knowledge, understanding and skills in response to conditions which are not entirely familiar or predictable, and to do so under pressure to an unknown audience. To do this effectively involves mental search and processing skills of a high order; skills that need practice throughout the course. Who better than Einstein to suggest how to tackle this? 'You only really understand something if you can explain it in a simple way.' A common strategy for checking understanding goes something like this: 'John do you understand that now? Fine, let's move on.' Another strategy might be: 'John, can you read your results to us please?' The problem with the first is that, when you ask a student this question, the answer is nearly always positive, whatever the true situation. With the second, apart from displaying an ability to read, John has not had to process any information.

In the review tutorials, my groups now keep the written products of their independent learning hidden from view for part of the time. With a little practice, it is possible to encourage a student-driven discussion, which might include a student presentation or demonstration, which can help students to come to terms with the depth of their understanding. Inviting them to reflect on their experiences and, together, to identify the strengths and weaknesses of their understanding, enables them to modify their written work in the light of the groups' experience. Discussing the development of learning skills becomes an integral part of the learners' experience of the subject; these skills are then acquired progressively, as and when needed. My students value this approach because they see its application to their exams, and have the time to spend on such activities because they are making more effective use of their independent learning time.

By sharing the construction of an agenda as the first step in a review tutorial, students know that their concerns will be dealt with in a supportive atmosphere. Because many areas of uncertainty will be common to the group, the students appreciate that they are not alone in struggling with an issue. By listening to my students' needs, I find that getting myself organized for a tutorial has become less a matter of preparing *my lesson*, more of preparing *their learning*.

(Robert Peers, Co-ordinator for Teacher Support,
Supported Self-Study Unit, Morpeth, Northumbria, UK)

MANAGING A MAJOR CURRICULUM INITIATIVE

Patricia Soper's description of reflection as the act of creating 'space in our heads to walk around an idea and look at it from various perspectives' is a valuable way of approaching the next contribution from John Stringer. As the Director of SATIS 8–14, he reflects on the challenges to be faced and lessons learned from managing and producing a major new science curriculum initiative, where the perspectives are provided by the large and diverse team of contributors and triallers.

SATIS 8–14: a science, technology and society project for the middle school years

SATIS is a project of the Association for Science Education which aims to put science and technology into a social context. The materials are low-cost, photocopiable and practical, and the SATIS 8–14 project follows other successful projects for GCSE and A-level students. All the SATIS materials have three essential components: they are written and tested by teachers, endorsed by experts in the field and they are active and engaging curriculum materials.

SATIS for 8–14-year-olds has taken three years to develop. The final result will be 150 active units, TV and radio links, a data disc, a poster, video and a picture pack. As well as five part-time editors, over 300 volunteer writers and specialist advisers have been involved, 200 trial schools, and over twenty local groups, together with over 800 people on a mailing list.

The project aims
- to make science and technology accessible to all pupils;
- to inform the work of non-specialist teachers in primary schools;
- to develop the cross-curricular work of secondary teachers;
- to acknowledge and support good liaison practice between phases.

Practicalities and challenges
A number of important objectives became apparent as the project pro-gressed, including the importance of involving a wide range of volunteer authors – both from education and from the professions and industry. We were looking for both a range of expertise, originality and the credibility that comes from classroom trialling and professional endorsement. Most mainstream science schemes have familiar styles and objectives. SATIS aimed at fresh approaches, techniques and skills. These resulted in materials that include process science, structured discussion, illustration, writing to a purpose, handling and displaying data in a wide range of ways, applying information technology, and communciating and recording using tech-nology. Practical examples include board games, role play, simulation, ques-tionnaires, data logging, and debate – among many others.

There was a recognized need among teachers for a wide variety of flexible and adaptable material to help them with science and technology and a need for accessible, friendly, teacher notes. We took as much care with the teacher notes as with the pupil materials so that they were easy to use.

Reliability was important so that the real experiences of trial schools were highlighted to give the materials practicality and credibility.

The work sheets were designed to be used either as photocopies or as teacher support since bulk photocopying might prove too expensive. It is expected that teachers will adapt and personalize materials.

Practicalities – the lessons to be learned
We learnt a number of lessons from establishing and developing this national project.

A large number of locally based groups are difficult to maintain and were most successful where they were led by a local enthusiast. The aim was to engage teachers and others across the country in developing mater-ials; they might then represent regional interests, as well as throwing the ideas net widely. In Northern Ireland an active group, with advisory team support, grew strongly both specific to the area and of general interest; while several determined attempts to establish active groups in Scotland (where the whole professional development and meeting scene is com-pletely different) failed to result in regionally produced units. We found that the local enthusiasts were critical; no amount of help from the centre could maintain a group without them.

Producing a resource that uses a range of media is difficult in practice. The demands and schedules of making broadcast resources are quite different from those of the published page.

Meeting National Curriculum demands and the raised expectations of teachers while still retaining some freshness and originality is hard. We achieved it through the encouragement of a huge number of original ideas; the fifty units in Box 2 – for Key Stages 2 and 3 – have some 200 individual parts, each with a trialled activity. There were 123 authors, 200 trial schools, and around twenty local working groups on this box alone. Ultimately, quality dictated whether the unit crossed the many fences to publication.

The project had to sell into a difficult market where teachers lacked both the money to buy materials that were not seen as mainstream and the timetabled time to use them. The decline in the advisory teacher service robbed us of key people who would have encouraged innovation.

How far did we achieve what we set out to do?
The material is of high quality in both its accuracy and its presentation.

We delivered a wide range of strategies from laboratory experiments to board games and including cartoons, stories, quizzes, models, etc.

The interest and enthusiasm of a great many people was maintained throughout. Many attended weekend meetings to initiate ideas, to maintain their interest, and to plan dissemination of the projects. A newsletter kept them all in touch with the project's development.

SATIS 8–14 has received excellent reviews. Teachers who see it want to use it. We have achieved many of our original aims.

(John Stringer, Project Director of the ASE Early SATIS (8–14)
Project 1985–93, Barclays Venture Centre, University of
Warwick Science Park, Sir William Lyons Road, Coventry, UK)

REFLECTIVE DIARIES

Dennis Fox, in his capacity as course leader on a professional training course in primary science, was faced with the challenge of determining (and then delivering) the nature, level and format of science needed for course participants to realize the potential of their primary-aged pupils in science. He reflects on the use of reflective diaries and in doing so establishes a relationship between reflection and action in the operation of his course.

Reflections into action
These are my reflections about a course in which I set up a procedure to enable and encourage the participants to reflect on their experiences each week and to share these reflections with each other. These shared reflections then formed part of the basis for developing involvement and progression through subsequent weeks.

It is all very well to encourage end-of-course reflections. These are important for looking at a course in its entirety. However, these do not provide an opportunity for course members to own and take some control of the consequences of their reflections. So this was an attempt to set up a system for integrating reflection with action which would affect the day-to-day life and operation of the course.

The course was an in-service course for primary school teachers and most of the participants had some responsibility for co-ordinating science in their schools. We met for one whole day in most weeks of the school year.

An important feature of the programme was a personal diary which each course member kept throughout the course. About fifteen minutes at the end of each day were left clear for a time for personal reflection on the day's events and these reflections were written up individually in the diaries. Each diary had a personalized drawing on the cover, but no name so that when I collected the diaries at the end of the session they were anonymous. Yet when I placed the diaries on the table for collection at the next session the owners could easily identify their own diaries.

The purpose of collecting the diaries was twofold. First I wanted access to the diary entries so that I could respond and demonstrate to the course members that their reflections were producing action on my part. Second, I wanted to feed back to them their reflections so that they all had access to the reflections of everyone else. In this way each diary entry was produced *individually* but it became part of a *group record*.

The diary entries for each week were analysed and a feedback sheet was prepared for the following session. Usually the individual items fell into three or four categories and the feedback sheet consisted of a reprint of all the diary items collated under the common category headings. It was thus very easy to see where the main areas of interest or concern were and it was possible for each course member to see his or her own items related to similar items from the diaries of others. I had encouraged the course members to express their worries and concerns so that these could be brought into the open and addressed and so that they could recognize that there were probably similar areas of concern amongst the other course members. You can see below that these concerns fell into three categories – worries about time commitments, concern about the difficulty of the subject matter and concern about its relevance to their day-to-day lives in the classroom. By collating the various diary items under common headings, I was able to show people that their individual concerns were widely shared and I was able to make a response which was intended to be reassuring and to show that I was hearing what they were saying.

On some occasions the diary entries were simply a response to events of the day. On other occasions it seemed useful to focus most of the responses on a particular issue. For example the applicability of some of the material to the primary classroom was a recurrent issue. A phone call from a headteacher to complain about this provided an opportunity to focus more specifically on the issue in the diaries for that week. I suggested that the diary entries might be in the form of a response to the headteacher. Rather to my surprise this produced a stream of entries showing the extent to which course members were becoming able to work through their own concerns about this issue:

I can fully understand concerns about the classroom relevance of the course. It is something the course tutors and course members are very aware of and I can assure you that the course is of great value to the participants.

I am finding considerable personal value at the adult science level.

I am more aware of scientific thinking.

Before starting the course my confidence and enthusiasm for science was nil and now I feel excited and extremely motivated to learn more about science.

I think that you are ignoring the personal development of your member of staff.

I used to think science in the classroom was about chaotic experiments that never worked. Now I see science as real. It's the earth around us and not an isolated experiment.

I am encountering a wider range of science topics than I had expected.

It gives us a good all-round grounding in a number of scientific issues.

When these comments were fed back to the course members the following week they provided a very good basis for discussion about the nature of personal and professional development through courses such as this.

It was interesting that one particular element of the course (earth sciences) consistently attracted appreciative comments in the diaries. In follow-up discussions the course members were able to appreciate that the geologist who taught that session had a far deeper understanding of geology than the level at which she was presenting it to them. They were able to reflect on the extent to which her success in presenting material at their level was determined by her own much deeper specialist knowledge. In fact one of the most valuable parts of the reflective process was the insight it gave these teachers into the problems and feeling of being students. Many of them commented that they could now view the experience of their pupils with more empathy.

Although the system was devised primarily to link reflection with action, it became clear that the reflective process stimulated by the diaries was also effective in helping the course members to clarify and articulate their own developing concepts and feelings – and not simply those concerned with science in the primary classroom.

Tutor comments
The feedback sheet was produced by collating the diary entries from the first session of the course. Students' diary entries are in italics to distinguish them from my comments.

Many of you expressed concern about the amount of work that seemed to be demanded and the amount of time you didn't have.

Apprehensive about being able to do all the work that is expected of me and keep my teaching job going and the family on the rails – when will the airing cupboard ever get emptied?

I feel I cannot tackle all that I am expected to do on the one study day and I don't know what will have to give.

Concerned about the quantity of work – unsure if I can meet this commitment.

I am worried about my study skills – I need more of a push.

Apprehensive about the assignments because of the time I don't have.

Concerned about the third assignment – sounds a bit daunting – I hope my normal classroom science will be acceptable.

*I am looking forward to having done the first assignment and not having made a complete * * * * * of it.*

My comment: The course is structured so that you can put a lot of time and effort into it – or very little; it's up to you. The more time and effort you are able to put into it, the more you will get out of it. Only you can decide how much you can afford. It will depend on your own priorities – both in terms of things which compete for your time and effort and in terms of the importance to you of what you get out of the course.

Many of you expressed a concern about the depth/complexity/difficulty of the material:

The level of science/understanding was way over my head – put me off science rather than encouraging me towards it.

The physics stuff still confuses me.

I felt overwhelmed by the mathematics.

Became daunted by what seemed to be the technical depth of the content.

Worry that they will think I am thick because I may not understand.

Worry that people will be trying their hardest to explain and I still won't understand.

Just as I began to get a glimmer of understanding we whizzed on to something else.

I am looking forward to having my intellectual darkness lightened but you will have to go much slower and at a lower level.

I've been thoroughly confused and I'm sure I've got more brain cells through all the thinking I've done.

My comment: The course is designed for people with very varied science backgrounds. If you have a very weak background you won't be left to struggle but you will have to be realistic about the progress you can expect to make. You won't be able to get as far (for the same effort) as someone who initially knows more science. If you have a stronger background you should be able to consolidate and extend this without going over lots of old ground.

Some of you were concerned that you were not always able to relate the content of the course to what goes on in your classroom. There was some understandable ambivalence about relating personal development at your own level to professional development as a competent teacher of young children.

At first I was concerned that the course would have little relevance to me as a classroom teacher although I was looking forward to a learning experience at my own level.

What use is the periodic table in the classroom?

Enjoyed the session on rocks because the pace was right and in a context which I could relate to the classroom.

The moon exercise was quite hard to understand. Why couldn't we do something we could try out in the classroom?

Initially disappointed that things were not all school or class based – but realized that sessions were designed to heighten my scientific knowledge.

I am concerned about my ability to set up experiments in the classroom – I never seem to have time to organize such things.

My comment: Does the following analogy help? If you are taking your class on a residential visit to a new area, you will need a good O.S. map of the area. You might also prepare a very simple sketch map for the children to use. No one would suggest that a children's sketch map would be sufficient for you as a teacher to find your way around the area and plan and supervise suitable activities for the children. This course aims to provide you with a good quality map of science and to help you develop the skills to use it.

Although you were apprehensive about some of the difficulties, without exception you were positive about this and looking forward to meeting the challenge:

One of the most useful courses I've attended in that it's helped me to stop and think a bit more about science.

It's what I want. I need to know what I'm teaching and this has to be done at my level.

I want to learn and pretend I'm a scientist.

I feel this is going to benefit my personal development.

Enjoyed having to think and work things out.

I'm excited about being a good science co-ordinator because no-one's ever told me what to do before.

Finally a comment one of you made about the group:

I enjoyed the group – active and dyanmic without any abrasive characters.

So did I!

(Dennis Fox, Department of Primary Education,
Nottingham Trent University)

(Acknowledgement: Kath Green, Department of Primary Education, The Nottingham Trent University, first stimulated my interest in the use of this kind of student diary.)

EXHIBITING SCIENCE

As Head of Interpretation and Education at the Science Museum in London, Graham Farmelo reflects on the difficulties encountered, and the opportunities seized upon, as the museum strives to change its rather staid image while maintaining its academic reputation.

Contemporary science exhibitions at the Science Museum

'Damp and dusty places' was Mrs Thatcher's disdainful description of museums in the early 1980s. More recently, most museums have been working to improve on their dowdy image, striving to realize their potential in the leisure market while consolidating their academic reputations. The Science Museum in London, a centre for scholarship and one of the ten most popular tourist destinations in the UK, has long been seeking to reconcile the two objectives. It has been well pleased recently with the success of Science Box, a new series of temporary exhibitions on contemporary science, aimed at non-specialist visitors, particularly families.

The series of exhibitions was planned partly in response to the crying need in the Science Museum – and, to be fair, in most other museums – for material that is genuinely contemporary. It is expensive to keep galleries up to date and museums, notoriously conservative institutions, are reluctant to chance their arm by taking risks with exhibitions that respond to the previous week's hot news. Museums tend to respond to news of ten years ago, not of last week. Apart from the book-on-a-wall displays in Paris's La Villette and, elsewhere, a few notice boards of scrappy press cuttings, no major museum or science centre in the UK and North America features a regular programme of exhibitions devoted to contemporary science.

Science Box, then, had no precedents. From the outset, it was intended that each of the exhibitions would be prominently located for three months in the museum's front concourse, to catch the eye of visitors. Each exhibition would be produced to the museum's uncompromising academic standards and presented within a special flexible framework, consisting of a modular structure based on carbon fibre rods that form a skeleton which houses replaceable graphic panels. With government support for museums falling each year, projects like this are not now possible without sponsorship: the Science Box programme has been possible only because of the support of Nuclear Electric plc, which contributed £250,000 towards the first seven exhibitions.

Recent research has indicated that the public are surprisingly interested in science. Even news of sport appears to be less interesting than new developments in medicine! It was, none the less, not as easy as it might seem to select topics for Science Box. Exhibitions normally work best when they are based, first, on impressive objects that can be seen only in museums and, second, on 'hands-on' exhibits, known in the trade as 'interactives'. This immediately favours technological topics, principally concerned with artefacts, rather than the ideas of science. The crucially important debate on whether global warming is a serious environmental issue would, for example, be a difficult subject to address in an exhibition whereas the design of, say, a new electric car would be potentially much easier to present.

The choice of the topics of the first three Science Boxes has reflected this concern to base the display on important objects. The first in the series of exhibitions opened in April 1992 and concerned DNA fingerprinting, a subject rarely out of the news. The display included the first DNA fingerprint, all the apparatus required to take an actual fingerprint, and one of the largest samples of DNA ever featured in public. These, together with carefully prepared text, some interactives and a touch-screen display comprised the exhibition which proved to be very popular with visitors. Research showed that some 84,000 people stopped to look at the display and that 66 per cent understood it at the level intended by the exhibition planners.

In addition to the main exhibition, Science Boxes are complemented by printed materials, produced for school and for the public, and public programmes that usually include lectures, demonstrations, films and drama presentations. The second exhibition, which concerned the applications of lasers in everyday life, was presented in the summer – when visitor numbers are particularly high throughout the week – so it was economical to organize a particularly rich programme of events.

The subsequent programme of Science Box has continued in this ambitious spirit. The choice of topics continue to be diverse – the ozone hole, passive smoking and the Olympic gold-medal-winning Lotus bicycle. By evaluating each exhibition with respect to its stated aims, the Museum is able to gauge the success of each one and to learn from experience. Among the key lessons so far have been the importance of: featuring at least two interactives, using small amounts of jargon-free text, ensuring a spacious exhibition structure and of featuring a visually appealing object in the path of the visitors to attract the potentially indifferent towards the display.

It would be unfortunate if this popular and unique enterprise were to be accessible only to those who can visit London. Touring is, however, very expensive: not only are finances required to duplicate the exhibition structure, considerable staff resources would also be needed to staff and maintain it. For this reason, Science Box would have remained in the capital if the government had not funded a year's touring, in which the DNA exhibition will visit Loughborough, Birmingham, Edinburgh, Liverpool, Jodrell Bank and Cardiff. If science news is as popular as the surveys say, this unique road show should reach a very wide audience.

(Graham Farmelo, Head of Interpretation and Education,
Science Museum, London)

CONCLUSION

As evidenced by the range of contributions here, the act of reflecting on one's practice is not easy and is interpreted to mean very different things depending on the different perspectives of the professional contributors. We have observed them employing a wide range of descriptive, analytical and evaluative skills as they reflect on their practice.

Making one's reflections public is shown to be particularly difficult, involving a good deal of personal risk in questioning established practice and framing problematic or puzzling aspects associated with it.

In this article we have seen amongst other examples, reflective journals or diaries being used to conduct professional dialogue between leaders of in-service training courses and participating students, reflection being used as a form of post-event audit of problems overcome and lessons learnt through directing a large-scale project, and reflection as a means of motivating post-16 students to prepare their learning from self-study science A-level materials.

Reflection is shown as a technique for extending museum workers' perceptions of the intriguing and challenging task of reshaping museum exhibits.

Victoria Marsick and Karen Watkins (1992) showed that reflection in the workplace raises some fascinating issues surrounding the challenge of facilitating reflective practice as a central aspect of workplace training which has been generally seen as an expert-directed activity.

They argue that the idea of reflective practice is compatible with the notion that employees at all levels of corporate organizations are empowered to identify and solve problems – and can assist workers to 'take more responsibility for daily decision making related to their immediate tasks' (Marsick and Watkins, 1992, p. 9).

Interesting evidence of reflective practice occurring through programmes of continuous learning in widely differing companies shows how important reflection has been in establishing new, often job-related learning approaches to training and development which have broadened companies' traditional focus on training.

An eight-point framework for effective continuous learning established by Marsick and Watkins synthesizes many of the ideas and techniques alluded to in this article by our contributors:

(1) **Clarify** the thinking and reasoning we bring to the situation and make it explicit.
(2) **Open** yourself to questions about what and how you are learning.
(3) **Notice** feelings, fact and intuition about the context.
(4) **Test** hunches before acting.
(5) **Investigate** many points of view.
(6) **Name** the problem, and then continue to rename it.
(7) **Undercover** values, beliefs, assumptions and norms that guide thinking and actions.
(8) **Experiment,** and in so doing, seek reality-based feedback.

Similarly, Marsick and Watkins introduce challenges faced in implementing reflective practice in the workplace that have figured prominently in our case studies. These include the problem of individuals lacking the skills for continuous learning, the challenge of encouraging peers to provide feedback to promote many different viewpoints, and linked to this the fact that work situations are not always set up physically or psychologically for feedback. We see a recurrent theme emerging, as Marsick and Watkins discuss:

> Another difficulty is that adults have worked hard to become who they are; continuous learning demands that they continuously unlearn past lessons

and become a new practitioner which leaves them vulnerable. Since work environments have not traditionally tolerated mistakes, the consequences of being a continuous learner may be serious. Continuous learners ask questions and challenge the beliefs of others in a way that may be misperceived as threatening. We should not also forget that people conditioned to be passive do not become proactive overnight.

(Marsick and Watkins, 1992, p. 12)

Our contributors have helped to illuminate the telling difference between having experiences in science education, analysing and understanding these experiences and learning from them, and in the process, categorizing their practice in terms 'useful for (themselves and) others' (Stones, 1992, p. 298).

They have shown that reflective practice – in its many different guises – can be a powerful tool for distinguishing between experiencing something and learning from it.

REFERENCES

Argyris, C. and Schön, D. (1974) *Theory into Practice: Increasing Professional Effectiveness*, San Francisco, Jossey-Bass.

Lewis, L. and Dowling, L. A. (1992) Editorial. *Adult Learning*, Vol. 3, no. 2 (January).

Marsick, V. J. and Watkins, K. E. (1992) Continuous learning in the workplace, *Adult Learning*, Vol. 3, no. 2, pp. 9–12.

Schön, D. (1983) *The Reflective Practitioner: How Professionals Think in Action*, New York, Basic Books.

Soper, P. (1992) Resistance, re-examination and resolution: the three R's of my reflective practice. *Adult Learning*, Vol. 3, no. 2 (January).

Stones, E. (1992) *Quality Teaching: A Sample of Cases*, New York and London, Routledge.

Waterhouse, P. (1990) *Classroom Management*, Stafford, Network Educational Press.

2.2

Detecting reflection-in-action among preservice elementary science teachers

Allan M. Mackinnon

This paper presents an analytic, exploratory study into the manner in which preservice elementary school teachers think about their early science teaching performances. The technical term for the particular kind of thinking that is sought is 'reflection-in-action', a term put forth by Donald Schön (1983) in his recent and promising conceptualization of the nature of professional thinking.

The study took place about a practical teaching exercise that occurred in an elementary science methods course. Third-year education students taught science lessons to grade four, five, and six pupils in a Canadian urban upper middle class school. The research problem was to determine whether Schön's conceptualization of reflection-in-action is applicable and appropriate to studying the way in which methods students make sense of their teaching performances. The study entailed the development and assessment of a 'clue structure' (Roberts and Russell, 1975), or set of criteria, for detecting reflection-in-action. Techniques of clinical supervision were utilized to guide the study of teaching, thus the approach entailed the analysis of clinical supervision dialogue. The study begins, then, with the assumption that the process of reflection, seen as part of Schön's view of professional action, is the same as the process of reflection as it emerges in the clinical supervision process. Excerpts of supervision dialogue from one supervision session with one of the education students are presented, together with a detailed analysis illustrating the use of the clue structure in detecting reflection-in-action.

THE DEVELOPMENT OF TEACHER CONCERNS

In order to establish the context for the study, it is helpful to consider a conceptualization by Fuller and Bown (1975) regarding the process of becoming a teacher. According to this conceptualization, beginning teachers typically change their 'teacher concerns' as they move through preservice to inservice teaching:

From *Teaching and Teacher Education* (1987) Vol. 3, no. 2, pp. 135–45.

Preteaching concerns – Fresh from the pupil role, education students who have never taught are concerned . . . about themselves. They identify realistically with pupils, but with teachers only in fantasy. They have not experienced the realities of the teaching role. Education courses which deal with the teacher's realities seem to them 'irrelevant'. The identification with pupils manifests itself at the beginning of observation, when they are often unsympathetic, even hostile, critics of the classroom teacher whom they are observing.

Early concerns about survival – At first contact with actual teaching, however, education students' concerns change radically. Their idealized concerns about pupils are replaced by concerns about their own survival as teachers. They are concerned about class control, their mastery of the content to be taught, and evaluations by their supervisors. They wonder if they will ever learn to teach at all. This is a period of great stress.

Teaching situation concerns – Concerns about limitations and frustrations in the teaching situation, about the varied demands made on them to teach, not just survive, are added on to self-concerns. Education students who are teaching now become concerned about methods and materials which were the focus of education courses taken previously. They find they learned content well enough to reproduce it on an exam but not well enough to explain it to someone else, to answer questions, or to give examples.

Concerns about pupils – Preservice teachers express deep concerns about pupils, about their learning, their social and emotional needs, and about relating to pupils as individuals. But they may be unable to act on these concerns. Flooded by feelings of inadequacy, by situational demands and conflicts, they may have to lay aside these concerns until they have learned to cope with more urgent tasks, such as being heard above the din.

(Fuller and Brown, 1975, pp. 38–9)

In previous empirical work with student teachers, Fuller (1969) found no evidence to support the proposition that beginning teachers are concerned with instructional design, methods of presenting subject-matter, assessment of pupil learning, or tailoring content to individual pupils. Yet these matters are typically dealt with before student teaching in education courses. Although her study involved education students only during their practicum experiences, Fuller drew insightful implications for their methods courses:

Information about concerns during this pre-teaching phase may actually be of more interest to many teacher educators than information about concerns during student teaching. First actual teaching, though stressful, is generally reported to be of more interest and benefit than other experiences offered in teacher education programs. Lack of interest is a problem before, rather than during student teaching.

(Fuller, 1969, p. 219)

The practical problem occurring in methods courses, as pointed out by this conceptualization, is not unfamiliar. It seems fair to say that method students often attend to matters that are of more concern to them than the theoretical perspectives of their instructors. Will they be liked by their students? Can they control a class? Is there any hope of getting a job? Their preoccupation with 'preteaching concerns' and 'early concerns about survival' may indeed inhibit their understanding of pedagogical theory. A goal for teacher educators may therefore be to help preservice teachers overcome their self-concerns so that they might develop concerns about pupils. A more fundamental goal would be to create practical contexts to serve as foundations from which methods students might better understand theoretical perspectives about teaching methodology.

Assuming that actual classroom experience would enhance the development of teaching situation and pupil concerns, and that theories of pedagogy might be better understood through the examination of practice itself, a logical approach toward a solution of this problem would likely entail the inclusion of school-based experience in the methods course. Furthermore, educational researchers might strive to operationalize the blend of theory and practice in methods courses by studying the stages through which beginning teachers move in learning to reflect upon their practice.

Implicit in the conceptual orientation of this work is the assumption that a particular kind of thinking about teaching will enhance the process of becoming a teacher. Not only is there a need for a practical context in which methods course material can be embedded, there is also a need for methods students to understand that context. Here, teaching is regarded as a practical, disciplined art. Good teaching depends upon insight, and insight comes from reflection. It follows that there is a need for an appropriate conceptual framework that will drive reflection among preservice teachers, detect it, and allow investigators to research it.

REFLECTION-IN-ACTION

In *The Reflective Practitioner: How Professionals Think in Action,* Donald Schön (1983) has presented a conception of 'knowledge-in-action' which challenges the traditional school of thought regarding the nature of professional knowledge – what he calls 'Technical Rationality':

> According to the model of Technical Rationality – the view of professional knowledge which has most powerfully shaped both our thinking about the professions and the institutional relations of research, education and practice – professional activity consists in instrumental problem solving made rigorous by the application of scientific theory and technique.
>
> (Schön, 1983, p. 21)

Schön refutes the notion that a science-like corpus of knowledge can 'drive' practice, and that it can lead to predictability and control in practical affairs:

> Among philosophers of science no one wants any longer to be called a Positivist, and there is a rebirth of interest in the ancient topics of craft, artistry and myth – topics whose fate Positivism once claimed to have sealed. It seems clear, however, that the dilemma which afflicts the professions

hinges not on science per se but on the Positivist view of science. From this perspective, we tend to see science, after the fact, as a body of established propositions derived from research. When we recognize their limited utility in practice, we experience the dilemma of rigor or relevance. But we may also consider science before the fact as a process in which scientists grapple with uncertainties and display arts of inquiry akin to the uncertainties and arts of practice.

(ibid., pp. 44–9)

In reconsidering the nature of professional knowledge, Schön honours the practical competence of professionals in divergent situations, and searches for 'an epistemology of practice implicit in the artistic, intuitive processes which some practitioners do bring to situations of uncertainty, instability, uniqueness, and value conflict' (p. 49):

> When we go about the spontaneous, intuitive performance of the actions of everyday life, we show ourselves to be knowledgeable in a special way. Often we cannot say what it is that we know. When we try to describe it, we find ourselves at a loss, or we produce descriptions that are obviously inappropriate. Our knowing is ordinarily tacit, implicit in our patterns of action and in our feel for the stuff with which we are dealing. It seems right to say that our knowing is *in* our action.

(ibid., p. 49)

Schön is more interested in the *process* of professional decision making than in the decisions themselves. He conceives of 'reflection-in-action' as a means by which professional knowledge is put into play, in terms of both 'problem setting' and problem solving:

> In real world practice, problems do not present themselves to the practitioner as givens. They must be constructed from the materials or problematic situations that are puzzling, troubling and uncertain. When we set the problem, we select what we will treat as the 'things' of the situation, we set the boundaries of our attention to it, and we impose upon it a coherence which allows us to say what is wrong and in what directions the situation needs to be changed. Problem setting is a process in which, interactively, we *name* the things to which we will attend and *frame* the context in which we will attend to them.

(ibid., p. 40)

According to the model of reflection-in-action, when a practitioner sets a problem in a situation, 'fundamental principles', that are 'closely connected both to his frames and to his repertoire of exemplars' (p. 317), are brought to bear on the situation. For Schön, fundamental principles represent theory, or conceptual apparatus, *in use*. The practitioner engages in a 'reflective conversation' with the practice situation. Past experiences are brought to bear on the situation; frames are imposed and bring to attention certain aspects of phenomena; problems are set and actions that entail certain solutions are formulated. What the practitioner 'sees' in the situation depends fundamentally on his or her conceptual repertoire and the way in which the reflection proceeds.

Referring to the clinical supervision of methods students for a moment, it is plausible that problem setting is one of the activities in which the supervisor and the student engage as they discuss teaching performance. As the discussion proceeds, and the student confronts new representations of his or her classroom practice, he or she is faced with a new task. The supervisor must, as Schön would say, *reframe* the problematic situation:

> The teacher [supervisor], who attributes the student's predicament to his way of framing the problem, tries to make sense of the problematic situation he is encountering at second hand. The situation is complex and uncertain, and there is a problem in finding the problem.

> Because each practitioner treats his case as unique, he cannot deal with it by applying standard theories or techniques. He must construct an understanding of the situation as he finds it. And because he finds the situation problematic, he must reframe it.

> (*ibid.*, p. 129)

The second element of reflection-in-action consists of experiment, played out to discover what consequences and implications can be made to follow from the reframed problem:

> In order to see what can be made to follow from this reframing of the situation, each practitioner tries to adapt the situation to the frame. This he does through a web of moves. Within the larger web, individual moves yield phenomena to be understood, problems to be solved, or opportunities to be exploited.

> (*ibid.*, p. 131)

Finally, reflection-in-action involves a reflexive interchange between the practitioner and the situation:

> But the practitioner's moves also produce unintended changes which give the situation new meanings. The situation talks back, the practitioner listens, and as he appreciates what he hears, he reframes the situation once again.

> (*ibid.*, pp. 131–2)

Schön's conceptions of problem setting and reframing are particularly useful when taken to the context of preservice teacher education. It is reasonable to suspect that through reflection methods students will come to new understandings of the effects of their teaching practice, and that the moves made in doing so match the elements of Schön's conception.

The process of supervision could be said to involve a three-way 'reflective conversation' among the teacher, the record of his or her teaching, and the supervisor. Schön speaks of the reflective process as being cyclic in character; it uncovers new understandings of events, which in turn, fuel further reflection:

> In this reflective conversation, the practitioner's effort to solve the reframed problem yields new discoveries which call for new reflection-in-action. The

process spirals through stages of appreciation, action, and reappreciation. The unique and uncertain situation comes to be understood through the attempt to change it, and changed through the attempt to understand it.

(ibid., p. 132)

Beyond the matter of coming to appreciate and understand events in a 'new light', the reflective practitioner engages in moves that have to do with the choice of action that will be taken. These moves comprise the rigour of the practitioner's 'on-the-spot experimenting':

When the practitioner sees a new situation as some element of his repertoire, he gets a new way of seeing it and a new possibility for action in it, but the adequacy and utility of this new view must still be discovered in action. Reflection-in-action necessarily involves experiment.

(ibid., p. 141)

While the experimental aspect of reflection-in-action is recognized as being integral to the day-to-day work of practitioners, the present paper focuses on *problem setting* and *reframing*. These are the categories that address the epistemological features of 'seeing' possibilities for action in practical situations. By definition, problem setting and reframing are the beginning points of reflection-in-action.

To summarize Schön's conception of reflection-in-action, it is worth noting the characteristics that markedly distinguish it from the traditional view of professional knowledge. Schön draws our attention to the dichotomies on which Technical Rationality rests: the separation of means from ends, of research from practice, and of knowledge from doing. According to the model of reflection-in-action, practice *is* a kind of research. In their problem setting, practitioners frame the means and ends of their action interdependently; what they do in certain situations depends on what they 'see' in those situations, namely the practical problems that they set and frame.

METHODOLOGY

The task pursued next is to demonstrate the linkage between Schön's theoretical perspective and actual events in the clinical supervision of methods students. This has entailed developing and assessing a 'clue structure' for detecting reflective activity on the part of methods students as they examine their own teaching performances. Before presenting the clue structure and demonstrating its use, it is appropriate to elaborate upon the methodology utilized in the analysis of data.

Initially, the data for this study consisted of transcriptions of five lessons that were taught by methods students, along with the discussion of those lessons that ensued between the investigator (clinical supervisor) and each person who taught. The data were collected in late October and early November of 1984 during the latter part of the methods course, just prior to the students' first practicum.

The analysis of the data was modelled after an approach put forward by Roberts and Russell (1975) which draws on 'informal philosophical analysis' (Kneller, 1966) to examine practice. Informal philosophical analysis is concerned with systematic conceptualization of terms employed to discuss important events in practice, and it is grounded in a demonstrable linkage between theoretical perspectives and issues of everyday life. Thus, in educational research, informal philosophical analysis is rooted in the events of educational practice itself, and indeed the products of informal analysis may comprise the bases from which implications for educational practice may be derived. The Roberts/Russell approach first draws on a systematic theoretical perspective as the source of an 'analytical scheme', or set of categories for the analysis, and then proceeds to develop a 'clue structure', that is a set of criteria for identifying instances of events.

Development of the analytical scheme

The analytical scheme was developed theoretically from two of Schön's categories: *problem setting* and *reframing*. Problem setting, in summary, is the process by which the practitioner identifies the problematic phenomenon of the situation to which he or she will attend, and frames the context in which he or she will attend to it. Reframing is 'seeing' in the situation new particulars that gave rise to new understandings of the problematic phenomenon, as well as new possibilities for action in the situation.

When shifted from Schön's contexts (architecture, psychiatry, and town planning) to the present context of teacher education, the initial theoretically derived analytical scheme required refinement. Two categories, adapted from Fuller and Brown's (1975) developmental conceptualization of teacher concerns, were added to Schön's two categories: (1) the notion that in becoming a teacher, education students learn to interpret classroom events from pupil-centred perspectives, rather than perspectives that are teacher-centred, and (2) the point that preservice teachers rely on personal experience as a student to assist them in assembling meaning from these pupil-centred perspectives.

Development of the clue structure

Upon inspection of the data, it was clear that 'acts of reflection' (consistent with Schön's theoretical formulation) had to be distinguished from 'acts of rationalization' on the part of the methods students. The latter consist of moves undertaken to justify, or defend, a particular teaching behaviour. Acts of rationalization were common to all five of the methods students, particularly during the initial stages of discussion about their teaching performances. Acts of reflection are very different in nature. They involve moves undertaken to play out the implications derived from various perspectives, or theoretical lenses, employed to make sense of the methods students' teaching experience.

Acts of reflection were seen to occur in three phases, which may collectively be referred to as a 'cycle of reflection'. As the data were analysed, the cycle of reflection became more and more evident in the supervisory dialogue and, eventually, the conceptualization of the reflective cycle served as the basis from which the clue structure was developed.

The reflective cycle was conceptualized, in the main, to deal with repeating patterns of 'negotiation about practice' that can be seen in clinical supervision dialogue. The cycle consists of three phases, which are quite distinct in character, but which lead into one another in a regular fashion. It should be made clear that these phases are analytic devices, and that therefore they do not always occur in groups of three and only once in a cycle. They are qualitatively different components of reflection in clinical supervision discussion.

Phase I – initial problem setting

In Phase I of the cycle an 'initial problem' is constructed from the preliminary analysis of a teaching episode. The problem will usually be shaped and somewhat changed by the end of the cycle, thus the qualifier 'initial'. The teacher or the supervisor can begin this phase by calling to attention certain aspects of the teaching, or of the classroom events more generally, which are problematic. When the problematic phenomenon is articulated by the teacher, self-concerns are sometimes exposed in the process. However, this is more evident at the beginning of the supervisory discussion. The framing of the initial problem allows the teacher to formulate a *conclusion* (1) about the problematic phenomenon, as well as an *implication* (1) for future practice. This sets the discussion up for the second phase of the reflective cycle. (The significance of the designation '(1)' is to mark the conclusion and implication as initial.)

Phase II – reframing

In this phase, the problematic phenomenon is re-examined from one, or perhaps several theoretical platforms. Reframing does not usually occur only once, but several times. Often, counter examples are constructed and contrasted to the problematic phenomenon. In addition, there is usually a shift from teacher-centred interpretations of classroom events, to interpretations that are pupil-centred. As the consequences of certain pupil interpretations are played out, the teacher is sometimes requested to reflect on his or her personal experience as a student to help make sense of the pupils' perspectives. Sometimes the supervisor offers anecdotes from personal experience to make a point. The result of the reframing process is a deeper understanding of the problematic phenomenon, based on the insights derived from the alternative perspectives and theoretical platforms used to examine it.

Phase III – resolve

The resolve is the product of all the work done in phase two. A new *conclusion* (2) about the problematic phenomenon is formulated, and a new *implication* (2) is often derived.

The reflective cycle occurs within an 'episode' of dialogue, which is that portion of the discussion devoted to a particular topic, such as classroom management, pacing, questioning, or an incident in the lesson.

The clue structure

The clue structure for detecting reflective activity in supervisory dialogue has been crafted from the concept of the reflective cycle and refined through repeated application to the data. There are four clues, which are stated here in the form of questions:

> *Clue 1:* Can the phases of the reflective cycle be 'seen' in the dialogue? *Is there a period of reframing activity?*
> *Clue 2:* Is there evidence of a change in the perspective from which a classroom phenomenon is viewed? Specifically, *does the teacher make a shift from using teacher-centred to using student-centred interpretations of the classroom event?*
> *Clue 3:* Does reframing result in a change in the conclusions about the problematic phenomenon or in the implications that are derived for practice? That is, *is there a change in the 'I should haves'?*
> *Clue 4:* In the course of reframing, does the teacher draw from his or her personal experience as a student to make sense of the pupil's position?

ANALYSIS: USING THE CLUE STRUCTURE

Excerpts of a clinical supervision discussion with Wendy are presented to show how the clue structure was applied and tested. First, it will be useful to look into the introduction of Wendy's lesson, which she taught to a class of grade five–six students in an elementary school. The lesson, which dealt with environmental factors, began with a review of the previous day's activity when the elementary students conducted an experiment to determine what type of light conditions isopods prefer:

3 Teacher: Okay, I see you've already been peeking in there. That's part of our project (refers to the buckets of pond water). That's all right. You've been looking at environmental factors I've been told. Does anyone want to tell me what an environmental factor is? Yes?

4 Student: Air pollution.

5 Teacher: Air pollution, okay.

6 Student: Water pollution.

7 Teacher: Sorry?

8 Student: Water pollution.

9 Teacher: Water pollution, okay, I think you were perhaps using isopods. Were you working with isopods? What sort of environmental factors did you find? Yes, Harry?

10 Harry: That they like going to corners and, usually, dim parts of the runway.

11 Teacher: So what's the environmental factor?
12 Harry: That they like going to dim parts.
13 Teacher: The dim parts. Yes?
14 Student: Isopods prefer finer sand and dimmer parts.
15 Teacher: Uhmm uhmm. Anything else?
16 Students: (silence)
17 Teacher: Would there be any other environmental factors that you can think of? No? Is there anything else here Tom?
18 Tom: Uhmm, well . . . the babies aren't used to the dim light and so they move to the light. And . . . I don't know.
19 Teacher: Anything else? No? Okay, we're going to look at environmental factors in a little bit different way.

The clinical discussion about the introduction of the lesson is presented next in order to display for the reader how the clue structure is used to detect the three phases of the reflective cycle and reflective activity in the supervisory dialogue. The dialogue is broken up into segments to allow for analytical comments to be made in the text (T = (Teacher) Wendy, C = Clinical Supervisor):

39 C: Okay, well let's begin just where you begin speaking here on page (85), #3. The kids were peeking in the buckets just while Mr. X was introducing you, is that right? Did you want to read out loud, or would you like me to?

40 T: Whatever.

41 C: Okay, 'I see you've already been peeking in there . . . that's part of our project. That's all right. You've been looking at environmental factors I've been told. Does anyone want to tell me what an environmental factor is? Yes?' And the student says, 'Air pollution.' And you say, 'Air pollution, Okay.' And another student says, 'Water pollution.' 'Sorry?' 'Water pollution.' 'Water pollution, Okay. I think you were perhaps using isopods. Were you working with isopods? What sort of environmental factors did you find? Yes Harry?' 'That they like going to corners and dim parts of the runway.' 'So what was the environmental factor?' 'That they like to go to the dim parts.' 'The dim parts. Yes?' Does anything cross your mind yet?

42 T: Do you want me just to cut in on you as you're going along?

43 C: Yes.

Reflective cycle: Phase 1 – initial problem setting

44 T: Okay. Well the first thing I notice is that I say 'Okay' far too often . . . which I wasn't aware of. But when I started this, I was very unsure how to open the lesson. How to . . . other than just say, 'You've been talking about environmental factors', I really didn't feel that I had a good opening line. And I find this all the way through. Like, I wasn't listening all that closely to what the kids were saying. Like, my response to them . . . I *was* listening to them, but I didn't respond in that manner.

45 C: Why do you say that?

46 T: Well, there's one instance that I noticed later on when I cut in on a

student as he was talking. But that was when he had answered with exactly what I was looking for.

47   C: And you got excited.

48   T: Yes. But I found I was repeating the students' answers quite a bit. Now, whether that's wrong or right, *I thought I should have tried to get the kids to say a little bit more.*

49   C: Why would you want to do that?

50   T: To clarify their meaning to both myself and the rest of the class, and try to see why they were coming up with those answers.

51   C: Now, can you see an example here on the page that would illustrate that?

52   Well, Okay, with these first two – air pollution and water pollution – I understood where they were coming from, but whether the rest of the class did or not . . . And that wasn't what I was looking for; that's why I brought up isopods.

53   C: Oh I see. So 'air pollution' and 'water pollution' really didn't . . . really weren't examples of environmental factors?

54   T: They weren't the ones I was looking for. I wanted to get them on to thinking about the light, and what they had been doing with isopods.

55   C: Did air pollution and water pollution, given as examples of an environmental factor, satisfy what you expected them to know about the word, or the term 'environmental factor'?

56   T: I didn't expect them to come out with things like that.

57   C: Yes, neither did I.

58   T: I found that several times throughout this . . . that they had a lot more knowledge than what I would have expected them to have at that stage.

59   C: Was that scary for you?

60   T: Yes, definitely.

61   C: I guess on the one hand you want them to tell you what they know, but you want to be able to handle it at the same time.

62   T: That's right.

63   C: And to sort of shape it into the meaning you want. Okay.

64   T: Again, I can see some of this causing me to be uneasy because I didn't know what they'd covered already, or what they'd had previously.

65   C: Sure. Actually, right now in terms of your development, you know very little about kids compared to what you will know about them.

66   T: As far as what they learn in school. Also, down here where the one fellow said that the isopods like to go to the dim parts, I think in that case . . . because that was pretty close to what we are looking for, *I should have gotten him to give a little bit more than that.*

67   C: How could you have done that?

68   T: Right now I honestly don't know. Perhaps get him to explain it in a different way or . . .

69   C: Okay.

This first portion of the dialogue illustrates *Phase I* of the reflective cycle – the *initial problem setting.* First, in utterance 44, Wendy *Frames the problematic phenomenon:*

Like, I wasn't listening all that closely to what the kids were saying. Like, my response to them . . . I *was* listening to them, but I didn't respond in that manner.

Second, Wendy's initial view leads her to name an *implication* (1) for practice in utterance 48, and again in utterance 66:

. . . I thought I should have tried to get the kids to say a little bit more.

Finally, in utterance 54, Wendy states her *conclusion* (1) about the problematic phenomenon, namely, that the students did not supply the examples of environmental factors that she was looking for.

Reflective cycle: Phase II – reframing activity

Now let us return to the discussion of the lesson, which moves into *Phase II* of the reflective cycle – the *reframing activity*:

70 T: On page (86), #12.
71 C: Right. I'm just looking up into the discourse that happens just before that point. To just briefly summarize it, you ask for examples of environmental factors, probably to get to their understanding of the term or the concept. And they give you things that you weren't expecting . . . and you go with flow. 'Air pollution, Okay.' Someone else says 'Water pollution.' Do you see what I mean? And then you make an adjustment . . .
72 T: To get them back on track.
73 C: To get them back on track. So, 'I think you were perhaps using isopods. Were you working with isopods?' They must have nodded their heads, right? 'What sort of environmental factors did you find? Yes, Harry?' So we're back on to environmental factors and isopods, in the context of isopods, and we're looking for light, moisture, temperature and things like that.
74 T: Actually just light. They hadn't done the other two.
75 C: Okay. 'They like going to the corners and usually the dim parts of the runway.' Well, I suppose what he said isn't really an environmental factor is it?
76 T: No. I was trying to get him to tell me . . . not where they had gone, but . . .
77 C: But to just use the word 'light'. And so what's wrong with what you did? 'So what's the environmental factor?'
78 T: And he just repeated what he had said before, basically. Except he did shorten it. I suppose I was still concerned at that time . . . I was still very nervous at that time and I was trying to get him to say 'light' and nothing else, sort of thing.
79 C: Well, you see it's not as bad as you think . . . I don't think. He's talking about their activity and you want him to say 'light'. 'So what was the environmental factor?' You're focusing him in and then he repeats the same thing.

In the passage above, the supervisor has introduced Wendy to a different way of viewing the problematic phenomenon. Although he does not explicate the difference, he judges the teaching performance in the introduction of the lesson favourably. This he does by focusing, in utterance 77, on Wendy's question, 'So what's the environmental factor?' He bases his judgement on the intention of the question, namely to have the student identify the environmental factor as 'light'.

Reflective cycle: Phase III – the resolve

The reframing activity continues later on in this episode, but in the next short passage, Wendy moves directly into *Phase III* of the cycle – the *resolve*:

80   T: Well, actually, when he answers he does say that they like to go to the dim parts, so . . . seeing it now like . . . *he has picked out what I was looking for.*

81   C: Okay. (pause). And things continue to flow along quite nicely. You're shaping the ideas. I think, quite nicely. 'Teacher: the dim parts. Yes?' And then, 'Isopods prefer finer sand and dimmer parts.' And then the 'Anything else?', and silence after that. How do you read that?

82   T: (pause) I don't remember from the actual time. Uh. . . .

83   C: It was sort of like . . . that was it. They'd given you everything that they had. 'Would there be other environmental factors that you could think of?' Tom says. 'Well the babies aren't used to the dim light and so they move to the light. And I don't know . . .'

84   T: *I actually think I should have left it the way it was instead of, you know, kept pushing for something else . . . for them to say, 'light' and nothing else.* And I think that's . . . from my understanding in looking at it now . . . that's what I was doing. I didn't accept what they said about going to the dim parts. I wanted them to explicitly say 'light' and nothing else.

In this portion of the discussion, Wendy has formulated a new *conclusion* (2) about the problematic phenomenon in utterance 80, as well as a new *implication* (2) for practice in utterance 84. This does not necessarily mean that she has used the supervisor's frame (utterance 77) to do so, but rather that the supervisor's reframing has triggered Wendy's own reframing of the problematic phomenon.

Thus far, the analysis of the supervisory dialogue has illustrated the use of *Clue* 1 and *Clue* 3 of the Clue Structure: That is, the three phases of the reflective cycle are evident in the dialogue (Clue 1), and there is a change in Wendy's 'I should haves' (Clue 3). The remaining two clues will be illustrated in the final proportion of discussion in this episode, which begins with the supervisor resuming the reframing activity:

85   C: Well do you think that you pushed them too hard?

86   T: Actually I don't think so, no. Because they didn't . . . they didn't react badly to it or anything. They were still all with me and everything at the time, so . . .

87   C: Do you think that it's important to push them a little bit?

88 T: In some cases, yes.

89 C: Well, you want to deliver sort of a challenge, don't you? Give them something to do and have a worthwhile purpose for them doing it? I don't know if they'd like it very much if you gave them all the answers.

90 T: No, no. Certainly not. I can see that.

91 C: In fact, that might really backfire, you know. If you were to give them all the answers.

92 T: It would be boring for them.

93 C: Let them off the hook a little too easily. What do you think would happen?

94 T: I think they'd get distracted very easily. They wouldn't, on their own . . . they wouldn't develop because children usually have that curiosity for starters . . . it's teachers who end up stifling it in them. That's my personal opinion, however.

95 C: What makes you say that?

96 T: Why do I say that?

97 C: Your own experience?

98 T: My own experience, yes.

99 C: What happened?

100 T: Nothing in particular that I can remember, but I know that I was very enthusiastic when I started school, and I was until about junior high.

101 C: Uhmm, uhmm.

102 T: And then I had a lot of old teachers who really didn't care what you were doing . . . and . . . I used to get away with a few tricks . . . you know, you'd hand in an assignment with the middle part missing out of it and they'd never notice.

103 C: Oh heck. Gee whiz.

104 T: And I found that they weren't interested in what you were doing. They had their list of what to get through and that was it. And they really didn't care how they did it. That sort of really turned me off for a while.

105 C: They didn't challenge you.

106 T: No, not at all.

In this passage, the supervisor began the reframing activity with Wendy's *implication* (2), which she stated in utterance 84. There she said that she should not have 'pushed' the students to say 'light' and nothing else. The supervisor's frame had to do with challenging students, and he equated this with the 'pushing' metaphor. Wendy reflected on her own personal experience as a student in order to support her claim that when teachers do not challenge, they end up stifling children's curiosity. The passage thus illustrates the use of *Clue* 4 (reflecting on personal experience as a student). Let us now return to the discussion for the remainder of the dialogue concerning the introduction to Wendy's lesson:

107 C: Okay, well I like what you're doing here . . . pushing them a bit. And to be honest with you, that . . . you know that your questioning technique is quite clear . . . I think the questions are clearly delivered.

And when something isn't quite right, and you want to communicate that you're pushing . . . that comes across quite clearly to kids. I think due to the evidence we have here. They are actually satisfying your push. Do you know what I mean?

108 T: Uhmm, uhmm.

109 C: A lot of times beginning teachers have problems with questions. They find that their questions aren't explicit enough . . . that the meaning of the question is slightly ambiguous, and the kids struggle to find out what it is that the teacher wants. And so quite often you'll find that a beginning teacher will ask a question and then there's silence. Nobody knows what he wants. So he repeats it in a different way . . . see? Well, that's not really happening as far as I can see anyway in this first part.

110 T: Is that a bad thing to do though?

111 C: To rephrase? Well it's not a bad thing to do . . . I think it's a good thing to realize that the question has been ambiguous . . . in which case it's an excellent thing to do . . . rephrase the question. But I think it's better if you can anticipate . . .

112 T: And avoid that for starters.

113 C: And avoid that, yes. But I don't see a problem with your questioning here. Perhaps you'll want to keep that in mind and raise something later on if you want.

114 T: Okay.

115 C: Let's just continue then. 'Anything else? No? Okay, we're going to look at environmental factors in a little bit different way.' Now the lesson sort of shifts here doesn't it?

116 T: Uhmm, uhmm. That was the beginning of my introduction . . . what I was going to be going into.

117 C: So, in the terms we've used in class, you've done your 'hook' – you've hooked up to what the kids have done previously in class. So you have them set for the lesson, right? Now, you were wondering a minute ago about your opening statement . . . 'You've been looking at environmental factors, I've been told.' Well, this whole little episode has occurred in 20 or 30 seconds . . . somewhere in there. And I think it's a nice little link . . . they're hooked right into the frame of mind that they left their last class with. And now you're ready to begin. I guess what I mean to say is that *perhaps it would be more useful to think of the entire piece of talk and how it functions, rather than just your opening comment. Okay?*

118 T: The whole introduction then.

119 C: Right, the train of thought. But let me just get this straight. When you began the introduction to this lesson, were you satisfied that the kids knew what an environmental factor is?

120 T: Yes.

The discussion moved on to another portion of Wendy's lesson at this point, thus the cycle of reflection dealing with the lesson introduction came to a close. The use of *Clue* 2 can now be illustrated by reviewing some of Wendy's utterances that occurred along the way. Clue 2 is concerned with whether there is evidence in the discussion that the teacher shifts from using teacher-centred to using student-centred interpretations of classroom events. In this cycle of reflection Wendy did make such a shift in regard to her views about students 'getting the point'. First, from the teacher-centred interpretation, Wendy's conclusion was that the students did not get the point. Notice, again, utterance 66 from Phase I of the cycle:

> . . . Also, down here where the one fellow said that the isopods like to go to the dim parts, I think in that case . . . because that was pretty close to what we were looking for, I should have gotten him to say a little bit more on that.

Later, in Phase III of the cycle, Wendy achieves a new interpretation (utterances 80 and 84):

> Well, actually, when he answers he does say that they like going to the dim parts, so . . . seeing it now . . . he has picked out what I was looking for.

> I actually think I should have left it the way it was instead of, you know, kept pushing for something else . . . for them to say 'light' and nothing else. And I think that's . . . from my understanding of it now . . . that's what I was doing. I didn't accept what they said about going to the dim parts. I wanted them to explicitly say 'light' and nothing else.

Finally, at the end of the episode (utterance 120) when the supervisor asked Wendy if she was satisfied that the students knew what an environmental factor is, she said, 'Yes.' These data suggest that Wendy has achieved her new view by shifting to the pupils' perspective in her interpretation of classroom events.

CONCLUSIONS

This study began with concerns about the experiences of preservice teachers in an elementary science methods course. It was argued that there is a need in the methods course for (1) practical teaching exercises that might better operationalize the blend of theory and practice, and (2) a way of conceptualizing how methods students make sense of such exercises. A central theme of the latter has been the movement made by beginning teachers in their interpretation of classroom events from teacher-centred perspectives to perspectives that are pupil centred. Schön's formulation of reflection-in-action has been engaged to conceptualize the shift of perspective that can be seen in a clinical supervision context.

The development of professional competence in teaching is seen by this investigator to be related in part to the habit of reflecting on practice. The habit of reflecting on practice is, in turn, marked by a willingness to examine and re-examine teaching experience from a variety of perspectives and theoretical platforms; it is not the case that the practice of teaching can be informed by one 'right' perspective, or by an overarching theoretical stance. Thus, the 'hidden curriculum' of the clinical supervision of methods students might be seen as provoking the habit of reframing classroom phenomena, particularly from plausible pupil-centred perspectives.

The analysis has led to several conclusions. Generally, Schön's ideas regarding reflection-in-action provide a useful way to interpret how preservice teachers make sense of their early teaching performances. One of the underlying themes of the study is that reflection should not be confused with rationalization. *Problem setting* and *reframing* are the categories that alert us to what reflection looks like. Furthermore, the concept of the reflective cycle, which focuses Schön's ideas on the context of teacher education, together with the clue structure presented for detecting reflection-in-action, provides a way of thinking about reflection among beginning teachers. The analysis of the data shows that problem setting and reframing (Phase I and Phase II of the cycle of reflection) *can* be seen to occur in the discussion with Wendy. The claims are (1) that the clues are faithful to Schön's work, (2) that they do, indeed, detect reflection in clinical supervision dialogue, (3) that the concept of the reflective cycle and its associated clue structure are applicable and appropriate to studying reflection among preservice teachers, and (4) that preservice teachers *can* reflect, given the proper situation (in particular, the occasion to teach, the transcript and the supervisor). The conceptualization of the reflective cycle, then, together with the clue structure for detecting reflection in clinical supervision dialogue, is put forward here as a way to provoke and to study reflection-in-action on the part of methods students engaged in the clinical analysis of their own teaching.

REFERENCES

Fuller, F. F. (1969) Concerns of teachers: A developmental conceptualization. *American Educational Research Journal*, Vol. 6, pp. 207–226.

Fuller, F. F., and Brown, O. H. (1975) Becoming a teacher. In K. Ryan (ed.), *Teacher Education* (pp. 25–52). National Society for the Study of Education, 74th Yearbook, Part II. Chicago, University of Chicago Press.

Kneller, G. F. (1966) *Logic and Language of Education*. New York, John Wiley.

MacKinnon, A. (1985) Detecting reflection-in-action among preservice teachers enrolled in an elementary science methods course. Unpublished master's thesis, University of Calgary, Calgary, Alberta.

Roberts, D. A., and Russell, T. L. (1975) An alternative approach to science education research: Drawing from philosophical analysis to examine practice. *Curriculum Theory Networks*, Vol. 5, pp. 107–125.

Schön, D. (1983). *The Reflective Practitioner: How Professionals Think in Action*. New York, Basic Books.

2.3

The importance of reflection in improving science teaching and learning

John R. Baird, Peter J. Fensham, Richard F. Gunstone
and Richard T. White

INTRODUCTION, NATURE AND PURPOSES OF THE STUDY

This is a three-year naturalistic case study of educational improvements through individual and group change. Teachers, students, and academics joined to research ways of improving the quality of teaching and learning in science classrooms. The main participants were 13 student science teachers, 14 novice and experienced science teachers, 64 science students from grades 8 through 11, and the authors. The three major aims were:

(1) **Teachers and teaching/learners and learning**
    To know more about what it is to be a teacher of science and a learner of science, and the mechanisms that underlie science teaching and learning.
(2) **Change**
    To know more about the processes by which individuals change with experience. Particularly, to explore the effects of a change whereby teachers and students assume greater personal awareness, responsibility, and control over their practice.
(3) **Facilitating change**
    To know more about appropriate and productive research methodologies for exploring Aim 1 and facilitating Aim 2.

First we describe the conceptual bases of the study, in which we emphasize the central role of reflection in determining its design, execution, and outcomes. Then follow findings that we obtained from the preservice and in-service components of the study using two major types of reflection – reflection on practice and phenomenological reflection.

Finally, the results of the study are interpreted in terms of the cognitive, metacognitive, and affective development of the participants.

[For the purposes of this article we are focusing on experienced science teachers.]

Abridged from *Journal of Research in Science Teaching* (1991) Vol. 28, no. 2, pp. 163–182.

CONCEPTUAL BASES OF THE STUDY

Three major fields of theory and research relevant to science teaching and learning are metacognition, constructivism, and the nature of individual change. Work of the past decade shows how closely these fields are related.

Metacognition refers to a person's *knowledge* of the nature of learning, effective learning strategies, and his/her own learning strengths and weaknesses; *awareness* of the nature and progress of the current learning task (i.e., what you are doing and why you are doing it); and *control* over learning through informed and purposeful decision making. Early studies attempted to promote metacognition in reading (e.g., Brown, 1980). Later ones showed that metacognition could be achieved in science classrooms, and resulted in improved cognitive and affective outcomes (e.g., Baird, 1986). Better metacognition, however, did not occur easily. Students and their teacher all had to expend time and effort on personal intellectual development. They needed support from the researcher to maintain their effort and to reach their goal.

In the same period as the studies of metacognition, researchers in many countries probed individuals' conceptions of scientific concepts and phenomena and found that ideas contrary to those of scientists were common (White and Tisher, 1986). Further, these alternative conceptions resisted attempts to change them (Champagne, Gunstone, and Klopfer, 1985; Gauld, 1986). The attempts indicated that time, effort, and support are three necessities for change.

The efforts to change students' beliefs brought out clearer understandings of the role of personal change in the improvement of science teaching and learning. A key notion to emerge is that individual learners construct their own understandings of concepts, principles, phenomena, and situations. Existing beliefs and attitudes influence strongly the constructed meaning. Osborne and Wittrock (1985) and White (1988) describe constructivism and conceptual change more fully.

The present study developed from our realization that constructivism complements metacognition in effecting personal change. Adequate metacognition empowers the learner to undertake the constructivist processes of recognition, evaluation, and revision of personal views. Hence we inferred that one reason for the lack of success in attempts to bring out conceptual change is that the strategies paid insufficient attention to assisting the learners to become sufficiently metacognitive for them to control the nature and direction of change.

Most prior studies of metacognition or of conceptual change refer to changes in students. They do not consider or report changes that may occur, or may be necessary, in the teachers. An exception that had a strong influence on the present study is the Project for Enhancing Effective Learning (Baird and Mitchell, 1986). In this long-running naturalistic case study, teachers and students studied ways by which students can assume more responsibility for and control over their learning. The study showed that changes in the metacognition of students could occur only after changes in the teachers' attitudes, perceptions, conceptions, and abilities; that is, development of teachers' meta-cognition must precede that of their students. A second insight gained from this study is that a method of collaborative action research is effective in promoting teachers' intellectual development (Baird, Mitchell, and Northfield, 1987). The method requires different types of participants (teachers and academic consultants) to bring different perspectives and skills to the combined group. Through discussion, the group generates tentative principles of theory and methods of practice that possess face validity from both perspectives. The participants decide on actions, then document and reflect on outcomes. The procedure supports change by the sharing of the endeavour.

The studies of metacognition and conceptual change, and the insights from the Project for Enhancing Effective Learning, led us to adopt an integrative perspective on change. The perspective includes a holistic approach to the study of individuals, research based on personal and professional reflection, and convergence of process and outcomes in teaching and learning.

A holistic approach follows from the perception that metacognition and construction of meaning are intertwined. The meaning that any learner derives from a lesson depends on a number of factors: the person's attitudinal state; perception of the nature, purpose and progress of the lesson; existing knowledge; and decisions about what to do as learning proceeds. Attitudes, abilities, and knowledge are all involved in the processing of information. To attend to only one of these aspects would be to cripple the study.

Similarly, we needed to attend to personal reflection as well as professional. Most action research involves reflection on practice (Elliott, 1988). It is tied to the specifics of classroom content and context. Though that is valuable, we sought a more complete picture of the development of teachers, so we planned to complement it with personal reflection – in which the individual concentrates on his/her more general life experiences as a teacher, learner, or researcher. Van Manen (1984) describes this type of phenomenological reflection.

The need to study processes and outcomes of teaching and learning together follows from our perceptions that teacher change precedes student change and that metacognition is linked with the construction of meaning and with conceptual change. Just as we should consider each learner holistically, so we should look at the processes and outcomes of teaching and learning together.

The integrative perspective on change, which we formed from considering the research on metacognition and conceptual change and particularly from the insights derived from the Project for Enhancing Effective Learning, directed the style of our investigation of the three major aims. We used collaborative action research, placing a strong emphasis on personal and professional reflection, with three groups: one of student teachers with the academics training them, a subset of that group (in subsequent years) as they began full-time teaching, and some experienced science teachers with their pupils.

The holistic principle and knowledge that metacognitive development takes time meant that the work with the three groups would go on for months.

Therefore we were committed to convenience rather than random samples. We had access to 13 student teachers who were about to begin a year of preservice training in education. All had science degrees. Two of their teacher educators were included in the study. Together the student teachers and the teacher educators would engage in continual guided reflection of both types – phenomenological reflection and reflection on practice. This group constituted the first component of the study: reflection during preservice training of science teachers. The second component relates to the induction and in-service phases of teaching. During their first two years of full-time teaching, three members of the student teacher group continued the collaborative reflection begun in the first component. The second component also involved 11 practising science teachers in three schools who collaborated with the authors for more than two years of phenomenological reflection and action research.

School students were important contributors to the second component of the study. Their numbers varied across the three years covered by the study, but in the middle year there were more than 300 students (in grades 7 through 11) who participated in classroom action research on ways of improving their interest, enjoyment, and understanding in science, while 64 students from grades 8 through 11 collaborated more intensively by joining in protracted and systematic phenomenological reflection.

Both strands of research – phenomenological and action research – employed a variety of data-gathering procedures appropriate to naturalistic interpretive research. The teachers kept diaries, completed periodic written evaluations, and entered into regular interviews and discussions about collaborative research. The students completed written evaluations and questionnaires. They also participated in classroom discussions and regular individual and small-group interviews. Although the major responsibility remained with the teachers, the authors shared the planning of lessons. They also observed and audiotaped classroom interactions and participated in teacher group meetings to review progress and findings.

The authors checked both their interpretations of events and their conclusions with the teachers and the students. In such extensive and subjective research such triangulation is essential. [. . .]

RESULTS AND INTERPRETATION: SCHOOL SCIENCE TEACHING AND LEARNING

Earlier, we asserted that progress towards the three project aims required two strands of research, both based on reflection. Whereas the preservice component of the study centred mainly on phenomenological reflection, in the induction and in-service component we encouraged participants to engage in reflection on practice as well. The practising teachers' reflection of both types deepened over the first two years of the project. In the second year, school students became participants in the phenomenological research, and important collaborators in joint research on classroom practice.

CONFIDENTIAL - DO NOT GIVE YOUR NAME

We would like you to consider <u>today's lesson in science</u>, and answer the following questions.

1. What did you do? (that is what <u>the topic</u> that you were learning [teaching]?)

2. Why were you doing this topic?

3. How did you go about learning [teaching] this topic? (i.e. what <u>activities</u> did you do in order to learn [teach] it?

4. How well did the lesson go: (Answer 'yes' or 'no', and give reason).

    (a) Was it successful - did you [the students] understand the work.

    (b) Was it clear [to them]?

    (c) Was it an enjoyable lesson [for them]?

Figure I   Questions asked of students and, in brackets, teachers, on the response form, three lesson trialling

Some findings regarding reflection on practice as part of on-going classroom action research

Of the various aspects of the reflection on practice over the first two years of the project, we have selected for mention only three episodes which relate to collaboration between teacher and students in reflecting on, and acting to improve the quality of, teaching and learning in science classrooms.

The first episode, entitled a 'three lesson trialling' of shared reflection on classroom practice, occurred in the project's first year. Baird et al. (1989) describe the detail of this procedure more fully, but it involved the teacher, each student, and a participant observer (consultant) independently preparing written responses to the four questions shown in Figure 1, near the end of each of a sequence of three typical science lessons.

The consultant collated the students' responses and presented the collated data to the teacher. The teacher and consultant then explored similarities and differences between the teacher's and students' perceptions of the 'what', 'why', 'how', and 'how well' of the lesson. Subsequently, teachers wrote answers in their diaries to the questions 'Was the trialling a successful learning experience for me?' and 'Is the procedure an acceptable and appropriate research method for teachers?' This procedure was adopted by 11 of the project teachers with their science classes, which ranged from grades 8 to 11.

While the teachers and the consultant derived numerous benefits from the procedure, it proved rather unsettling for the teachers. In the words of one teacher, it was 'another humbling experience'. Many students seemed to have little idea of the answers to such questions as 'Why were you doing the topic?',

What I think of science

Question 1   What did you learn about in science over the last week?

About Ferns, Algae, Lichens, and plantlife.

Question 2   Consider your science lessons over the last week.

		A lot	A bit	Not much	Not at all
(a)	How much did you **look forward** to your science lessons?		✓		
(b)	How much did you **enjoy** them?		✓		
(c)	How **interesting** was the work you did?	✓			
(d)	How **hard** did you work?		✓		
(e)	How much did you **understand** of what you were doing and why you were doing it?	✓			
(f)	How much do you **like** your teacher?	✓			
(g)	How **important** is the work you did for you and your future?		✓		
(h)	How much did you **think carefully** about what you were doing?			✓	

Figure 2   One grade-8 student's completed 'shared perceptions' form (student version)

Question 3

(a) What was the **best** thing about science lessons last week?

We could go outside to study plants and didn't have to stay in the classroom all that much.

(b) Why do you think this?

Because somtimes it gets boring just sitting at a desk listening to a teacher tell you about it. This way you can find out for yourself.

Question 4

(a) What was the **worst** thing about science lessons last week?

Having to draw all the different types of algae etc.

(b) Why do you think this?

Because we were only see what they look like not finding out what parts of the plant were which eg leaves roots etc.

Question 5

(a) Do you think Mr.   is teaching science well?

yes

(b) Why do you think this?

Because he lets us work by ourseules and dosen't interrupt while we are working. Also if we ask him a question he will always answer it so we understand it.

Question 6

(a) Do you think you are learning science well?

yes

(b) Why do you think this?

Because I can mostly understand what is being taught.

Figure 2   continued

and their ratings for question 4 (see Figure 1) were often quite negative. Also, there was often considerable disparity between the teacher, consultant, and student responses to questions 1, 2 and 3. However, all the teachers valued the experience. They believed that it had made them reflect more deeply about their practice, and that this enhanced reflection had led to positive change in their classroom attitudes, awareness, and actions. A few representative teacher responses were:

> I found talking about the lesson afterwards was valuable. It pointed out to me that the kids should know why they are doing what they are in the lesson, and also that they should enjoy the lesson. It was enlightening to read the summation of students' answers to the questions . . . It made me think about why I was doing a particular section of work.

> It made me realize that the students should be more involved in verbalizing their thoughts and that, perhaps, I was 'dominating' the procedure.

> During the time that I was working with (the consultant) on the three lessons, I was more conscious than usual of needing to have a *very* clear idea of exactly (a) what I hoped to achieve during each lesson, and (b) what I expected students to do for each lesson. I believe that I have become more conscious of this in my lessons since.

In the second year of the study, this procedure was modified by having teachers and students complete a 'shared perceptions' form (Figure 2) near the end of selected lessons. This time, the consultant reported the teacher's responses and the collated student data to the teacher and students *in class* so

Categories of teacher change

1. More clarity of instruction and direction.

2. More activeness and variety in work to be done.

3. More structure/monitoring of classwork and more control of behaviour.

4. More (equal) collaboration between teacher and students.

Categories of student change

1. More independence/initiative/activeness.

2. More attentiveness/application to the work.

3. More responsibility/accountability for work done.

4. More cooperative/supportive/courteous attitude.

Figure 3 Categories of change agreed to by teachers and students, 'agreement for change' procedure

that everyone had the opportunity to participate in a general discussion about the results and possible interpretations. These discussions, carried out in a supportive, constructive atmosphere, helped identify some of the lesson features and classroom practices that diminished students' enjoyment of, and level of application in, science lessons. These features then became the basis for the third episode of this shared reflective process. This episode was entitled the 'agreement for change'.

The agreement for change started with an extended classroom discussion between teacher and students. In this discussion, all class members identified and agreed to three changes that the teacher would make and three changes that the students would make in science classroom behaviours. Selection of particular changes was based on the extent to which teacher and students believed that such changes would enhance students' enjoyment and application. Overall, this procedure was undertaken by 12 teachers and 316 students in 14 classes over grades 8–11 at five schools. Figure 3 lists the major categories of change agreed to by teachers and students.

After entering into such joint agreements, the teachers and students attempted to institute the changes. The progress of the agreement was monitored by means of a form that the teacher and each of the students completed after various periods of time. One student's completed form is shown in Figure 4.

To complete Section A of the form, the student (or teacher, for the teacher version) had to remember the changes that both teacher and students had agreed to make. Then, in Section B, students responded as to whether they believed that they and the teacher had fulfilled the agreement during the previous week's science lessons. Students then evaluated the extent to which they believed that the teacher's, and their own, changes had affected their enjoyment of the lessons, how hard they had worked, and the extent of their understanding of the work.

While there was some variation in the nature and extent of change among the different working groups, the procedure was very successful overall. Depending upon the group, the agreements lasted up to 14 weeks. In sum: (a) students remembered the agreed-upon changes – a median of 92% of all students (range 53%–100%, *by class*) remembered at least two of the teacher changes, and a median of 85% of students (range 52%–100%) remembered at least two of their own changes; (b) students believed that teachers were acting to make changes (median 'yes' responses to question 3(a) – see Figure 4 – was 86%) (range 57%–100%); (c) of the students who acknowledged teacher change, approximately 55% median (range 21%–100%) believed that these changes had improved their enjoyment and understanding of lessons; (d) students believed themselves to be attempting to enact the changes (median 'yes' response to question 4(a) was 80%; range 47%–100%); (e) of the students who were acting to change, many of the perceived benefits related to increased enjoyment (median 47%: range 26%–92%), working harder (median 54%, range 22%–83%) and, very importantly, understanding more (median 58%, range 27%–91%).

<u>CONFIDENTIAL</u>   **Name:**
                              Date: *2 . 9 . 88*

Year 9 Agreement on Science Teaching and Learning

Weekly evaluation form

A. <u>The agreement</u>

1. <u>Mr _____</u> has agreed to attempt to make 3 changes to the way he teaches your science lessons. What are these 3 changes?

      1. *more variety* ✓
      2. *clear instructions* ✓
      3. *simple language.* ✓ $\frac{3}{3}$

2. <u>You</u> have agreed to attempt to make 3 changes to the way you learn in your science lessons. What are these 3 changes?

      1. *ask more questions* ✓
      2. *get set work done* ✓ $\frac{3}{3}$
      3. *help friends* ✓

B. <u>This week's results</u>

3 (a)   Did you notice <u>Mr _____</u> making any of his 3 changes in <u>this week's</u> science lessons? (Answer 'Yes' or 'No) *YES*

  (b)   If you answered 'Yes', - what changes did you notice?

      the clear instructions
      & simple language.

Figure 4   One grade-9 student's completed 'agreement for change' form

(c)   How would you rate the effects of his changes in (b) on:

* **My enjoyment of the lessons**:

I enjoyed the lessons **more than normal** as a result of his changes   ☐

His changes had **no effect** on my enjoyment of the lessons   ☑

I enjoyed the lessons **less than normal** as a result of his changes   ☐

* **My understanding of the lessons**:

I understood the lessons **more than normal** has a result of his changes   ☑

His changes had **no effect** on my understanding of the lessons   ☐

I understood the lessons **less than normal** as a result of his changes   ☐

---

4. (a)   Did **you** make any of your 3 changes in **this week's** science lessons?
(Answer 'Yes' or 'No') *yes*

(b)   If you answered 'Yes' - what changes did you make?

to support friends

(c)   How would you rate the effects of these changes on:

* **My enjoyment of the lessons**:

I enjoyed the lessons **more than normal** as a result of my changes   ☐

Figure 4   Continued

My changes had <u>no effect</u> on my enjoyment of the lessons ☑

I enjoyed the lessons <u>less than normal</u> as a result of my changes ☐

✱ <u>How hard I worked during the lessons</u>:

I <u>worked harder</u> than normal as a result of my changes. ☐

My changes had <u>no effect</u> on how hard I worked. ☑

I worked <u>less hard than normal</u> as a result of my changes. ☐

✱ <u>My understanding of the lessons</u>:

I understood the lessons <u>more than normal</u> as a result of my changes. ☑

My changes had <u>no effect</u> on my understanding of the lessons. ☐

I understood the lessons <u>less than normal</u> as a result of my changes. ☐

5.   What did you <u>enjoy most</u> about science this week?

Discussing the work

6.   What did you <u>enjoy least</u> about science this week?

preparing for the test.

Figure 4 Continued

It should be noted that while these responses were subjective perceptions by the students, in most cases they were corroborated by their teachers, who also recorded improvements in these aspects of classwork.

Why were these agreements so successful? Some main reasons appear to relate to the constructive, cooperative nature of the joint endeavour, the pursuit of concrete goals important to the participants, and the clear indications of progress or lack of it. Students and teachers were working as teams, where everyone understood and had agreed to the nature and purposes of the activity. There was clear and balanced accountability for failure to enact the agreement (e.g., students could constructively direct a teacher's attention to a change that the teacher had failed to institute during the period, as could the teacher do the reverse). Conversely, there were concrete and relatively short-term rewards for success at making changes.

These three episodes, culminating in the 'agreement for change' procedure, demonstrated the efficacy of individual and joint reflection on practice for improving classroom teaching and learning for the participants.

Some findings regarding phenomenological reflection – teachers

Since the preservice component of the study had demonstrated the value of phenomenological reflection for personal intellectual development, we encouraged it in the in-service component. The teachers undertook protracted and systematic phenomenological reflection by answering, about once a month for up to nine months, six questions about their 'lived experience' of science teaching and learning. Figure 5 shows one completed form.

Teachers varied in the number of forms they completed, and in the insightfulness of their answers. Of the 14 teachers, 11 filled in more than one form, and four filled in more than five. Periodically, we held informal discussions with teachers to discuss their perceptions of the questions and the nature of their answers.

Most teachers appeared to benefit from repeatedly reflecting on the questions, some very much so, as their answers to question 6 show: 'What has answering the five questions above made me do/think about?' Examples:

Whether I practise what I preach. Am I really aware of my students' perceptions of science learning?

Consider the reasons why I teach and what students probably feel about the subject.

It has made me focus on the important aspects of motivation and interest.

How my enthusiasm and approach obviously affects the students' behaviour – I must *act* enthusiastic regardless of the way I *feel*!

The underlying goals of my work. Strengthened my resolve that my style of teaching is more likely to achieve my goals than previous styles.

<u>CONFIDENTIAL</u>

Name.........................

Date........................

Please answer each of the questions by thinking deeply about
<u>YOURSELF</u>

Answer in terms of <u>how you are now.</u> (-not as you think things
should be, or how they are for other people).

<u>For me</u>;

1. <u>What is it, to be a science teacher?</u>
    *It is to be a person with a poorly defined task. This lack of
    definition, particularly in regard to the operation of the task,
    can be extremely frustrating for the new teacher in terms of
    knowing how to go about achieving goals and in terms of evaluating
    ones performance. At the same time this lack of definition is a
    wonderful blessing as it gives me almost total authority over how
    I teach science. This is not necessarily a good thing for my
    students or any others for that matter.*

2. <u>What is science teaching?</u>
    *It is attempting to create an environment(s) which allow,
    encourage and assist students to better understand their world <u>and</u>
    (more importantly) gives them skills with which to better answer
    their own questions (a very crude attempt at saying assist them to
    become better learners). At the same time science teaching is
    bringing to students' attention, issues which are likely to be
    important to them now or in the future*

3. <u>What is science learning for my students?</u>
    *At present a fairly exciting time (for most) in which they have
    the responsibility for achieving goals by which ever methods they
    choose. For others a time in which they have greater opportunity
    to do less (due to the nature of the teaching approach). For all
    - a poorly defined task during which they are frequently uncertain
    of what is expected of them.*

4. <u>What is the most important pay-off in science teaching?</u>
    *Helping students to be better learners and part of this being
    their expressions of seeing this as a positive thing.*

5. <u>What is the most important cost, or worst aspect, of science
   teaching?</u>
    *Uncertainty of how one is performing, i.e. lack of professional
    feedback and the consequent difficulty to motivate oneself.*

6. <u>What has answering the five questions above made me do/think about?</u>
    *Reflect on the objectives of my professional task, in particular
    the importance of helping students to become better learners. It
    is a helpful tool in my development. It also serves as a reminder
    of the underlying objectives of my task - something which, despite
    its fundamental importance seems to be lost in the crowd of more
    pressing day to day concerns of teaching.*

Figure 5   A teacher's completed phenomenonology form

CONFIDENTIAL

Name: ....

Date: ....

Please answer each of the questions by thinking deeply about YOURSELF. Answer in terms of how you are now (NOT as how you think things should be, or how they are for other people).

1. What is it, to be a science student? (Base your answer on how you feel)
    For me, it is: *just another subject at school that I have to go through. Although I may learn different things in science than in any other subject it is still just a compulsory subject at school that everyone has to do.*

2. What is science learning? (Base your answer on what you do)
    For me, it is: *answering questions, doing assignments, having class discussions, doing some prac experiments and finding out about things that don't really interest me at all.*

3. What is the most important pay-off in learning science? (Base your answer on what you get out of it most)
    For me, it is: *when we do things about nature, for example: plants, animals, the earth. I think the more people know about the natural part of life, the better.*

4. What is the worst aspect of learning science? (Base your answer on what you dislike most)
    For me, it is: *having to sit through science when we are doing a totally boring topic, e.g. machines, electricity.*

Figure 6   A grade-8 student's completed phenomenology form

Some findings regarding phenomenological reflection – students

A total of 64 grade 8–11 students at two schools volunteered to participate in a process of phenomenological reflection similar to that described above for the teachers. Periodically, over six months they completed a form similar to that of the teachers. Figure 6 shows a completed form.

Over the six-month period, most students completed approximately three forms. Also, the consultant interviewed the students from three to seven times each, individually and in groups, about their general ideas and beliefs and their particular responses to the questions on the form.

Many of the students found reflection beneficial. At the end of the procedure, 21 students at one school were interviewed individually about their perceptions of the effect of the procedure on them. Of these 21 students, 12 asserted that completing the forms and having the discussions had helped them. Five other students were also positive, but somewhat less definite. Fourteen of the students believed strongly that it was important for them to be reflective in their classwork, and 10 of these believed that they had been moved to this view by doing the project activities.

CONCLUSIONS

Taken overall, findings from the study illuminate each of the three aims given in the introduction. These findings include the following.

Aim 1: Teachers and teaching/learners and learning

The phenomenological reflection provided insights into the personal experience of teaching and learning that are unobtainable by other methods. These insights highlight the singularity and complexity of factors that influence the teaching/learning approach, progress, and outcomes.

The findings from the phenomenological research assisted interpretation of the extensive data set arising from the collaborative-action research. In the latter research, teachers and students worked together to explore aspects of science teaching and learning and to devise ways of changing classroom roles and responsibilities to preserve and develop desirable cognitive, metacognitive, and affective outcomes. The research has generated significant gains in the levels of satisfaction and performance of both teachers and students.

Aim 2: Change

The changes referred to above have led students to accept a greater level of accountability and responsibility for their own learning. The improved intellectual competence and classroom intellectual performance of students associated with enhanced metacognition has been more than matched by enhancement in teachers' self-perceived and actual metacognition. Teachers have changed to become more perceptive, resourceful, and purposeful classroom practitioners. The manner of development of teachers' expertise in teaching and ability-to-research teaching and learning in their classrooms is in accord with constructivist principles of attitudinal and conceptual change.

Aim 3: Facilitating change

For teachers and students, change occurred in both general intellectual development and in specific task competencies. For both types of improvement, the opportunity for intensive, regular reflection was crucial. The nature and extent of change depend on the exercise of certain responsibilities by different members of the collaborative group. One measure of the extent of change was the transfer of many of those responsibilities from the authors to the teachers and students themselves.

In particular, findings from the study affirm the importance of two key aspects of the integrative perspective on change: the need for personal and professional reflection and the facilitation of reflection through collaboration. It appears that both types of reflection are necessary and mutually facilitating for enhancing professional expertise through enhanced metacognition.

One interpretation of this finding relates to science teachers' conceptions of *cause* in science and in science teaching and learning. Conceptions of cause that pervade science and much school teaching and learning of science are often monistic (focus on unity) and absolutist (invariant). That is, there is striving to discover the *one* correct explanation of a particular scientific phenomenon, the *one* most elegant procedure for testing an hypothesis, and so on. The veracity and applicability of such explanations or procedures are taken to transcend time, context, and, for some 'universal laws', content. Unlike science itself, however, cause in teaching and learning is unlikely to be unitary and invariant. It is much more likely to be multiple (pluralistic) and content-, context-, and time-dependent (relativistic). For example, most teachers would acknowledge that the success of a particular lesson is influenced by the nature of the content *and* the time of day, *and* the ambient temperature, and so on.

Conception of cause is particularly relevant to the nature of successful teaching – one of the objects of the current research. In order to become successful, science teachers may need to apply this pluralistic, relativistic conception of cause to their own development. Conceptions of the nature of successful teaching as law-governed and generalizable need to change to ones which view it as developing in a constructivist manner through a process of individual reflection on personal life experiences (i.e., phenomenological reflection). Results from the phenomenological strand of the current research indicated such development can occur. *Collaboration* fosters reflection by providing a means of exchange of information and resources, and by affording support during the demanding and unsettling change process.

REFERENCES

Baird, J. R. (1986) Improving learning through enhanced metacognition: a classroom study. *European Journal of Science Education*, Vol. 8, no. 3, pp. 263–282.

Baird, J. R., Fensham, P. J., Gunstone, R. F. and White, R. T. (1989) Teaching and learning science in schools: a report of research in progress. Unpublished monograph, Monash University.

Baird, J. R. and Mitchell, I. J. (eds.) (1986) *Improving the Quality of Teaching and Learning: An Australian Case Study – the PEEL Project*. Melbourne, Monash University.

Baird, J. R., Mitchell, I. J. and Northfield, J. R. (1987) Teachers as researchers: the rationale: the reality. *Research in Science Education*, Vol. 17, pp. 129–138.

Brown, A. L. (1980) Metacognitive development and reading. In R. J. Spiro, B. C. Bruce and W. F. Brewer (eds.), *Theoretical Issues in Reading*

Comprehension. Perspectives from Cognitive Psychology, Linguistics, Artificial Intelligence and Education. Hillsdale, NJ, Erlbaum.

Champagne, A. B., Gunstone, R. F. and Klopfer, L. E. (1985) Effecting changes in cognitive structures among physics students. In L. West and L. Pines (eds.), *Cognitive Structure and Conceptual Change.* Orlando, FL, Academic Press.

Elliott, J. (1988) Teachers as researchers: implications for supervision and teacher education. Invited address at the annual conference of the American Educational Research Association, New Orleans, April 1988.

Gauld, C. (1986) Models, meters and memory. *Research in Science Education,* Vol. 16, pp. 49–54.

Osborne, R. J. and Wittrock, M. C. (1985) The generative learning model and its implications for science education. *Studies in Science Education,* Vol. 12, pp. 59–87.

van Manen, M. (1984) Practising phenomenological writing. *Phenomenology and Pedagogy,* Vol. 2, no. 1, pp. 36–69.

White, R. T. (1988) *Learning Science.* Oxford, Blackwell.

White, R. T. and Tisher, R. P. (1986) Research on natural sciences. In M. C. Wittrock (ed.), *Handbook of Research on Teaching,* 3rd ed. New York, Macmillan.

2.4

The 'practical theory' of teachers

Gunnar Handal and Per Lauvås

In this [article] we will introduce the [following] *thesis* [. . .] and a strategy for counselling with teachers. Then we will establish some of the *pre-conditions* which we think are important for understanding and eventually accepting the thesis.

> *Thesis:* Every teacher possesses a 'practical theory' of teaching which is subjectively *the* strongest determining factor in her educational practice.
> Counselling with teachers must consequently originate in each teacher's practical theory, seeking to foster its conscious articulation, and aiming to elaborate it and make it susceptible to change.

To give meaning to this thesis, however, it is necessary to look in more detail at the meaning of the term 'practical theory' as it is used here.

THE CONTENT OF THE 'PRACTICAL THEORY'

The term 'theory' commonly refers to an interrelated set of hypotheses or statements which can be used to *explain* or understand phenomena or situations, or to *predict* what will happen when certain conditions or premises exist. This is the scientific use of the term. What might be the proper use of the term in education is a disputed question which we, however, will not discuss here.

[In the present context] 'practical theory' refers to a person's private, integrated but ever-changing system of knowledge, experience and values which is relevant to teaching practice at any particular time. This means, first of all, that 'theory' in this sense is a personal construct which is continuously established in the individual through a series of diverse events (such as practical experience, reading, listening, looking at other people's practice) which are mixed together

From Handal, G. and Lauvås, P. (1987) *Promoting Reflective Teaching: Supervision in Action*, SRHE and Open University Press.

or integrated with the changing perspective provided by the individual's values and ideals. In this way, a 'practical theory' may be regarded as a complex 'bundle' of all these elements. It is also worth stressing that it is indeed a *practical* theory, primarily functioning as a basis or background against which action must be seen, and not as a theoretical and logical 'construct' aimed at the scientific purposes of explanation, understanding or prediction.

Although such 'theories' held by different people may have a high degree of similarity, there will always be a personal or individual aspect to them. Personal experiences in practical teaching situations (as teacher or as pupil) will differ from person to person, even though the same general kind of experience is common to many individuals. The books read or the lectures listened to may be identical for many students at a teachers' college. Nevertheless, the knowledge gained, and the meaning and the consequences extracted from these sources, will vary among them. Consequently, we do not have in mind just one or even a few 'theories' that people who teach hold and which guide their practice. We use the term 'practical theory' to refer to the indefinite number of 'bundles' of knowledge, experiences and values which have been and are continuously established in people, related to teaching (or to educational practice generally).

It is probably necessary to go a little further into this concept and – for analytical purposes – to dissect it, trying to identify more clearly its elements as well as their interconnections. For analysis, let us establish three components included in this 'practical theory':

- personal experience;
- transmitted/mediated knowledge, experience and structures;
- values (philosophical, political and ethical).

Personal experience

All young people and adults have experienced educational situations, at least as pupils being educated, taught or trained; many also have had further experience as educators, teachers or trainers. Consequently, we have all experienced practice which was, variously, successful, dull, terrifying, rewarding, difficult, and so on, and have – to a variable extent – drawn personal conclusions as to why things were experienced as they were. These experiences, conclusions and hypotheses accumulate and form part of our practical theory. In formal teacher training, specific situations are set up to provide experience in the kind of teaching for which the training officially prepares. At a minimum, such teaching practice will give the 'raw experience' of having taken part and performed a role in teaching situations. At its optimum, it will also give rise to an understanding of the situation and of the student teacher's own role in it, of why things went as they actually did; and even an understanding of more general phenomena in education, seen in the light of this particular experience.

Experience of this kind may – according to Bateson (1972) – lead to learning at different levels. At the first level, we learn what to do in similar situations; in other words, we learn the content of the 'lesson'. At the second level, we learn a lot about the relationships and structures which are implied but not explicitly stated. We learn about ourselves as persons, about the roles we are expected to play, and so on. Often, this kind of learning is both more subtle and more fundamental, and, accordingly, well worth taking into consideration when looking into a person's practical theory.

The quality of the experience we get out of a teaching/learning practice varies considerably. It may add much or add little to our personal practical theory. If what happens in the actual teaching practice is elaborated after-wards, preferably in the light of one's own and other people's experience and knowledge, there is good reason to believe that the *understanding* added to the practical theory will be richer than if the practice is only experienced and not explicitly reflected upon. It may be helpful to notice that the concept of 'praxis', as used by the 'Frankfurt School', consists of two constitutive el-ements of *action* and *reflection* upon action. To put it another way: some fishermen are said to have twenty years' experience of fishing; others have only one year, experienced twenty times. The latter have never reflected enough on their practice to actually learn from it. Could the same also be said about teachers?

Transmitted knowledge, experiences and structures

In addition to what we directly experience ourselves, and thus can use as material for our theory building, we pick up and include other people's experiences and knowledge as well. The visiting teacher who comes to our staff meeting to describe his way of teaching a particular subject or topic, the course-book put together by experienced authors, the research report from an educational development programme, the ideas about ways of dealing with pupils who have learning difficulties communicated by a colleague over a cup of tea in the senior common room – all these are sources upon which we draw to expand and 'fortify' our 'theory'. In none of these cases is our own immediate personal experience in a practical situation involved, al-though relating to such experience may make these contributions more meaningful and valuable.

Included in this component are also those structures which are transmitted to us in the form of concepts, theories, commonly held beliefs, and so on, whether they are transmitted by persons, by the media or by way of the material world surrounding us. When the word 'teacher' in common language is meant to indicate a person who transmits knowledge to someone else, we have an example of language structures which influence our practical theory, as in the structuring effect of a specific theory of motivation or a prejudice about race relations. Through their influence on our practical theory, they affect our actual practice.

Values

Our own values, or ideas of what is good and bad in education as well as in life generally, are probably strong determining elements in our practical theory. We may have a preference for a competitive or a co-operative relationship between people. We also have specific attitudes to authority. We have different ideas concerning the value of classical subjects as opposed to training for mastery of daily-life situations as the appropriate 'content' for education. All this will no doubt have a strong influence on the way our personal practical theory is constituted – and, accordingly, on our teaching practice. The values in question may be of a more general ethical or philosophical nature concerning the 'good life' (for instance, that a meaningful life is preferred to an abundant life), they may be political values (like ideas about democracy, the distribution of values, freedom and the power of influence) or they may be more directly related to education (like equality of educational opportunity, the right to receive teaching in accordance with one's culture, and so on).

Integration of the elements in a practical theory

The brief comments and examples which appear under the last three headings may lead us to believe that this complex entity labelled 'practical theory' is in fact a simple phenomenon, neatly subdivided into three categories available for inspection. This is far from the truth. The division above is meant only for analytical purposes. The different 'parts' of the theory are – in reality – intimately interwoven and impossible to identify as isolated categories in a person's practical theory. They are influenced by – as well as influencing – each other in the continuous modelling and remodelling of the theory.

Not all the elements have necessarily the same weight or importance in the integration process. This is probably best illustrated by looking at the influence of values on the two other categories. Values, as we know from psychology, heavily influence our perceptions of things we experience ourselves, as well as what we perceive and accept in ideas presented by others. We sort out, delete and integrate, interpret and distort received impressions on the basis of what we hold to be good and right. A similar structuring effect on our new experiences (personal as well as mediated) is created by our earlier experiences.

This leads us to perceive and use the knowledge transmitted to us from others in the light of what we value, as well as in accordance with the perspective created by earlier experiences. Thus the values we hold will – directly and indirectly – have a dominating effect on the structuring of our practical theories.

On the other hand, we experience our own practical efforts very much in the light of structures, concepts and theories transmitted to us, in such a way that this may even lead us to change our values and beliefs to some extent.

Another relevant distinction worthy of note is the one made by Ryle (1945) between 'knowing how' and 'knowing that'. The distinction implies a difference between theoretical knowledge about a phenomenon or a procedure (for instance teaching) and practical knowledge as to how to perform or to act (for instance, again, in teaching). It is indeed possible to know a lot *about* an activity without being able to practise it oneself.

A person's practical theory – it will be seen – may be balanced so far as these forms of knowledge are concerned, or it may be heavily 'overloaded' towards one of them.

If, for instance, the practical theory consists excessively of 'knowledge that', this may be due to the fact that it is based more on mediated knowledge transmitted from others, and less upon personal experience in relevant practical situations. For counselling, this means that a certain part of the basis for the theory – in this case the experiential part – ought to be favoured. If the opposite emphasis of the theory is the case, counselling should provide possibilities for the teacher to put her practical 'know-how' on a footing of more generally acknowledged concepts to make the total, integrated content of her practical theory more valuable. Ryle's pair of concepts thereby helps us to realize again the importance of the necessary dialectical relationship between action and reflection in any individual's production of authentic knowledge.

Some other concepts may be helpful in understanding this complex integration of elements into a practical theory. We have adopted them from Arfwedson (1985) who is, in turn, indebted to Bernstein (1971), Lundgren (1972) and Sarason (1971). They say that the teacher is dependent upon a *code* (principles for ordering their conception of the school) which, in each particular situation, will determine the way they perceive the school-world around them (*perception of surroundings*). This perception, again, gives rise to their particular way of *acting*, which in turn may lead to experiences contributing to either a confirmation of (or a change in) the *code*. The code is therefore a product of both former and new experiences as teacher or pupil – and accordingly a product of socialization. What goes on around the teacher in the educational world (*in the context*) is experienced in the light of her present *code* in such a way as to fit into her *perception of the surroundings*. In order for her to develop further, and to change her code, counselling may be needed as a productive element in the school situation, questioning the code and confronting it with conflicting evidence as to its adequacy.

Another term comparable to our 'practical theory' is *'strategy'* in the way it is used by Stenhouse (1979). He too stresses the integrated character of any valid basis for action established in the teacher's thinking, comprising knowledge from philosophy, learning theory, developmental as well as social psychology, and sociology – as well as practical experience. Stenhouse, however, does not include our kind of value element in his concept of a teaching strategy, leaving out, to our mind, an important element in the integrative structuring of the strategy – or of the practical theory, as we prefer to call it. In sum, we must regard this practical theory as a dynamic and ever-changing 'bundle' of these elements based on both practice and what, in other uses of the word, might be referred to as 'theory', integrated within a value-perspective.

Practical theory as an individual or collective entity

Up to now we have referred to the practical theory as the individual teacher's construct, upon which their practice is based. In our context this will also be the predominant perspective. However, we think it is possible to apply the term even when we are dealing with *groups* of teachers and the basis for educational practice that they share. In counselling with, for instance, the staff of teachers at a particular school (or with a faculty of teachers in a university department), this is an important use of the term to bear in mind.

Just as a particular teacher may be said to have developed at a given time a practical theory for teaching, a group of teachers, working together in an educational institution, may have had experience shared between them, as well as shared knowledge from readings, lectures, courses, and so on. They may, in addition, have some values which are central to them all and around which their collective practical theory is integrated. In reality, however, such collective practical theories will in many cases be quite rudimentary, owing to the fact that only a small part of the educational practice in schools is shared. It is, in fact, possible in many types of schools for teachers to go on practising side by side, on the basis of quite different practical theories, without too many conflicts between them. It is an accepted part of educational tradition that teachers are allowed a great deal of 'professional freedom' in their work. From the pupils' point of view, however, such discrepancies in practical theories among their teachers may be quite an exhausting element in their school experience. They are the ones who constantly have to adjust to differences in practice due to differences in the theories which prescribe that practice.

In schools where teachers have sought and found co-operation (or have been 'forced' to co-operate because of an open-plan school environment) the situation may be different. Co-operation provides mutual insight into one another's practice, and may give rise to questions and discussions about the reasons underlying such practice. For any kind of co-operative teaching to develop, some collective practical theory must be established among the partners in the enterprise. This may happen as a result of complementary domination and submissiveness without any explicit discussion and decision-taking between the teachers involved. It may, however, also be the result of a long and continuous dialogue on the educational questions involved, resulting in the development of a collective practical theory that is shared among the co-operating. It goes without saying that this is not an easy, conflict-free process. Rather, it is likely to be demanding and controversial, as differences in experiences, knowledge and values have to be resolved (at least to some degree) for the group to arrive at some viable collective basis for their work. Counselling which tries to help the members of the teaching team become aware of the differences between them, as well as aware of the contradictions implicit in the situations in which they work, may be helpful in the development of such a collective basis for action.

Here we are dealing with a similar phenomenon which Arfwedson (1979) has referred to as a *collective code* as opposed to an *individual code* for each teacher.

It will not be possible in all cases for, let us say, the total staff of teachers in a school to agree on a collective practical theory which embraces all of them and, at the same time, includes enough common knowledge and values to be productive in practice. A minimum requirement in such situations, however, ought to be that the different prevailing teaching practices, as well as their related practical theories are *known* to the different members of staff, so that they can be taken into consideration in the overall planning and implementation of the work of the school.

It may be useful at this point to refer to authors like Lortie (1975) and Sarason (1971) with regard to the present status of such collective practical theories. When teachers as a group have not succeeded to any extent in establishing a collective theory for their work, this is very much due to the fact that such success presupposes some collective insight into practice as well as collective reflection upon it. This pre-condition, however, involves more time devoted to working together at school than has traditionally been required of teachers. Becoming engaged in a practice of this kind would mean reducing the freedom of the individual teacher to plan and reflect, and would accordingly mean placing a personal constraint on the normal work of that teacher.

In most of what we shall be writing about further on, we return to the counselling of individuals to improve their individual practical theory. We regard it as important, therefore, to refer to collective practical theories as relevant entities in counselling with groups as well [. . .].

THE INFLUENCE OF A PRACTICAL THEORY ON TEACHING PRACTICE

At this point there may be good reason for asking ourselves the question 'What are actually the important "governing factors" for educational practice?' Are we governed to a large extent by our ideas of good teaching, our theory, ideals, thinking and planning – in short, by our practical theories – or are other factors more influential? What about the social pressure stemming from our colleagues or from the pupils and their parents? Or what about the influence of the 'frame factors' such as the curriculum, the architecture of schools, the rules and regulations enforced upon us from above, the resources we have at our disposal, and so on?

When asking teachers about the factors which influence the character of their teaching practice most strongly, we often receive answers indicating that frame factors and social factors – particularly at a local level – are perceived by the teachers as more influential than their own 'practical theory'. This has also been empirically demonstrated in Sweden (Arfwedson 1985). From a Marxist point of view, it might be valid to consider the practical theory as an ideological entity established to make the structurally and materially governed practice meaningful and acceptable to the actors concerned and to society.

Whatever our theoretical framework, it is possible to support the statement that work in schools is strongly influenced by factors outside the command of the individual teacher or group of teachers. We concur with this view and accept the research and theory illustrating and demonstrating it.

So why focus so strongly on working with teachers' practical theories – with their minds – as we are doing in this book, when mind probably matters less than matter? We think there are good reasons to do so.

Firstly, although the frame factors of different kinds have a strong impact on educational practice, these factors are also 'moulded' through the way they are interpreted and understood by the teachers who are doing the teaching. Although the architecture of the school and the size, form and equipment of its rooms will definitely limit forms of teaching, we still see that different groups of teachers are able to utilize such potentials rather differently. They seem to 'see' and understand their surroundings differently, thus psychologically operating in different environments although these may be quite similar materially.

Arfwefdson (1985) has shown that the 'code' of teachers – their principles for interpreting the world around them as well as for acting in it – is influenced by the context in which the teachers work. Although this is true, it may also be possible to influence the individual code or the school code through the introduction of systematic counselling – for instance in the way introduced in this book – as a 'context factor'. To summarize, the frame factors do not only govern teaching directly, but mainly indirectly through the way they are interpreted and understood by the teachers working within them.

Secondly, the frames imposed on the school by forces outside it still leave quite a sizeable 'free room' open for the decision of the teachers. Within this free room the teacher has the option of making choices and decisions, and – as demonstrated by Berg and Wallin (1983) – most teachers do not utilize this freedom to its full extent. Rather, many of them stay within frames and limits imposed on them by their own lack of imagination, knowledge of alternatives, and so on. This free room, consequently, is an important part of the arena for counselling, where change is possible through the changes of teachers' individual and collective practical theories without entering into conflict with limiting material and structural frames.

Thirdly, counselling can assist in the process of making frames of different kinds visible and apparent to teachers. Making such factors conscious is at least a step in a process whereby they may eventually be changed, if that is considered necessary. Changes of this kind, however, will rather be a result of political or organizational work than of the individual work of teachers in their daily teaching.

Consequently, we do not deny the effect of frame factors in influencing strongly what happens in teaching. On the contrary, for reasons given above we *also* find it important to work with the minds of those who interpret the frames in daily life, who act with some freedom within the imposed framework and who may even be actors in the everlasting battle to decide which frames to impose on the school.

When focusing on working with teachers' practical theories, it is important to bear in mind that we are working within the set of mental 'brackets' outlined above. We do not claim that teaching can only – or even mainly – be changed by changing teachers' minds through their practical theories, and this is our main focus, in this text.

THE DEGREE OF CONSCIOUSNESS ABOUT ONE'S PRACTICAL THEORY

It is necessary to emphasize that, by saying 'all teachers have a practical theory', we here literally mean all those who set out on the task of teaching others, whether they have any professional training for it or not. That means that we include students at a teacher-training institution the moment they first meet a class of pupils, as well as fully trained and experienced teachers who have been practising for years. We also include those who teach only as a minor part of their vocational function, e.g. people from different professions who take on a teaching role as part of, or in addition to, their ordinary jobs. Hence, the 'theory' we speak of here is not something reserved for trained and certificated teachers in the profession, being the result of their official preparation.

From a casual inspection only, it is noticeable that this practical theory is not only different as far as content is concerned. It differs also in its degree of *elaboration*, as well as in the extent to which it is *consciously* held by the teacher concerned.

In instances when the role of a teacher is performed we can see that there is a very limited consciousness of the practical theory underlying teaching practice. Some will even deny having such a theory, and will therefore be unable to formulate important parts of it. Still, some sort of theory exists in their thinking and will influence the way they teach, even though this influence may be less than conscious. Their values, their own experiences in similar situations of what 'works', as well as what counts for them as knowledge about teaching, will form a basis which influences what they actually do in their own educational practice.

Even teachers who recognize that they have a practical theory which determines their work will often have problems trying to formulate it. The composite nature of the 'theory', which we have tried to describe above, and the fact that it is not an explicit set of rules or prescriptions but is rather a 'bundle' of knowledge and evaluations makes formulation of it difficult in any simple, straightforward terms.

For many teachers – or teachers-to-be – the degree of elaboration of their practical theory (or its internal consistency) is not very high. Knowledge based on quite different sources, and with mutually inconsistent assumptions underlying it, may exist side by side and influence different parts of one's practice. This may be difficult to accept, as we have already pointed to the complex dynamic and integrating tendency which we encounter in the establishment of a practical theory. We believe, however, that this lack of consistency may be due to the fact that the knowledge, experience and values involved are often only partly understood and therefore poorly integrated; the basis of or assumptions underlying such knowledge is not readily apparent to the teacher. This knowledge is probably taken too much at face value and will, consequently, not be properly integrated. This will lead to inconsistency in the 'theory' which, again, will produce inconsistent or incompatible practice.

An important aim in counselling with teachers is, in our opinion, in making the practical theory of the individual teacher more conscious and elaborated. This implies:

- helping the teacher realize what kind of knowledge and values underlie her practice;
- clarifying the reasons and justifications of significance to her;
- confronting her knowledge/values with alternatives outside, or already imbedded in her practical theory; and
- facilitating the teacher's own identification of internal contradictions and conflicts within her own practical theory.

For a teacher to become capable of expanding and refining personal practical theory, it is a great help to make that theory visible and accessible in its existing form.

FOCUS IN COUNSELLING: DEVELOPMENT OF PRACTICAL THEORY

In our perspective, counselling deals with the development of the theory behind action, and does not focus primarily upon 'visible' teacher behaviour. An example may explain why.

Mrs Higgins, the geography teacher, receives in her class five students coming on teaching practice from the nearby college: John, Nanette, Fiona, Mark and Leslie. She wants them to learn how to teach map-reading and tells them to practise a technique of leading the whole class in reading the map by means of the teacher's presentation on an overhead projector. When actually implemented, this advice soon demonstrates that John is able to perform this kind of teaching with ease. He also understands and accepts Mrs Higgins's reasons for using this method, namely that the pupils have to get it right the first time when they start their map-reading in order to avoid misunderstandings and later re-learning. Nanette is also able to practise the kind of teaching required because it has been spelt out in some detail, but she has no understanding of why this might be a good way of doing it. She could, consequently, do it again in another teaching situation, but it might well be a situation where the technique would be absolutely irrelevant. Fiona, however, understands well, and accepts the reason for choosing the method and where and when it might be applied, but she is not yet able to perform in this role with ease. She is still a bit confused in her handling of the technical equipment, goes a little too fast in her explanation, but will certainly be able to master the technique, given a few more chances to practise.

Mark, on the other hand, masters the technique immediately and finishes his lesson smoothly, but he does not agree with Mrs Higgins's reasons for choosing that way of teaching. He keeps this to himself, and carries out the teaching as instructed. Finally, Leslie objects openly to Mrs Higgins on the same grounds as Mark, and decides to attack the teaching task quite differently: she leaves it to pairs of pupils to try finding out things from the map as a source of information. She also gives reasons for this alternative method, referring to her own way of looking at knowledge and her ideas about motivation in learning.

Several points can be made on the basis of this description of a practical situation.

Similar kinds of teacher behaviour may be the result of rather different practical theories, as in the case of John and Mark, who both perform well but on the basis of different practical theories.

Quite different ways of teaching may also be the result of similar practical theories, as is shown by Mark and Leslie, who would agree to a large extent about what would be the right thing to do in this particular teaching situation. However, they *act* here quite differently, evidently because Mark's theory also contains a tendency (or value) – to conform or act as instructed, if it is unavoidable. There is reason to believe that they would teach in very much the same way if they were left on their own.

Neither Fiona nor Leslie carried out the teaching successfully, judged by Mrs Higgins's standards; but, on looking back, we see that there are very different reasons for their 'failure' – to be found in the realm of practical theory and in their consciousness of it.

A lot of the counselling that goes on in the practical part of teacher training focuses on training student teachers to master methods or techniques without giving sufficient attention to the underlying practical theory upon which this practice is based. According to our ideas of counselling, this means concentrating on overt student behaviour rather than on building the practical theory of the teachers involved. This emphasis may lead to some apparent short-term effectiveness, but not to the development of really professional practice in the long term. We think that Dewey, many years ago, pointed to the same truth in this quotation (1904, p. 28):

> . . . criticism should be directed to making the professional student thought-ful about his work in the light of principles, rather than to induce in him a recognition that certain special methods are good, and certain other special methods are bad. At all events, no greater travesty of real intellectual crit-icism can be given than to set a student teaching a brief number of lessons, have him under inspection in practically all the time of every lesson, and then criticize him almost, if not quite at the very end of each lesson, upon the particular way in which that particular lesson has been taught, pointing out elements of failure and success. Such methods of criticism may be adapted to giving a training-teacher command of some of the knacks and tools of the trade, but are not calculated to develop a thoughtful and independent teacher.

One cautionary note, however, is necessary at this point. The focusing in counselling on development of the teacher's practical theory does not, of course, preclude working on the mastering of techniques and methods for use in teaching. Every teacher needs to master such 'knacks and tools of the trade', and this accordingly must be part of a professional training. The important thing is to ensure that this part of the training takes place within the proper perspective – that of developing the understanding of teaching through the development of the teacher's practical theory. What is mastered in the area of techniques must be connected to, and integrated within this vital theory.

Summing up, we may say that the same teaching practice may reflect rather different practical theories (in content and degree of consciousness) and that similar practical theories may result in quite different practice. The training in practical ways of teaching does not, therefore, necessarily lead to a concomi-tant change in the practical theory underlying teaching behaviour. The chance to practise teaching is a necessary but not at all sufficient element in teacher training. Consequently, focusing training on the mastery of specific techniques must not be confounded with counselling, as we use the term. In order to improve the chances of changing teaching practice through counselling it is certainly the 'theory' underlying that practice which must be focused upon.

WHO IS RIGHT?

What now of Mrs Higgins's practical theory? Because *she* has one as well, of course. We have seen that it did not correspond to Mark's and Leslie's. Which of them is the 'right' one? Some of you will already have agreed with Mrs Higgins, while others will be backing up Leslie. And this is only on the basis of the very limited information we have given in the example. Further clarifica-tion might change the picture, but still we would be likely to have different opinions about who was 'right'. One alternative, in deciding, would be to give the 'right' to Mrs Higgins. After all, she is the counsellor in this situation, she has many years of experience and is the one who has both authority and authorization for the job. The problem, however, is that Mr Ross, who teaches geography in the neighbouring school, and who also receives students on teaching practice, would go along with Leslie in her view and support her solution and its justification. In this case, we must probably lean on real scientific educational theory to solve the conflict. What does research say? Again the problem is that research is not unambiguous. We might find research showing that the mastery of a task is more quickly achieved when the correct performance is shown and the learner is trained to copy it. We may, on the other hand, find evidence that pupils who get a chance to explore their way into a new area are more highly motivated, learn more and with better retention than those who are led through the content step by step by the teacher. This may lead us to look in more detail at the evidence to see if the tasks or learning required are of a different nature in the two situations; whether what is meant by 'mastery' or 'knowledge' is different; or whether there are concomitant learning results (like, for instance, a development of dependence/independence) that also occur in either of the situations and that we would welcome or regret. There might be more to learn both for Leslie and John – and probably also for Mrs Higgins and Mr Ross – by looking into, as well as behind, the immediate reasons *why* we want to teach and why we actually teach the way we do. At least we would then be operating on the level of practice theory, where the *reasons* for our practical are to be found, even though they are sometimes hidden, unconscious and poorly organized.

The *immediate* problem in counselling (and even more so in evaluation) in teaching may seem to be to decide on who is to be the master – who has the right to say what is 'right' or 'wrong'. However, the way we see it is that the *real* problem in counselling is to learn how to allow the counsellor and the teacher to go together into the realm of 'what to do and why to do it' in order to explore the appropriate basis for action and the knowledge, experience and values supporting or contradicting different solutions. The aim of such an exploration is not to find out *who* is right, but to learn more about ways of thinking and acting in education in order to develop our own practical theories, to make them more consistent and to ensure that the use of them is a more conscious use. Lewis and Miel (1972, p. 234) put it this way:

> . . . there is an increasing agreement in the profession that there is no single best way to teach; there are many ways. The important thing is to help the teacher to become self-propelling and self-actualizing.

It should also be noted that what is meant by 'good teaching' is most certainly a controversial question. We may limit ourselves to evaluation in accordance with immediate criteria of effectiveness, in relation to limited objectives for a particular lesson; or we may see teaching against the background of what is good and therefore needed in a wider societal context. In taking the latter perspective, we may also differ in our criteria depending upon whether we are complying with the officially stated needs of society or whether we have a critical attitude towards those needs. Whether teaching is 'good' or not can thus be measured against very different standards: these ought to be discussed in counselling to make teachers aware of them, rather than making teachers conform to one standard by concealing the alternatives.

What we have just said might imply that we think that one kind of teaching is as good as another so long as the teacher is able to justify it in consistent terms. We don't. Both of us have our own preferences for 'the right way' in particular situations, and we sometimes even have difficulties in providing a solid justification for them. Two lines of argument have to be followed to explain this. The first we choose to call 'the-nature-of-education-argument' and the other is named 'the-what-do-I-do-when-no-one-is-watching-argument'. Let us follow them briefly before we return to the position of the counsellor in counselling practice.

The question of the *nature of education* is certainly a risky venture for anyone who is not a trained philosopher. So this is not going to be a thorough philosophical discussion of the question, but rather a brief sketch of some central points. Education is certainly no 'natural phenomenon'. It is on the contrary an artificial, cultural creation, which – even though it exists with similar functions in all cultures – takes on different shapes, aims and ideals from culture to culture and from time to time. The education in medieval schools for the aristocracy was quite different from that in today's state schools for the majority. The schools for teenagers in Newcastle-upon-Tyne, in Leningrad or in Guatemala may have striking similarities but still represent quite different ways of looking at education. Even within one country you will find quite different conceptions of the school and the way it ought to be run, which results in quite different teaching practices. What is 'good education' or 'good teaching', therefore, must be related to the group for whom it is sup-posed to be good (teachers and/or students, groups in society, and so on), as well as to some ideal of what is really 'good' for this group, and to the reasons why this is so.

Of course, it is possible to come to some sort of agreement on what we, in a particular society and at a particular time, should establish as our teaching system. On the one hand, this will only be an agreement at a high level of generality which will need a lot of further interpretation by teachers and school authorities. On the other hand, this is always an agreement reached under particular social and historical conditions which are subject to change and development. Even within settled periods between any formal changes in the framework of a school, changes in teaching ideals as well as in conceptions of what constitutes 'good teaching' may occur. Given this perspective, we find it difficult to base either teaching about teaching or counselling with teachers on a determinate model of 'good teaching', which is conventionally that assumed by those who work within teacher-training and which is used as the criterion against which teaching practice is evaluated. On the contrary, we consider it reasonable to focus upon an improvement in the teacher's conscious knowledge, about the relationship between what the teacher does in practice and the reasons for it, in order to become increasingly aware of her own theory and able to judge alternatives in a way which makes both rejection of them as well as revision of their own theory possible. In other words: for a teacher to be able to take a conscious stand in any future conflicts regarding her teaching practice, she must have already internalized such conflicts and learnt to handle them, and not been merely taught specific 'correct' solutions to them.

Consider also the dependence of teaching on situational factors which are constantly changing. Good teaching does not come about in one way only. Given a certain group of pupils, a certain 'history' of what has just happened, a specific attitude existing in the group for the moment, and so on, the best way to teach a particular problem in mathematics may be quite different from the best way in some other situation. In addition, the personality of the teacher, the strong and weak points, what treatment the class is used to and the prevailing attitudes in the culture around the school are factors influencing what it might be 'right' to do. Still, among all this multitude of situational elements, a teacher must find a way to implement what has been established as her aims and objectives (at least in a long-term perspective) in accordance with the chosen philosophy. Even when this means that the teacher must *act* quite differently in different situations, she must be continually pursuing the same aims and keeping in line with her ideals. In other words she will try to teach according to a strategy, not just utilizing specific tactics or techniques more or less mechanically. To do this, she needs insight and understanding and the habit of continually investigating what she really wants to achieve, how she is trying to bring it about and what experiences she is gaining. Teaching is an activity where there is no single way to the goal, but a very large number, and where many of these ways will suffice in any specific situation with its particular characteristics. This line of argument may well lead us to be classified as value-relativists. Maybe this is a fair description. We mean that, in a field like education, it is important to have people working who are aware of the background of what they are doing, and who are able to change and adjust both their 'theory' and their practice in the light of new evidence, and reflect upon what really happens around them in the classroom, the school and society. Teachers who have learnt only to accept one model of teaching as the right one will more easily run the risk of either becoming rigid and static in their teaching or becoming passengers on any educational bandwagon that happens to pass by their school. Many different ways of teaching may be 'right', depending upon the time and the place in which it takes place, the elements to be found in the immediate situation, the aims which are being pursued and the ethical, political and educational values that the teacher is trying to implement.

Perhaps this represents an extreme view on our part, compared to other members of the educational profession, who will probably take a less relativist stand in this matter. Some will say that educational theory has to be far more prescriptive than we allow. Others will claim that educational practice itself offers the advice which we argue is needed in our type of counselling process.

Our stand – which no doubt reflects relativism and a disbelief in the direct application of educational theories or directives derived from day-to-day teaching practice – implies a belief in the vital importance of the teachers' professional judgement.

The other line of argument we suggested above was that dealing with the question 'what-do-I-do-when-no-one-is-watching'. We think this concerns the relationship between action itself and the basis for action. In teacher-training it is possible, and to some extent fairly easy, to get student teachers to model prescribed teaching behaviours. This is done in many teacher-training programmes and has been a tradition for some time. Examples may be found clearly in, for instance, micro-teaching programmes, where teachers are trained to perform specific techniques (like formulating questions to pupils or securing responses from a majority of the pupils in the classroom, and so on). This is done by means of bits of practical teaching in 'micro' situations (micro as far as the task, time and number of pupils in the 'class' are concerned). The session is recorded on videotape and then played back to the teacher practising, preferably with a counselling teacher also watching and commenting. After the playback and counselling, the actual teaching sequence is repeated in order to get an improved result. The tasks and techniques selected for this sort of training are decided upon by those in charge of the programme and – at least sometimes – are based upon some theory or less systematic opinion as to what are considered important techniques to be mastered in teaching. This approach, of course, also rests upon values, knowledge and experience; and is subject to the same relativistic verdict as *any* theory.

Techniques learnt in this way may well be used in further teaching by those who have been trained to master them; but – in our experience – only to the extent that the teacher in question has accepted them as *hers*. This acceptance may, of course, be due to the fact that there are no alternatives that seem applicable in her teaching, or to mere belief in authority, rather than to thorough understanding of and agreement with the thinking behind the technique. If the techniques are not accepted, however, there is no reason whatsoever for the teacher to continue using them in further practice. The stronger the pressure is, in the training situation, to teach according to specific prescriptions (for instance through the use by tutors of a strict grading or evaluation system), the easier it will probably be to make the teacher conform to the rules while in training. However, the chances that teachers will continue to teach this way in their further vocational practice will be hardly likely to correspond to the certainty ensured by pressure during their training. Apart from the fact that they have had a chance to practise a certain way of teaching and will possibly resort to it where there is a lack of alternatives, teachers, like most other people, will be more likely to act according to their own beliefs or in their own interest, when not being watched, than to do what they have been told.

A reservation at this point is, nevertheless, essential. We do not consider educational situations as 'free' ones where the actors may do as they please. On the contrary, we regard teaching as an activity which is to a large extent framed by rules, regulations, structures (material and social) and resources. Still, there is a great freedom left to the teacher as a professional person to act as an individual, particularly when there is interest in exploiting the 'free space' within the system. And it is within this space where there is freedom for various practices that we maintain that teachers will prefer to act according to the conviction, knowledge and experience which is their *own*, a part of themselves, rather than to follow prescriptions given by others, the value of which they do not accept. The possible exception may be the extremely conforming teacher who is happiest looking for models in figures of authority. In our opinion, the school should certainly not base itself on this kind of teacher in the way it sets up its counselling system and procedures.

It is sometimes wise – although it may at the same time be a frightening thought – to consider the relative shortness of the period a teacher is in a formal training situation, compared to the length of time in real teaching. With an active vocational career of, say, forty years, the training period of three or four years is only a tenth of the vocational period – the tip, as it were, of the iceberg. Considering that counselling, in the form here described, is itself only a small part of the activities offered during training, one should probably not over-state what can actually be learnt as a result of teaching practice supported by counselling. The consequence for us of this consideration is to focus counselling on helping the teacher to develop independence and reflection *on her own*, together with an inclination to continue the development of her practical theory – again *on her own* – by the systematic integration of practical experience, transmitted knowledge and reflection upon both within an overall value perspective.

The same problem can be regarded from another point of view – that of educating for innovation. Stenhouse, in his inaugural lecture on research as a basis for teaching (1979, p. 11) says:

> Teachers must be educated to develop their art, not to master it, for the claim of mastery merely signals abandoning of aspiration. Teaching is not to be regarded as a static accomplishment like riding a bicycle or keeping a ledger, it is, like all arts of high ambition, a strategy in the face of an impossible task.

We agreed with his notion that teaching must – throughout a career – be the development of a type of practice, not a falsely assumed mastery of it. Counselling must take this into account and aim at supporting the teachers' development. With reference to Abelard, Stenhouse (1979, p. 1) quotes the ideal of setting out 'to learn the wisdom which we do not possess'. If this is a task for practising teachers, counselling must be a help to them, not a hindrance, on their difficult way towards it.

Continuing from these two lines of argument, even if we do not think that *any* way of teaching is as good as any other, we still prefer to base our counselling with teachers on a thorough discussion or dialogue with the teacher about the basis for her practice and relationship between this basis and what the teacher does or plans to do. Even though we are pretty sure *ourselves* what we would prefer to do in a given practical teaching situation, we do not think it either *right* or *wise* to establish our solution (however well based in 'theory' we think it is) as the model to be followed. This is particularly so in counselling with *teachers*, considering the nature of the field in which they are working, although our thinking has relevance in other counselling situations as well.

We are, however, touching here upon a very delicate point in our argument – one which has certainly been pointed out by some of our students. It is that, as you yourself, in the role of counsellor, have your own practical theory, aren't you more or less bound to impose it on the teacher? This imposition may, of course, be done so subtly that in practice neither party will be aware of it, and it may thus be just cleverly disguised manipulation. The risk is certainly there. To us, it is of vital importance to try to avoid it.

There is, it must be said, an inevitable tension involved in counselling. On the one hand, the counsellor may act completely on the basis of the teacher's own intentions and practical theory without expressing his own views or practical theory at all. On the other hand, he may force his own theory and ideals upon the teacher, either directly through manifest pressure or by subtle manipulation.

This is probably a major problem in counselling, whatever strategy is applied. As a counsellor, you will always be in a powerful position. You may find yourself enforcing your theory directly or you may find the same happening by manipulation. However, we believe both tendencies should and *can* be reduced.

The teacher must be able to go to the counsellor as a detached professional person. At the same time, she must be invited to relate herself to his theory, continuously and openly, as an alternative theory to learn from, relate to and even reject. This means that the counsellor and the teacher must know and realize the difference between *persuasion* and *conviction* (Hellesnes 1975). The first is limited to talking someone into a new position either by virtue of one's authority or by arguments which may seem to be acceptable but which in fact are not really shared by the one who is being persuaded. This is a superficial change of position which will not result in a lasting change of practice, but only in an apparent change. Conviction, however, leads to the real acceptance of a position based on a recognition of the value of the arguments supporting it.

In practical counselling, accordingly, care must be taken to keep this distinction clear in the minds of those involved. Just as it is right that the counsellor should argue, comment, present alternatives, make his own position clear, and so on, it should be equally clear that it is up to the teacher to integrate, disregard, connect, change or keep her own practical theory and make her own decisions about her practice.

One important reservation has to be made. The relationship between the teacher and the counsellor is not a totally symmetrical one with both participants in equal positions. And, at least in a training situation, an extra responsibility rests with the counsellor which, in certain situations, may lead him to object that some teacher-decision is being put into practice. He may, for instance, find the practice suggested unethical in relation to pupils. However, this is something that should be stated frankly and not disguised as an artificial 'consent' between the teacher and the counsellor. The asymmetric relationship in this situation must be declared in order to establish a proper subject–subject association between the two participants. A real dialogue presupposes a clear understanding of the relationship between the teacher, the counsellor and the teaching (the subject matter of the counselling process).

We confess that there is a great risk to be run at this point of our becoming totally idealistic and utopian. Will the strategy as described to this point have any chance whatsoever of withstanding the test of reality? Aren't there too many factors working against it, such as the lack of suitably qualified counsellors or the submissive role of the teacher being counselled, which is due to a long-lasting socialization, and so on? Certainly it can be admitted that it is a strategy which is demanding in many ways. But, on the other hand, to change or adjust existing practice a potent theory such as this is needed. Only then will it give firm direction to change. So, if we think the strategy is a good one, it is surely worth while to continue searching for ways of implementing it.

WHAT IS PRACTICE?

The emphasis so far on the practical theory of teachers as the focal point for counselling, as opposed to their teaching practice, may give the impression that this kind of counselling takes place in a purely theoretical sphere and will therefore be of interest more to theoreticians than to practising teachers. In the end the prime concern of the teacher is always: What am I going to *do?* Løvlie (1974), in an article on educational philosophy for practising teachers, and in another on the meaning of 'practice' (1972), has helped us clarify our position on this point. He illustrates the character of educational practice in the form of a triangle divided into three levels (Figure 1).

The P_1 level is the level of manifest *action*. This is where we operate when we walk into our classrooms and explain, ask questions, give assignments, motivate, evaluate or whatever. At the P_2 level, however, we are at a 'conceptual' level of *planning and reflection*. When I prepare myself for what I am going to do – thinking and wondering about how to do it, looking for ideas within my knowledge and experience, searching for guidance for decisions about what to do, as well as when I review what I have been doing today or recently, trying to

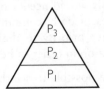

Figure 1   Schematic representation of educational practice

see what I can learn from it – then I wander around at the P_2 level. The P_3 level, finally, is the level of *ethical consideration*, where I find myself at times. Here I reflect in another mode, asking myself (and others) whether the way I teach is right or ethically or politically justifiable.

P_1 level: Take Mrs Howard for instance, the German teacher. She practises teaching German in her own individual way every year. When the term starts, she gives the pupils their daily homework of German grammar, then checks carefully every day to see whether they have really learnt what they were assigned. Those who have not done the work properly (and there are always some, as you know, who for different reasons have not) she makes a fool of them publicly in front of the class, in an ironic way, trying to make them feel embarrassed. In other words she 'puts them down' before the very eyes of their class-mates. And this is repeated until nobody will risk coming to her classes unprepared in German grammar.

P_2 level: The reason for this practice is that Mrs Howard has found from earlier experience that this is a method that really works. She has tried it out and refined it over the years. Besides, she has also found that there is good evidence in psychology that the social motive of peer-approval is a very strong one, particularly in pupils of secondary age; so she knows that her own practical experience has some scientific support. She has also found that those of her pupils who really do their grammar homework pass, with very good results, the kind of examination that is traditionally given. Some of them, however, whom she has met later on in their lives, complain that they did not feel competent in practical communication in German when they actually had to use the language.

P_3 level   In a discussion at a meeting in the German department at her school, she is questioned by some of her colleagues as to whether her practice could be considered ethically justifiable or not. They thought that it was not acceptable to treat pupils in the above way; that it was, at least, not in accordance with central values expressed in the aims of the school. Mrs Howard did not agree with this and referred to the effectiveness of the method. On the other hand, she said, she did often wonder whether it was right to put such a heavy emphasis on the formal aspect of German, but did so because the external examinations emphasized such knowledge. Certainly there was evidence that most of her pupils would need a mastery of practical language skills for the purposes of daily communication. She had, however, thought it right to give priority to the minority who needed good marks in the examination in order to be accepted at university.

From this example it should be possible to see that restricting the concept of *practice* to the P_1 level only – that is to what actually happens in the teaching situation – is an undue limitation of the scope of our concern with teaching practice. What actually happens must be understood and eventually questioned just as much at the P_2 and P_3 levels – in other words at the levels of what we have called the practical theory of the teacher. We therefore consider it essential that counselling with teachers be so arranged that all three levels of the triangle of practice are included in the discussion between the practising teacher and the counsellor.

A closer look at the kind of arguments that may occur at the P_2 and P_3 levels may further clarify our understanding and lead to the provision of a better background for analysis in the counselling session, both for teacher and counsellor. Again we lean on the terminology and analysis of Løvlie.

Plans or prescriptions for teaching practice, whether they are merely thought up by teachers on their way to school or found at leisure in extensive methodologies of teaching, consist in principle of what Løvlie calls 'practical statements'. Practical statements contain recommendations for educational practice in the form: 'If you want to achieve this and that, then you ought to do so and so.' Or they can be put in the personal form: 'As I want to achieve this, then I shall do it this way.' The form of such statements will in practice vary considerably. They may be lengthy paragraphs stating the results which one might be aiming at together with pages full of description of how to go about achieving these results. In principle, however, they follow the form above. In addition to this, both the individual teacher (at least when questioned about it) and the writer of the book on methods will give reasons and justifications for the practical statements included in the plans and prescriptions. These reasons will be of different kinds, and Løvlie suggests the following categories:

Theory-based reasons

These reasons refer to *theory* or empirical results which have been established by research. In the example featuring Mrs Howard, there is a reliance on this kind of reason when she refers to motivation theory and to knowledge from developmental psychology. Evaluation of reasons of this kind must of course, be made in relation to the scientific criterion of *truth*. Is it really like this? Does the theory refer to conditions in reality and is this reality comparable to the one in which we are teaching? Even so, as we have already seen, educational research offers competing truths which are both controversial and tentative and is, accordingly, questionable as the sole basis for action.

Practice-based reasons

These are reasons that refer to practical evidence about what *works* in teaching. The criterion referred to here is not truth but *applicability* or *effectiveness* in practice. Mrs Howard knows from experience that her method works, and will probably also be able to refer to colleagues who can support her observations. Whether she could find evidence in research or theory to support it or not would not alter the fact that the practice has proved to be appropriate.

Confronted with 'practical statements', the teacher will not only have to test their value in terms of their scientific truth. She must also evaluate them against the criterion of applicability. If someone suggests that groups of pupils with a high level of anxiety in test situations ought to be grouped separately in different classes and taught differently from pupils who are low on this trait, the teacher will not only (or perhaps not even primarily) be interested in checking this recommendation against theories about motivation and anxiety. She will, rather, have to consider if this is a practical suggestion that has a fair chance of working when confronted with all the other conditions which have to be considered when grouping procedures are established. On the other hand, when testing the 'practical statement' in this way against the criterion of applicability (looking for practice-based reasons from her own or other people's experience), she does not take into consideration the important ethical aspects of the problem. This is done, however, when it comes to the so-called 'ethical/political justification'.

Ethical/political justifications

At this point, we have to consider what are the *ethical* implications of the 'practical statement' in order to establish a basis for decisions of a *moral* nature. Mrs Howard is asked to give justifications of this kind for her practice at the meeting in her department, and is confronted with arguments from her colleagues which indicate a conflict between different values. At this point, Mrs Howard fails to appreciate what kind of justification is being asked for and supports her action with reference to her practice-based reason: it has proved effective. This is something which we often do, because we are not sufficiently aware of the distinctions between the different categories of argument described above. It is thus important to make these distinctions clear in order to improve the teacher's conscious refinement of her own practical theory; and, accordingly, it is something which ought to be emphasized in counselling with teachers.

SUMMARY

So we can end the excursion into the concepts and clarifications adopted from Løvlie. Returning to the concept of a practical theory, we can try to summarize it in Figure 2.

Teaching practice is more than what actually goes on in the direct encounter between pupils, content and teacher. It also includes the planning and evaluation activity which comes before and after this encounter, and refers both to the actions of teaching and to the underlying practical theory of the teacher concerned. Initially, we subdivided this practical theory into three components: (1) personal experience; (2) transmitted knowledge and experiences; (3) values. In the language of Løvlie, represented here through the triangle of practice, we have found that 'practical statements'

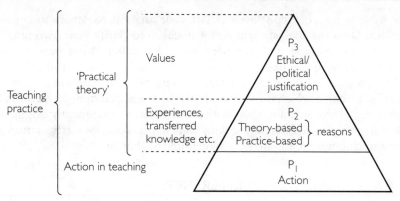

Figure 2   Relationship between practice and practical theory

(recommendations for educational practice) may be supported by reference to two levels of reasoning:

- practice-based and theory-based reasons, which is but another way of categorizing what we have called personal experience and transmitted knowledge, and so on; and
- justifications based on moral/ethical/ political considerations, or on what we have referred to as values.

The illustration above is, however, lacking in one important respect. It may give the impression of a freedom of action which we have already denied. A number of *frame factors* (resources, localities, material, rule systems, structures, and so on) impose restrictions on the 'free choice' of the teacher (but also offer possibilities!). These factors also influence the way experiences and knowledge are perceived and thus actively 'distort' the reflections on which we base our practice.

After this rather long excursion into a series of explanations of the pre-conditions for the thesis presented at the beginning of this article, we may return to the thesis itself to see if it has now been better established and whether it carries more meaning at this stage than it did when it was first presented. There may, at the very least, be a better basis now for accepting or rejecting it, or for putting it to the test of practical experience.

Notice what we have actually been doing during the preceding discussion:

- We have tried to establish *theory-based* as well as *practice-based* reasons or evidence for the thesis.
- We have, as well, tried to establish ethical/political *justifications* for it, based on value statements relating to education.

In order to give yourself personal experience in carrying out an analysis of such an argument, and thereby to make it more meaningful to you, try to go back and analyse the article in the terms given above (and elaborated in the previous section). Which of the given reasons and justifications do you find sufficiently well established, and which of them fail to satisfy your standards? What are *your* reasons for your conclusions? Put your analysis to others to get their reactions. Does the analysis help you – at least – to clarify your own practical theory for counselling with teachers, even if it differs from ours to some extent? What have you planned to do to clarify and expand it further?

Then go back to the focus on *thesis*: Every teacher possesses a 'practical theory' of teaching which is subjectively *the* strongest determining factor in her educational practice. Counselling with teachers must consequently originate in each teacher's practical theory, seeking to foster its conscious articulation and aiming to elaborate it and make it susceptible to change.

REFERENCES

Arfwedson, G. (1979) *Lärares arbete. (Teachers' Work.)* Studies in Curriculum Theory and Cultural Reproduction/5. Stockholm Institute of Education.

Arfwedson, G. (1985) *School Codes and Teachers' Work. Three Studies on Teacher Work Contexts.* Studies in Curriculum Theory and Cultural Reproduction/11. Stockholm Institute of Education. Malmö, CWK Gleerup.

Bateson, G. (1972) *Steps to an Ecology of Mind.* London, Intertext Books.

Berg, G. and Wallin, E. (1983) *Skolan i ett utvecklingsperspektiv. (The School in a Developmental Perspective.)* Lund, Studentlitteratur.

Bernstein, B. (1971) *Class, Codes and Control,* Vol. 3. London, Routledge & Kegan Paul.

Dewey, J. (1904) The relation of theory to practice in education. In *The Third Yearbook of the NSSE* (National Society for the Study of Education), Part 1. Chicago.

Hellesnes, J. (1975) *Sosialisering og teknokrati. (Socialization and Technocracy.)* Oslo, Glydendal.

Lewis, A. J. and Miel, A. (1972) *Supervision for Improved Instruction: New Challenges.* Belmont, Wadsworth.

Lortie, D. C. (1975) *Schoolteacher: A Sociological Study.* Chicago, Univ. of Chicago Press.

Løvlie, L. (1972) Universitetspedagogikk – eller debatten som ble vekk. (Teaching at Universities – or the debate that disappeared.) In Mediaas, N. *et al.* (eds.) *Etablert pedagogikk – makt eller avmakt?* Oslo, Universitetsforlaget.

Løvlie, L. (1974) Pedagogisk filosofi for praktiserende laerere. (Philosophy of education for practising teachers.) *Pedagogen,* No. 1, 22, pp. 19–36.

Lundgren, U. P. (1972) *Frame Factors and the Teaching Process: A Contribution to Curriculum Theory and Theory on Teaching.* Stockholm, Almqvist & Wiksell.

Ryle, G. (1945) Knowing how and knowing that. *Proceedings of the Aristotelian Society, XLVI,* 6, pp. 1–16.

Sarason, S. B. (1971) *The Culture of the School and the Problem of Change.* Boston, Allyn & Bacon.

Stenhouse, L. (1979) *Research as a Basis for Teaching.* Inaugural Lecture. University of East Anglia, Norwich.

PART 3: Science for All

Introduction

Elizabeth Whitelegg

The slogan 'science for all' has been a commonly used phrase since the 1960s and it has appeared in various forms in political speeches, reports from The Royal Society, UNESCO and education ministries of various countries. This section introduces the concepts behind the slogan and explains the rationale for the adoption of 'science for all' principles by educationalists both in Britain and internationally.

In the first article, Peter Fensham gives a broad overview of the 'science for all' movement and underlines the importance for everyone having access to a broadly based science education for a large proportion of his or her schooling. He considers various models of current practice in science education and examines these in the light of 'science for all' criteria. Finally, Fensham reflects on who the students of a 'science for all' curriculum actually are and why the science currently taught in schools has been inappropriate for many of these students. This theme is developed further in the articles that follow. Wynne Harlen considers the importance of scientific literacy for school pupils and advocates opening up the science curriculum and providing equal opportunities to study science for a wider variety of people. She focuses particularly on girls and offers some arguments for why they are underrepresented in science. Furthermore she presents suggestions for change via a curriculum that allows science processes to become a central learning strategy. In the next article, Reg Dennick considers the cultural specificity of Western science curricula and examines the debate between a multicultural science approach – one that aims to include examples of the uses of science from a variety of cultures so that tolerance and respect for other cultures is developed – and antiracist science which assumes that a racist ideology is embedded in the curriculum. The education of girls and pupils from ethnic minority backgrounds can be further disadvantaged if they are also socially deprived, and in her article Joan Solomon highlights the damage to pupils' learning brought about by social deprivation – damage that has far greater effects in terms of sheer numbers of pupils who experience deprivation than does disadvantage due to a pupil's gender or ethnic minority background. Social deprivation can result in

impaired language development and behavioural problems at school. Roy Purnell's article on special educational needs in science expands this area and
describes the development of special-needs education and the more recent
developments that relate this specifically to science.

Having examined the 'all' in 'science for all', the remaining two articles
consider aspects of further and higher education in science. Roger Blin-Stoyle
in his presidential address to the Association for Science Education in 1993
(reproduced here in slightly amended form) considers the changes that must
take place in post-16 education in England and Wales if we are to produce a
population that has a broad enough base of scientific and technological knowledge to meet society's future needs and to be compatible with the rest of
Europe where a less specialized science education at post-16 level is common-
place. In the final article in this section we return again to 'science for all'
criteria and present a case study of a course at The Open University that
attempts to offer broadly based science to those with no previous qualifications
in science. In particular, the OU course is examined in the light of some of the
criteria for a 'science for all' curriculum presented earlier.

3.1

Reflections on science for all

Peter J. Fensham

INTRODUCTION

In the 1980s 'science for all' emerged as the slogan that embodied a new challenge for science educators around the world. In 1983 UNESCO's Regional Office for Asia and the Pacific convened a small working party to prepare a case for *Science for All* (UNESCO, 1983), which was then endorsed by the regional ministers for education in 1984 as a top priority programme to further these aims in the next decade. In Canada a three-year study culminated in a report entitled *Science for Every Student: Educating Canadians for Tomorrow's World* (Science Council of Canada, 1984). In the USA, the then National Science Foundation (1983) published *Educating Americans for the 21st Century*, a plan to improve science education for all America's elementary and secondary students. Soon after this the American Association for the Advancement of Science (AAAS) established Project 2061, the first report of which was entitled *Science for All Americans* (AAAS, 1989). The Royal Society (1985) in Britain put out a short but startling manifesto, 'Science *is* for everybody'. It states that 'a proper science education at school must provide the basis for an adequate understanding of science . . . (which is then added to throughout life)' (The Royal Society, 1985, p. 2). This understanding, it goes on to say, needs to include not just facts but the methods of science and its limitations as well as an appreciation of its practical and social implications. This description of science is a clear statement of a priority that is repeated in all these national reports and it is this view of science that embodies 'science for all' as a new challenge to school science. Thus, the first objective in Canada's *Science for Every Student* is that school science should develop citizens able to participate fully in political and social choices facing a technological society.

In Australia, for various reasons, the slogan emerged in a more muted form because a question mark was added: *Science for Everybody?* (Curriculum Development Centre, 1988). One reason was the fact that the Australian

Adapted by the author from Science for all: a reflective essay, *Journal of Curriculum Studies* (1985) Vol. 17, no. 4, pp. 415–35.

debate explicitly included a tension not acknowledged in the other reports between the objectives they were advocating for school science. This tension is central to my discussion of 'science for all' in this article. I also point out that 'science for all students' is not entirely new, and that there is much to be learnt from the 1960s and 1970s when school science was at last a national priority in many countries. In the great surge of curriculum activity in science that occurred then, attention was focused initially on more specialized education in the sciences in secondary schooling. Many projects, however, were developed that did aim at more general levels of education such as primary and lower secondary. It was believed, and often stated, that learners at all levels of schooling would gain new excitement, new skills and new knowledge from the new curriculum projects and their new materials. With respect to the issue of 'science for all' at school in the 1990s, it would be foolish indeed to ignore the memories of these earlier attempts to do very much the same sort of thing. It is a lot easier now to be confident about what was, and was not achieved in these earlier efforts, than it is to be sure about what was really attempted and why it happened as it did. General consensus in a number of countries acknowledges three facts concerning the achievements of the 1960s and 1970s reform projects:

(1) A much better science curriculum and curriculum materials became available for those at school (at most about 20 per cent of an age group) from whom the future scientists and science-related professionals will be drawn.
(2) We have not yet achieved an effective science education in schools for the 80 per cent or so who most probably will not continue with any formal education in science after they leave school.
(3) The minority who go on from school to tertiary studies that are science – based are unrepresentative in a number of ways, such as gender and ethnicity, of those who enter schooling at the elementary or primary stage.

The above reports and their slogans of intention are evidence for the negative assessments in the second and third statements above. The first statement does, however, represent both a very considerable achievement and a great deal of useful experience from which we can now learn as we face the new tasks for science education.

SCHOOL SYSTEMS AND SCIENCE EDUCATION

The curriculum reform movement of the 1960s and 1970s has rightly been criticized for so often behaving as if schooling and science education take place in a social and political vacuum. When its rhetoric did acknowledge the social demands that science education was called upon to meet, it failed to distinguish between their curricular implications or to recognize that being in competition they can also conflict with each other.

In the 1970s sociologists of knowledge, sociologists of curriculum, and social analysts of the curriculum projects, derived from these reforms considerable evidence of the way in which a social demand in practice turned out to be both a resource for the development of a curriculum and a constraint on its particular form, its knowledge of worth, the styles of teaching it actually encourages, and the learners it will advantage. They point out that schools are established by societies in which various social groups have interests that such an institutional form of education can serve. The curriculum, in its parts and in its totality, is the instrument to serve these interests, and the field where the competition between these social interests in schooling is resolved. The sciences, particularly the physical sciences, in many societies, are gateway subjects that filter the relatively few students who are allowed to move into certain professions of high status, societal influence and economic security. Because of the societal power associated with these positions, we can call this a *political* interest in schooling. Again, industrial interests need a limited but definite number of persons with scientific skills and expertise to maintain and expand a variety of aspects of a society's economy. This is an *economic* inter- est. Scientists, particularly in research institutions and universities, are now a power faction in society with a major interest in *maintaining their discipline* as an élite and important field. They are thus keenly interested in having the schools begin the process of reproduction of the sciences as those in higher education define them. In addition, there are clearly many ways in which the *cultural* and *social* life of groups in society are now influenced by technology and by knowledge and applications from the sciences. Science education can assist these groups to have a sense of control rather than of subservience and to take advantage of what science has to offer them. The fascination of scientific phenomena and the role of human inventiveness in relation to them offer much potential for school education to meet the interests of its learners for *individual* growth and satisfaction.

A recurring example of the competition between social interests is how the curriculum of science education at school can serve the demand for scien- tifically equipped professionals and the demand for a more scientifically liter- ate population. The former demand, related to the political and economic interests and the maintenance of the discipline, is needed so that societies and economies can keep pace in a world where scientific knowledge and technol- ogy play rapidly increasing roles. The latter demand is more related to the other three interests mentioned above and is concerned with those who should benefit from the personal and social applications of science and who will be prepared to respond appropriately to the changes of a scientific or technologi- cal character that increasingly confront the society. Layton (1973), in *Science for the People*, provided a classic account of the competition between these interests in Victorian England, when an attempt was made to popularize science in basic schooling before it was available at higher levels to those who were to become the source of the scientists and engineers of that age. It may appear that the achievement of either of these two targets will also be a contribution to the other. That is, as the first target is met and exceeded, school science education is on the way to meeting the second. Or, if the second is met to any significant extent, the first will then follow. Just such a simplistic co-operative view of the interactions of societal demands and the curriculum of schooling operated in the reforms of the 1960s. The advocates of more general science education at that time attempted to participate in the opportunities for curriculum reform that were provided by the more powerful demand for more science specialists. Under the advice and guidance of well-meaning university scientists and encouraged by some slogans about the nature of learning that were current at the time, the 1960s' projects aimed at inducting all learners at school into the world of the scientist. Not surprisingly, it was the research scientist they chose as their model scientist. There was, it seems, a genuine belief that both targets would be met if all children, in appropriate ways for their level of schooling, were to learn some of the ideas and some of the ways that research scientists use to describe and explore the world. All (or as many as learned successfully) would thus have gained a degree of scientific literacy, and enough of them would be interested to continue on to become the future specialist workforce.

It is now clear that the apparent even-handedness in the statements of intent gave way in practice to the interests the first target represents. The first curricula to be redesigned, for example, in the USA, Britain, Australia, Canada, Sweden, Thailand, and Malaysia, were either for the upper secondary school or for élite secondary students – the very levels and streams which contained those from whom the specialist workforce would be drawn. By giving priority to the curricula for this minority of students, the projects were explicitly rejecting the interests of the larger target group for scientific literacy. Very few countries in the early 1960s had even a majority of each age cohort still in regular secondary schooling at the levels of these privileged sectors.

Both these target groups and the distinct goals they represent are again referred to in the rhetoric of the contemporary scene. The rhetoric for 'science for all', that is, for the second goal of the 1960s and 1970s is, however, much stronger and clearer than it was in the 1950s and 1960s, and the societal pressures for it to be achieved are much more substantial. Many countries now have a majority of each age group still at school (or are aiming to achieve this state soon) in the later years of secondary school and most of them will not go on to become scientific professionals. Problems of the environment are now inescapable concerns for all citizens, and this worldwide situation is a critical difference between the 1980s and the 1950s, the two periods leading up to these bursts of curriculum activity. These changes add strength to the claims of 'science for all'. Slogans, however, are powerful and effective because they are responded to readily. Agreement and responses to a slogan do not, however, mean that everyone attaches the same meaning to it. Roberts (1982) in Canada has contributed greatly to our understanding of how competing interest groups in science education perceive the idea of scientific literacy, and respond to its curriculum concerns. He argues that seven curriculum emphases can be found in the history of science education practice in elementary and secondary schools in North America. These are 'everyday coping; structure of science;

science technology and decisions; correct explanations; self as explainer and solid foundation' (Roberts, 1982, p. 246). It is not very difficult to associate most of these with one or more of the societal interests that have been described above. Only a few of these interests have been satisfied at any one time by the science curriculum. This impossibility of serving all interests with a single curriculum is consistent with what has emerged from the historical and sociological analyses of science curricula referred to earlier. It is a central plank for the discussion in this article.

THE MINORITY DEMAND

In many countries there has been a significant improvement in the supply of technological and scientific professionals over the last twenty years although concerns continue to be expressed about the qualities they have. Some forms of scientific specialization, for example biological sciences and medical sciences, are now so well supplied that there is a surplus beyond what the national economy can afford. In other countries there is a shortage in many of these science-based specialisms and overcoming this is still the top priority. It is important to assess some of the prices that educational systems have paid in giving priority to meeting this national need. The ultimate formal education of a nation's scientific and technological workforce is in the hands of universities, colleges or institutes of technology. These educational institutions form a hierarchy, the top of which is under considerable international pressure to conform to the production of graduates who share a common body of knowledge and associated practical skills or experiences. The rapid growth of scientific knowledge in the twentieth century has not led to a great diversity of content in the science courses at top universities or in the school systems that equip the minority of students who enter the tertiary hierarchy. Rather, certain specific conceptual content in each of the sciences has been consolidated as the knowledge worth learning. A basis for choosing this conceptual content for undergraduate science courses is, no doubt, that it is 'powerful' in the sense that a number of these concepts are ones scientists everywhere commonly use as they consider new phenomena and the problems posed by the applications of science or technology. Nevertheless, the learning of these concepts (and their precursors in school science) can take so much time that the excitement of contemporary science and its many interactions with society can be, and often are, overlooked and omitted.

Two basic questions face any national system of education when it gives a priority to the development of this type of professional élite. Who shall be permitted to enter the training group (remembering it involves not more than about 20 per cent of the age cohort)? What prior preparation will they be given? These tasks of selection and preparation change with time. In some countries they are associated with the middle levels of the secondary part of the education system. In some less developed countries they may even extend to the lower secondary levels or even down into the primary level. In a number of countries since the 1960s, the locus for these questions has shifted to higher levels as secondary education has become a mass phenomenon. Periods of economic growth and recession in the more industrialized countries have both led, for different immediate reasons, to greater retention of students in secondary schooling. In very few cases is there a degree of openness that enables direct entry into science and technological education at the tertiary level without prior membership of a group in secondary schooling that somehow has been 'selected' and 'prepared'.

The availability of science and technology courses via open-type universities in a few countries may be leading to exceptions, although it would be necessary to know how many of their students are in fact novices in these fields and how many graduate into the professions other than teaching, before these examples are established as real alternatives. A consequence of the clear messages the majority of each age cohort has been receiving at school, that there is only one route to these professions, namely success in these subjects at school, is that interest in such tertiary courses among the many mature-age students now entering higher education will be low.

The two tasks of selection and preparation are usually associated. That is, the content of science education deemed a suitable preparation for the science disciplines in tertiary education has also turned out to be a useful selective device since comparatively few students learn it successfully. Whether this low success is due to inherent difficulty in the content of science, or whether it is due to lack of interest among students is another issue. It is certainly possible to envisage alternative content for learning in school science education that would not serve the selection task in this way. For example, a course that focused on more relevant, practical skills of science and on scientific knowledge of direct use in everyday life may well achieve many more successful learners than are required. After all, a very wide spectrum of the school-leavers in many countries do now acquire the skills of driving a motor car – a much more complex set of skills and associated conceptual judgements than are required in many practical experiments in school science. The association of selection and preparation has, of course, some strange and disturbing consequences. For example, if a science education at school could be devised that most children were able to continue to learn with substantial success, it would not suit the selection task as we now understand it. Such a course may, however, have highlighted the interest of many more of the age group to consider seriously the scientifically related technologies and professions as possible careers. While failing to do the selection task, it may have broadened the size and the basic intellectual quality of the base from which selection would then be made. Because present science education is taught so sequentially, we know little about how students would cope with the conceptual learning in tertiary science if they began from a wide base of familiarity and confident accomplishment in more practical scientific knowledge. However, it is just possible that this base would be an even better preparation than the current narrow conceptual learning is.

A CURRICULUM FOR SCIENTISTS

The solution to the dual questions of selection and preparation has been found in most countries by the creation of a secondary school curriculum in the sciences that has the following characteristics:

- the rote recall of a large number of facts, concepts and algorithms that are not obviously socially useful;
- too little familiarity with many of the concepts to enable their scientific usefulness to be experienced;
- concepts that have been defined for high levels of generality among scientists without their levels of abstraction being adequately acknowledged in the school context, and hence their consequential limitations in real situations is not adequately indicated;
- an essentially abstract system of scientific knowledge with examples of objects and events to illustrate this system rather than those aspects of the science of factual phenomena that enable some use or control of them to occur;
- life experiences and social applications only as exemplary rather than as the essence of the science learning;
- the association of laboratory practical work with a belief that this activity enhances the conceptual learning rather than being a source for the learning of essential skills or the means of investigating new phenomena;
- content which gives a high priority to the quantitative, even in biology and chemistry where this priority is probably greater than it is for many practising biologists and chemists.

Such a school curriculum has no real discontinuity between what is regarded as knowledge of worth in specialist science education and the content of the school curriculum even down to the first years of secondary schooling. Furthermore, the conceptual and abstract nature of this chosen content lends itself to a sequential type of development in teaching and learning that inevitably provides for the selection task. A concept is introduced. It is then defined and its use illustrated. It is then further developed in a quantitative sense or by elaboration of its subcategories, etc. Examples include: the idea of acids as proton donors; acids and bases reacting as a conjugate system; pH as the measure of acidity; strong and weak acids, acidity and concentration equilibria.

If a learner loses motivation or fails for whatever reason to learn one stage, then it is almost impossible to recover. The sequences stretch on, only terminating when the curriculum says so, not because some investigation is complete. The learner is always dependent on the teacher or the textbook for the beginning, the end, and for what is 'correct'.

Furthermore, in many schools or educational systems reasonable achievement in the learning of science subjects is not sufficient to allow a student to continue in a science stream at school (particularly for the physical sciences). A high level of the abstract and sequential learning in mathematics is also necess-ary. Thus, the minority group in this concentration on sciences and mathema-tics has paid the price of being unable to study much of the humanities and the social sciences, the subject areas that more directly develop communication abilities and raise value issues.

The selection task influences science curricula in many ways. For example, quantitative aspects of chemistry (stoichiometry, etc.) are introduced com-paratively early although they are difficult to learn, and not essential to the learning of much of the inorganic and organic chemistry that follows. The use of mathematical hurdles has, in a curious way, allowed a not insignificant degree of social mobility into professions involving science and technology to occur. For some males this quantitative knowledge content with its abstract-ness and emphasis on algorithmic use has enabled them to overcome the advantage that certain socio-economic groups have in the more culturally and language-based subject areas. This effect is not an outcome of the deliberate use of curriculum for positive social reconstruction. On the other hand, we now also know a great deal about the way the above content of preparatory science is a major contributing factor to other groups of students who have been and are low participators or achievers in science.

The worst price of these solutions to the demand for scientific profes-sionals is that the majority of the school population learns that they are unable to learn school science. Furthermore, unless strenuous efforts are made to offer alternative forms of science, most students will identify science as presented at school as what science is. Science to most students becomes a subject that in some mysterious way enables a small group of their peers to become an élite.

One other unintended price arose from the implementation, rather than the development, of the 1960s' reform. Bringing senior school science 'up to date' and continuous with how the teaching of the sciences in university was being conceived and practised seemed a reasonable basis for the curricular reforms. The developers prepared materials that included a number of the elegant aspects of science such as the role of models, laboratory work as a process of both intellectual and practical enquiry, and macro – and micro – levels of considering phenomena. In the process of implementing these cur-ricula, the rubrics of preparation and selection, however, emphasized only some of this content and as a consequence it became the knowledge of worth. External examinations and selection procedures based on them converted the processes of teaching and learning the sciences into rather narrow first stages of an induction *into* the world of academic science. Learners became like novitiates being tested by the rigours of a journey the joys of which would only come much later. Their teachers' task was to try to bring them along the first stages of the long journey that they themselves had earlier successfully traversed for a few more stages. Furthermore, often the stages the teachers had reached did not include much of the 'surprises by joy' that give academic scientists such delight.

MISPLACED OPTIMISM

A most striking feature of the 1960s' and 1970s' projects was the optimism and enthusiasm of developers who undertook the task of providing a science education for a more general group of the school population. For example, those who were given the chances of sharing their subject with primary children for the first time took up their tasks eagerly. Some focused on important topics from the knowledge and content of science that they themselves had learnt in secondary school or at university and set out to rework them for presentation to these young learners. Others put an emphasis on the so-called processes of science. If only the pedagogical approach was cleverly enough designed, and if only the teachers could be encouraged to follow it faithfully, there was an optimistic belief that the mass of learners would learn, and find the same satisfaction in these topics that the designers had achieved through their own education in science. The pedagogical approaches they chose were often drawn from the nature of science itself – guided discovery, stages of development, etc.

The evaluations of the implementation of these development projects suggest that this optimism was rather naive and arrogant. Only a relatively small percentage of a population historically have sustained a fascination with scientific knowledge for its own sake. It was expecting rather too much that the designers and teachers of the 1960s and 1970s could produce such a revolution of interest in science as they defined it.

A CURRICULUM FOR ALL

If the 'science for all' of the 1990s is not to make the same sorts of mistakes it must not impose on the majority of learners a content and approach to science that is important to a small minority made up of science teachers, scientists and science curriculum developers. These persons, educated extensively in science, have learnt to look at the world and at schooling through eyes that are very conditioned by scientific knowledge. This was the educational process that separated them from the majority of their peers. Their very success in it makes it difficult for them to see science from the viewpoint of future citizens for whom science is only one aspect, albeit an influential one, of their lives in society.

For example, the person educated in science is likely to differentiate between science and technology. Many citizens draw no such distinction and give technologies as examples of science they have experienced or heard about. Again, those educated in science appreciate precise definitions and explanations while the others are more interested in information and how to apply it.

Progress with 'science for all' will require a radically different way of choosing content in science that is worth learning. If we are serious in our claims that science and our technological society affect and can contribute to the lives of all citizens, then it is some of these points of contact that must be identified. This will involve a view of science from a position in society rather than a view of society from within science itself. As young learners move through the years of schooling their experiences in society (home, local community, school, wider community, etc.) will change, and they will encounter a stream of situations in which science is a contributing aspect. Science curriculum developers as persons with a familiarity with the rich corpus of science, would then have the task of identifying and matching the appropriate science to this changing set of social situations. Non-scientists would be very important members of the curriculum teams for 'science for all'.

Science teachers, with their own confidence about learning science, would now in effect be couriers for their students between the corpus of science and their students, rather than inductors of them into its initial layers. The science they would bring would enable their students to understand and operate in their world better, and to believe increasingly that science and its applications in technology are great human inventions that can be drawn on or rejected for their own and society's well-being.

WHAT IS NEEDED IF 'SCIENCE FOR ALL' IS TO SUCCEED?

I have argued that the education in the sciences of an élite training group won in the last reform process against the science education of the majority in the competition between conflicting demands on school science. If the latter is to succeed it will be important that all the relevant knowledge we have gained since the 1960s is taken into account. Four types of this knowledge are discussed in the remainder of this article: organizational knowledge of curriculum, knowledge of how curriculum content can be defined, knowledge of who are the *all*, and knowledge of how teachers change.

Organizational support

If 'science for all' is to have status, worth and credibility with parents, learners and society more generally it will need structural supports in the organization of school systems and in individual schools.

Three organizational ways to support 'science for all' and to deal with the competitive power of the education in the sciences of the minority are already evident in some school systems: containment, core and options, and parallel curricula above the containment level.

Containment

An organization of containment means that the specific education in the sciences for the minority does not occur below an agreed level. Below that level studies in the sciences are aimed at the wide range of students and their curricula are determined on 'science for all' criteria. England and Wales, France and Thailand are countries that have now established this type of organization. Closer examination of the content of their national curricula for science up to the containment level would be needed to see what criteria were involved in its choice. Beyond these levels these countries have either two or three years of schooling for studies in the sciences curricula that are geared to the preparation of the science-oriented minority.

It should be noted that systems that operate a stream of education (in separate schools as in the Netherlands, or in the same school as in some Australian states) for the minority alongside another more general science for the majority are not examples of containment. Nor indeed does such an organization support the concept of 'science for all'.

Core and options

The curriculum can be organized as core studies plus options. Science with the characteristics of 'science for all' would be the core study for all students throughout their schooling. Additional units in the sciences would be available in the later secondary years for those who wished to prepare for science-based tertiary studies. An important corollary would be that tertiary institutions would make available bridging or introductory units in the sciences for students without the preparatory options. In a number of countries some tertiary institutions do offer these sorts of courses or they are available via open-learning programmes. Often these have come into existence because of a shortfall in their supply of students with traditional preparation rather than as a corollary of the changes in secondary schooling above. The USA is probably one of the few examples where optional units in sciences are available in some of its school systems, the successful completion of which lead to advanced placement in university. Many universities in the USA also offer introductory courses in the sciences, but a number of states are only now trying to establish a core of science for all students throughout high school.

A very common initial response to any suggestion that the particular science education of the minority should be contained or made optional, is that the approach would undermine the effectiveness of the supply of future professions in science-based fields. Accordingly, it is important to consider the possible or likely effects of these forms of organization. The evidence from existing practice is not decisive. Some countries begin the teaching of the selective and preparatory type of science early in the secondary years. Other countries already postpone the serious development of this type of science education until the third, fourth or even fifth year of secondary education. Examples of these patterns exist in some developed and some developing countries where supply has at times been both too low and too high. Where widespread retention in schooling is increasing and the supply is too small the case for containment at a reasonably high level seems compelling. An excluding type of science education with obvious cultural incongruities for the majority population would seem to be unhelpful to the expansion of the pool of learners from which the supply group is to emerge. Where retention is still low, early identification of potential members of a special science stream is more easily justified.

A final answer to the concern about supply clearly cannot be given because there has not yet been sufficient experience of containment that is underpinned by an effective 'science education for all'. If such a science education were to be really effective, then there is little doubt that the pool of students interested and successful in science would be larger than at present. With such a background of achievement and confidence, one or two years of deliberate preparatory education in the sciences should then be quite adequate for the needs of higher education institutions. Whether enough of this larger pool will choose this preparation will be more influenced by the financial and other prospects society offers to scientific professionals than by things internal to the education system.

Parallel curricula above the containment level

The existence of alternative curricula for science education above the level of containment can help in clarifying the purposes of science education. These exist already in a number of countries. In Thailand, for example, science is part of the school curriculum at every level. Students in the humanities stream of upper secondary schooling have to study physical and biological science for two years. This is a major advance on the situation in Australia, New Zealand, the USA and a number of other industrialized countries, where biology has been pressed into a role in which it is taken as a so-called science subject by non-science learners in senior secondary schooling. This limits the study of biology in schooling for the minority science stream and provides a very unbalanced education in science for most of its learners that gives them no confidence in the physical sciences. Since many of these learners become teachers in primary schooling the effect on them gets carried through to the next generation.

A number of countries have alternative courses of science education in their vocational upper secondary schools, or in the vocational streams of their comprehensive schools. Provided the content of these alternative science courses and their examinations clearly are different in emphasis and kind from the science subjects taken by the science minority, their existence certainly helps to indicate that there are and need to be different curriculum emphases for science education.

Content for 'science for all'

Below the level of containment, wherever it may be set, there are a number of years of schooling in which all or most of the children of a society should be offered a meaningful science education. Its content should be those aspects of science that will improve the quality of their life outside school and in the future.

Earlier in this article a number of characteristics of traditional education in the sciences were given. The converse of some of these, the official concern and intentions supporting 'science for all', and the 'view from society' mentioned earlier lead to a number of other characteristics that may be useful checkpoints for choosing this content:

- Its content should have immediate and obvious personal and social relevance to the learners. That is, it ought to stem from their existing knowledge and experience and relate to their impending social situations.
- Its learning objectives (practical skills and knowledge) should have criteria of achievement that most learners can realize at some level.
- Its broad themes, topics or issues should constantly be visible to make sense of the component parts of the learning.
- Its pedagogy should exploit the demonstration and practice modes that are inherent to much science and also to the cultural learning about natural phenomena and technologies that occurs before and outside schooling.
- Its learning of practical and intellectual skills and processes should flow naturally from the nature of the science topics rather than be a primary focus of the learning themselves.
- Its assessment should recognize both the learners' prior knowledge and all their subsequent achievements.

With such a set of characteristics the next step is to begin to identify content that may meet them.

Eight years ago when I first attempted to consider the appropriate content of 'science for all' (Fensham, 1985), there was little to go on besides the failures of the content that had been developed in the earlier projects. The unattractiveness and hence difficulty associated with the theoretical concepts and principles of school science have been mentioned above. If this was true at the secondary level it was even more evident at the primary level despite the clever materials and approaches that were devised by some American projects to teach a conceptual approach to these young learners. Failure of this science content had been almost inevitable since it was just what those who were to teach it had rejected or failed to learn in their own schooling.

More persistent and successful in pervading the intentional curriculum for elementary schooling in many countries was a content for science based on the so-called processes of science – observing, classifying, measuring, predicting, etc. In practice, the learning of this content has been little more successful. Even where it seems to have been achieved in primary schooling, it has been ignored and not reinforced by secondary teachers and society. Millar and Driver (1987) have helped these failures to be understood by critically reviewing the relationships between scientific knowledge and these processes from three perspectives. They argue that such a clearly defined set of processes does not actually exist as a describable method of science. Scientists do not just observe. Scientists look for some aspect that comes from their current view (conceptual) of the situation in question. Their instruments that extend their observational power have built into them the concepts and theories they have come to trust. Observing is concept exploration and hence is not a general or prior process. The second point these authors make is that the process view does not correspond with the way humans learn and store information. *Content*, in a conceptual sense, and *context* are important in a way that the process approach to science education has failed to recognize.

Fortunately, in the latter half of the 1980s some of the new science curriculum projects have established some promising new bases for the content of the science they will promote. 'Concepts in contexts' has become a very useful slogan to point to one of these new bases. Its keywords recognize the great deal that has been found out in the 1980s about how science is learnt (Gunstone, 1988; Osborne and Wittrock, 1985), and about the importance of taking the learners' situations (contexts) seriously.

The authors of the Salters' Chemistry Project (Salters' Science Course, 1987) add operational meaning when they say its curriculum starts with material and phenomena familiar to 13–16-year-olds from their own experience or from television, books, etc., and introduces concepts and explanations when they are needed in working on these everyday things. Industrial, technological, economic and social implications are thus central to the content of this chemistry.

This recognition of learners' real-world contexts in order for concepts to have meaning has led to very non-traditional names for blocks of learning. 'Clothing', 'drinks', 'warmth', 'buildings', 'keeping clean' are units of study in chemistry; 'transport', 'communication', 'bridges', 'living in air and water', and 'sports' in physics; and 'life support technologies', 'organ transplants', and 'bio-technologies' in biology. The material for these units include knowledge from sciences other than the one that is named as their subject field.

These contextual names have broad meanings and some developers have referred to *networks of concepts* in *networks of contexts*. This elaboration tries to emphasize that social applications of science are not isolated events but form part of a complex and dynamic social whole. Thus 'transport' or 'traffic' are better contexts to study than 'the lead accumulator' or 'the bicycle' as isolated technological applications of a chemical or physical concept. The idea of the two networks also helps to emphasize the linkages between the concepts and the contexts and between each other that we now know are so essential to learning.

Finally, when *context* and *concept* are both taken as seriously as science content, a new set of concepts emerges that may be a very important key to what 'science for all' needs to become. Projects in Canada and in the Netherlands have included socio-scientific concepts so that the realities of context can be studied seriously. 'Blood alcohol limit', 'toxic level', 'unit energy cost', 'risk of radiation' are concepts that are defined and even legislated by societies. They are what citizens need to understand. They are too scientific to be taught confidently by anyone other than science teachers. They are not purely scientific so they have not had a place in traditional school science.

At the primary level promising redefinition of science content is occurring as a result of the emergence of technology education and environmental education. Situations (contexts) that can be starting points for learning, such as common technologies (in actual or simulated kit form) and environmental ones, have a reality for the young learners and their teachers alike. The emphasis for the learning in the first case which becomes how the former work, can be used and modified to achieve useful ends. In the second it is an exploration of what the quality of environment is or could be, and how it is affected by the personal and social behaviours available to the learners and the teachers. Both approaches seek to build strong cognitive, affective and behavioural relationships between learners and teachers and what is being learned. As these develop, the introduction of the conceptual ideas from science or technology should occur with more natural ease than has hitherto been the case.

WHO MAKE UP 'ALL'?

The fact that the slogan is a call for 'science for *all*' is indicative that hitherto science education has not served the interests of all students. This is a consequence of competition between societal demands on school science and the associated curricular emphases that have determined the sort of science that is the knowledge of worth.

Much has now been discovered about some groups of learners who have been discriminated against by this science. The international achievement studies in science in the mid-1970s publicized the fact that in many countries girls participated and achieved less in science than boys. The publication in Britain of *The Missing Half: Girls and Science Education* (Kelly, 1981) and in the USA of *Women in Science* (Kahle, 1985) provided more bases for this concern and a response to it. Several curriculum approaches have been taken to remedy this bias. The first was to remove the often quite blatant gender imbalance in existing textbooks and other curriculum materials for science. Some progress has been made in the rewriting and choice of language, illustrations, the contexts in which phenomena are presented, and the applications chosen to illustrate concepts. The meanings of gender-neutral, gender-friendly or more importantly gender-inclusive are, however, still being uncovered as far as curriculum materials are concerned. The second approach has been to examine and change the way option and choice are built into the curriculum of schooling, particularly but not only in the later secondary years. At the classroom level, a number of studies have shown that teachers in Western classrooms allow and even encourage differential participation favouring boys in co-educational classrooms. Intervention studies in primary and secondary classrooms that set out to alter this teacher behaviour have reported success. At the school or system level, student choice in certain organizations of the curriculum can have a profound bearing on how the sexes participate in the science curriculum as has already been mentioned. Such choice opens school science to the gender biases in society about science. Japan, some European countries, and Thailand are countries that do not allow such open or spurious choice and require students studying science (or even all students) at these levels to include both biological and physical sciences in their overall curriculum of learning.

A spectacular outcome of this pattern of enforcing study has been reported in the Bangkok area of Thailand where girls and boys were participating in all three sciences equally, with the girls outperforming the boys in chemistry, and performing equally with them in physics (Klainin and Fensham, 1987).

The third approach has involved the contexts of science learning. This has led some of the new curriculum projects with a science–technology–society (STS) orientation to include more explicit personal and social aspects of science. These have been espoused by some educators who are concerned with the problem of gender and science. Some of them, however, have pointed out that gender concerns about girls and science should not mask the unpopularity of science among many boys at school. They have suggested that STS has the potential to have positive effects for more boys as well as for girls.

This possibility was taken a step further when the differential appeal of various contexts that have been used in physics curricula were explored in the Netherlands. It is not just a matter of adding an STS dimension, because there are a number of possible STS dimensions. They found that the widespread assumption that because boys at school more often already have technological careers in mind they will find technological topics of science satisfying, does have to be questioned. They did find gender differences in the positive responses to a number of topics, but that weather, traffic and music were satisfying to both boys and girls. Another subtle aspect of STS has been reported. If 'doubt' about the applications of science can be accepted as an integral part of the content of a science curriculum, then that type of STS curriculum is likely to have a receptive response from a wider cross-section of students.

These curriculum approaches have, however, so far been largely a means to an end: to induce girls into learning a science that is only marginally changed. Manthorpe (1982) argued a case for going further and replacing current school science, with its masculine emphasis, with a different sort of science. Work on the different interests and attitudes of boys and girls has been a helpful foundation for such changes. These studies suggest two ways learners can interact with the content of science curricula. These have been labelled 'analytical/ instrumental' and 'nurturative', picking up such juxtaposed pairs as 'interest in rules/interest in relationships' and 'interest in controlling inanimate things/ interest in nurturing living things'. Boys and girls are not, however, neatly distinguished by these two sets of characteristics. The evidence indicates overlapping distribution with more boys on the 'analytical/instrumental' side and more girls on the 'nurturative' one. Manthorpe's suggestion was a science that includes:

- a holistic view in which social, ethical and moral questions are unquestionably involved;
- a scientific community based on co-operation;
- respect for and equal valuation of different forms of knowledge – including the irrational and the subjective;
- placing emphasis on a rewriting of the intellect and emotion;

- a re-evaluation of the belief that the quality of life has priority over economics.

The McClintock Collective (1987) in Australia has produced curriculum materials and conducted many curriculum workshops for science teachers that are consistent with such a 'feminine' science curriculum. It is certainly different from present curricula and from the 'girl-friendly' ones that have been advocated. In a similar but even more extreme vein, there are arguments for a feminist science curriculum that would also be more humanist and thus more inclusive. The studies of gender and science and the emergence of curricula for science that are more gender inclusive have been important for 'science for all' but it is only a beginning. From this case it is clear that the target of 'all' will only be reached step by step as we identify groups who are disadvantaged by existing curricula and when more appropriate curricula to meet their needs are invented. As yet nothing like the attention that gender has received has been paid to ethnic, or socio-economic groups who are also now known to be low participators.

So much of modern science has been developed and described by European and North American male scientists that it inevitably reflects the thought forms and language of these countries. This means that it does not mesh very easily with other thought forms and languages which are different. The work of Wilson (1981) on the cultural contexts of science education began to tackle the complex issues in extending science education to the 'all' who make up some of these groups. Christie (1991) in a recent paper on aboriginal science in Australia highlighted the very great differences in metaphorical thought between these cultural groups and Western science when he described the significance of relations to the former compared with counting elements to the latter. Much more work will need to be done to free school science of its inherent cultural, ethnic and class biases.

TEACHER CHANGE

The key role of teachers in relation to materials in curriculum implementation has often been alluded to in relation to the failures of the 1960s' and 1970s' reforms. If 'science for all' in any of its stages of discovery and invention is to succeed, teachers will need an immense amount of help and support. Indeed the major part of the curriculum development resources will need to be devoted to teachers and not to materials production.

Fortunately, a great deal of attention has been paid to teacher change throughout the 1980s, and much of it has been in science education. The Secondary Science Curriculum Review, established in England and Wales in 1982, was essentially an exercise in teacher change. In Australia, Canada and England some successful examples have been reported of how long-term collaborative work between groups of teachers and science educators has led to major shifts in teaching from expository pedagogies to ones that are more effective for more learners.

In these and other countries exemplary teachers have associated teacher change, and considerable progress has been made on the elaboration of teachers' professional knowledge as a key factor in changing other teachers. There is no shortage of ideas for helping teachers change. All of the approaches acknowledge it is a slow process needing lots of support – only rarely is it rapid. If science is to be for more and more learners its teaching must, at every step, be conceived in a new way by more and more teachers. This will only happen if those calling for 'science for all' provide the support that teachers need.

REFERENCES

AAAS (American Association for the Advancement of Science) (1989) *Science for All Americans*. A summary report of Phase I of Project 2061. Washington, DC, American Association for the Advancement of Science.

Christie, M. (1991) Aboriginal science for the ecologically sustainable future, *Australian Science Readers Journal*, Vol. 37, no. 11, pp. 26–32.

Curriculum Development Centre (1988) *Science for Everybody? Towards a National Science Statement*, Canberra, Curriculum Development Centre.

Fensham, P. (1985) Science for all, *Journal of Curriculum Studies*, Vol. 17, no. 4, pp. 415–35.

Gunstone, R. (1988) Learners in science education, in P. Fensham (ed.) *Development and Dilemmas in Science Education*, pp. 73–95, London, Falmer Press.

Kahle, J. B. (ed.) (1985) *Women in Science: A Report from the Field*, London, Falmer Press.

Kelly, A. (1981) *The Missing Half: Girls and Science Education*, Manchester University Press.

Klainin, S. and Fensham, P. (1987) Learning achievements in upper school chemistry in Thailand: some remarkable sex reversals, *International Journal of Science Education*, Vol. 9, no. 2, pp. 217–27.

Layton, D. (1973) *Science for the People*, London, George Allen & Unwin.

Manthorpe, C. (1982) Men's science, women's science or science: some issues related to the study of girls' science education, *Studies in Science Education*, Vol. 9, pp. 65–80.

McClintock Collective (1987) *The Fascinating Sky*, Melbourne, Ministry of Education.

Millar, R. and Driver, R. (1987) Beyond processes, *Studies in Science Education*, Vol. 14, pp. 33–62.

National Science Foundation (1983) *Educating Americans for the 21st Century*. Report of the National Science Board Commission on Precollege Education in Mathematics, Science and Technology, Washington, DC, National Science Foundation.

Osborne, R. and Wittrock, M. (1985) The generative learning model and its implications for science education, *Studies in Science Education*, Vol. 12, pp. 59–87.

Roberts, D. (1982) Developing the concept of 'curriculum emphases' in science education, *Science Education*, Vol. 66, no. 2, pp. 132–60.

The Royal Society (1985) Science *is* for everybody. Executive summary from *The Public Understanding of Science*, London, The Royal Society.

Salters' Science Course (1987) Science Education Group, University of York.

Science Council of Canada (1984) *Science for Every Student: Educating Canadians for Tomorrow's World*, Ottawa, Supply and Service.

UNESCO (1983) *Science for All*, Bangkok UNESCO Regional Office for Education in Asia and the Pacific.

Wilson, B. (1981) *Cultural Contexts of Science and Mathematics Education*, Leeds, Centre for Studies in Science Education, University of Leeds.

3.2

Education for equal opportunities in a scientifically literate society

Wynne Harlen

The purpose of this paper is to link together three concerns in science education: ideas about the improvement of scientific literacy of the general population, equal opportunities for males and females in school science education, and proposals for an increased emphasis of process-based learning experiences in formal education. That the first two of these concerns should be linked ought to be self-evident, for it would not be possible to foster a scientifically literate population when half of that population is underachieving in their science education. If we think not so much of the justice of providing equal opportunities for women but, narrowly, of the value to society of increasing the level of public understanding, there are strong arguments for paying attention to how science can be taught in a way that increases rather than deters interest and scientific literacy in both sexes.

The importance of a scientifically and technologically literate population is being emphasized in all countries, since it is recognized that specialist scientists and technologists cannot operate without a knowledgeable supporting society. Layton, for example, commenting on the developments of the last 20 years, has observed that 'While new scientific knowledge and appropriate technologies clearly required specialised manpower for their generation, maintenance and growth, their local applications could not take root and be purposefully controlled in the absence of an informed public' (Layton 1986, p. 9). He goes on to say that the need for more scientists and technologists was the hallmark of the developments of the 1960s, while the need for a scientifically and technologically educated public is the hallmark of those of the 1980s. One of the signs of this has been the considerable increase in conferences, journals and other publications on these matters [e.g., The Royal Society 1985, 1986, CIBA Foundation 1987, Shortland (ed.) 1987].

However, the concerns to which these publications are addressed are not entirely new. They were eloquently expressed in 1972 in the UNESCO publication *Learning to Be* written by Faure *et. al.*, which included this warning:

From the *International Journal of Science Education* (1989) Vol. 11, no. 2, pp. 125–34.

Lack of understanding of technological methods makes one more and more dependent on others in daily life, narrows employment possibilities and increases the potentially harmful effects of the unrestrained application of technology – for example alienation of individuals or pollution will finally become overwhelming.

(Faure *et al.*, 1972, p. 66)

This quotation underlines the importance of not excluding women from the definition of 'public'. The dependence on others, the narrowing of employment prospects and the loss of feeling of control over one's life are suffered in greater degree by women in an increasingly technological age as a result of unequal opportunities for education in science and technology. Moreover, the voice of women in such matters as protesting against the less humane applications of science, urging measures to prevent pollution and emphasizing human values in decision-making is not being heard.

The third link in the chain of arguments presented here is the approach to science teaching. There is a strong case for arguing that process-based science is likely to be more stimulating to more pupils of both sexes than the presently predominating content-based approach. Further, because it conveys an image of science as imaginative and created by the human mind, it is more likely to be seen as interesting and relevant by girls. In presenting these arguments there is value in taking an international view, especially one that combines thinking from those developing countries that have moved so rapidly towards modernization and from those that have had the benefit of advanced technology for a longer time.

THE NEEDS OF A SCIENTIFICALLY LITERATE SOCIETY

A technological society requires both trained scientists and technologists and an informed, scientifically and technologically literate society. It is a challenge to the educational system to provide for both these needs and in doing so it is important not to separate the two at too early a stage. There is a tendency to consider that future scientists have to learn 'real science' while the rest concern themselves with the philosophy, sociology and social implications of science. However, just because future science and technology specialists require an understanding of advanced concepts and processes, they do not therefore have any less need than others for an appreciation of the relevance of science to everyday problems or for an exposure to the moral and ethical issues relating science, technology and society. This suggests that one solution is to provide a common curriculum both for future specialists and for others until a thorough foundation has been laid. Countries adopting this solution include Thailand, where all pupils follow a broad and integrated science curriculum through six years of primary school and three years of lower secondary school. A different solution is for there to be parallel science programmes in secondary schools. This need not be in the form of distinct courses, as has commonly been the practice in this country, but could take the form of modular programmes with students selecting several options from those on offer, with some modules being compulsory for all. A further and more innovative suggestion is made by Layton:

> Alternative versions, more appropriate to the aim of 'science for all', might include the history of the subject, the study of its applications or its related technology, its social or cultural impact, or its more existing recent and contemporary frontiers.
>
> (Layton 1986, p. 17)

However, Layton also points out that as long as the 'academic' learning in science enjoys its high status, bolstered by the examination system, it is unlikely that these alternative versions would be chosen whatever their educational value.

There are signs that give rise to greater optimism, however, that in many countries there is a serious attempt to overcome the problems of curriculum organization and competition; that there will be wider acceptance of science courses aimed at providing a balanced and relevant education for all pupils. What will such courses look like? To answer this question it is useful to begin by examining their aims and to come to their content later. The set of aims provided by the Secondary Science Curriculum Review (SSCR) combines statements relating specifically to science and others of a more general nature:

> The important aims here are those that look to provide adequate opportunities for all students:
> (1) to study the key concepts and principles of science as a way of looking at the world;
> (2) to study those aspects of science that are essential to an understanding of oneself, and of one's personal well-being;
> (3) to study the key areas of science and technology that relate to the world of work and leisure so that they are better able to participate in a democratic society;
> (4) to study key concepts that are essential to an understanding of the part science and technology play in a post-industrial and technological society;
> (5) to discuss, reflect upon and evaluate their own personal understanding of key scientific concepts, theories and generalisations;
> (6) to explore topics and themes which exemplify the limitations of scientific knowledge as an explanation of the human conditions.
>
> (SSCR 1987, p. 3)

Attention given in current curricula is restricted almost entirely to the first of these; it would indeed be revolutionary if equal attention were to be given to all.

Most sets of aims can be achieved through a variety of content and these are no exception. The criteria for choosing content selected by SSCR are the following:

> (1) the content included should maximize the possibility of teaching the processes, skills and attitudes important to science, and increase the competence and capability of pupils;

(2) it must be able to be taught to, and owned by, all pupils;

(3) the content should have some relevance and applicability. It must need to be known and be transferable to a range of contexts during and after school;

(4) the content must appeal to both male and female students, and to students of differing cultures;

(5) science content should be consistent with a broad and balanced science curriculum;

(6) the necessary teaching strategies and resources must exist to teach it;

(7) it must provide a basis for further study;

(8) it must take into account local circumstances.

(SSCR 1987, p. 10)

These are rather less specific with regard to relevance and application than the following set of criteria devised by the Asian Programme of Educational Innovation for Development (APEID), which are also described as criteria for the selection of content for 'science for all':

(a) it should be perceived by the learners as immediately useful in their real world or as having social worth by its economic or community value. In other words, it should lend itself to experiences and practical use that are meaningful to the learners;

(b) it should improve the living conditions of the learners, or increase their productivity, and contribute to the well-being of the community and to national development goals;

(c) it should be based on daily life experience of the learner's needs, relate to the resources of their real world, and must have obvious applications in their work, leisure or homes;

(d) it should include natural phenomena which will create wonder and excitement in the learners;

(e) it should enable learners to acquire and master useful and employable skills and intelligently to use these skills;

(f) it must consider cultural and social traditions, and seek to complement these and not clash with them unnecessarily;

(g) it should make the learner recognize and appreciate the importance of science and technology in national development; and

(h) it should enable the learners to utilize wisely the resources in the environment and to live more harmoniously with nature and society.

(APEID 1983, pp. 20–1).

There is more here that is relevant to technological education (technology interpreted as applications of science). A further significant difference between the two sets is the inclusion in the Asian list of reference to 'cultural and social traditions' highlighting the rapid rate of change in developing countries that can bring tradition and technological innovation into conflict with one another. In a muted form there is a parallel problem in relation to British citizens from other countries and the concept of 'multicultural science' is developing an awareness of this problem (Gill and Levidow 1987). The Asian list does not, however, include specific mention of gender differentiation as the SSCR list does, and it may be, that in this respect, some developing countries have still some way to go.

Both lists include reference to skills, but in the APEID list it is implied that these are 'useful and employable' and thus somewhat different in character from the 'skills and attitudes important to science'. The fact that one list mentions both scientific skills *and* the need to appeal to both female and male students, while the other mentions neither, is significant in the context of arguing that these are connected. In order to substantiate the claim that it is easier for a programme designed to develop process skills to appeal to girls as much as to boys than one which is concerned mainly with the understanding of content, it is necessary to discuss the role of process skills in learning science and the typical response of girls to conventional science.

PROCESS-BASED LEARNING IN SCIENCE

Process-based learning in science, contrary to some views, does not deny that science is about understanding the world around and developing concepts that help this understanding. It recognizes, however, that understanding has to take place from within the learner, that ideas which add to useful knowledge cannot be implanted from outside. It follows the same view of learning that is currently described as 'constructivist', in which pupils' existing ideas are recognized and taken as the starting point for learning; learning being seen as the change in these ideas (Harlen and Osborne 1985). In this view, development of ideas depends on pupils testing their ideas against experience and new evidence, a process that will involve observing, interpreting, hypothesizing, raising questions, communicating, that is, the *processes* of science. The ideas that emerge from a particular scientific investigation will, if the processes are carried out scientifically (for instance, taking into account all the available evidence, making justified predictions and testing them rigorously), be consistent with evidence so far encountered, even though they may not be more widely accepted. Successive testing of emerging ideas, as new experience is encountered, will give them a greater power to help in understanding a wider and wider range of experience.

It is useful to picture this learning as is shown in Figure 1. In this representation the initial ideas that can be linked are to the left and the result of the testing processes to the right. The result can be the same initial idea confirmed, or modified or rejected. If the idea is rejected a different existing idea has to be tried. The arrows represent the linking and testing processes and the diagram shows that they occupy a key role in the fate of the ideas. Whether or not modification or rejection of ideas takes place when it ought to, will depend on the way in which the processing of ideas and information is carried out, among other factors. Hence the argument for emphasizing the use of science processes and consciously developing them in science education.

An extension of this model suggests that if ideas are presented but the process skills are not adequate or are not used in relating them to experience,

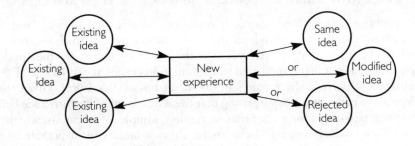

Figure 1   Schematic representation of the learning process

these ideas remain dislocated from experience and, if they have to be learned, it must be by rote. Such rote-learned ideas will not be used in helping the understanding of things around since they are not ones thought out and arising from previous experience. Unfortunately, much of science learning is of that kind for many pupils in their secondary education. Pupils learn to reproduce some of these ideas at the right time in order to pass examinations, but they are unconvinced about their knowledge, for they know that they do not understand. Attitudes to science are severely damaged by such experience; moreover it contributes to pupils' perception of science as concerned with facts and principles (some of which don't make sense to them) in which their role as learners is as passive receivers.

A quite different view of science emerges from the process-based approach to learning that has been described. Science is experienced as the construction of knowledge, knowledge that comprises ideas accepted as long as there is evidence to support them but which are open to change as necessitated by new evidence. Scientific knowledge can then be experienced and recognized as a product of human activity and thought. Later it will be realized that this means that it is not as 'objective' as is often supposed but it is indeed influenced by social and cultural values.

This view of science is surely more compatible with the aims of science education as suggested by SSCR and quoted earlier, than science as 'objective truth'. Further, learning by making one's own sense of the world through the use of process skills leads to competence. Quoting the SSCR Curriculum Guide 2 (SSCR 1987) further, there are three essential components of competence: ownership, transfer and decision-making. 'Ownership is important because it indicates that the learning taking place is intelligible, credible, fruitful and relevant to the youngsters concerned.' Of course the range and nature of the knowledge owned is also important; it is of no value to own trivial and irrelevant knowledge. The ability to transfer knowledge to new problems and to have a greater freedom of choice in making decisions depends upon having relevant ideas and information as well as process skills. Thus, an emphasis on process in learning is not a substitute, nor an alternative to, balanced content, but it is essential to the business of making that content 'one's own'.

GIRLS AND SCIENCE: A BRIEF SUMMARY OF THE PROBLEM

The 'problem' of girls and science is really one of girls and physics (and to some extent chemistry). In England and Wales, where pupils can choose not to continue the study of all the sciences after the age of 14, figures for the uptake of physics and chemistry, indicated by examination entries at age 16 and at 'A' level, show a massive discrepancy in favour of boys (DES 1985). Given this differential uptake, it is not surprising that the Assessment of Performance Unit surveys carried out in these countries on random samples of all pupils, whether or not they study physics and chemistry, show a large gap in performance between boys and girls at age 16 in these subjects. The implementation of the National Curriculum in England and Wales, from 1989 onwards, will require all pupils to study elements of all sciences up to the age of 16; this is likely to affect that part of the gap that is due to take up. However, this does not explain the fact that the gap between boys and girls is already there in physics at ages 11 and 13 (Johnson and Murphy 1986) when the differential uptake in studying the subject will not yet have operated. This is confirmed by the results of the first and of the second surveys of International Evaluation of Achievement in Science (Comber and Keeves 1973, Keys 1987, IEA 1988).

In seeking possible causes for these disparities between the sexes one must expect that multiple and combined influences will be at work. There is no simple cause–effect relationship. A range of factors is likely to be involved and a considerable amount of enquiry and research has shown which are the strongest contenders.

An explanation that was once popular, but has now been dismissed by most involved in this work, is the biological one. This suggests that there are inherent differences between the sexes in brain structure or capacity, particularly related to visual–spatial ability, where tests have sometimes shown boys to be superior in performance to girls. Three pieces of well-confirmed research evidence combine to demolish this explanation, however: first, the observed performance differences could equally well be a result of differences in treatment of boys and girls in their early years; second, supporting the first point, the difference is not found in all cultures (Maccoby and Jacklin 1975); and third, when deliberate attempts are made to improve spatial abilities girls respond in the same way as boys (Cohen 1983).

The factors that deserve more serious consideration are socially determined. They have been well covered, in publications edited by Kelly (1981 and 1987), under the headings of the masculine image of science, the reinforcement of sex-linked personality characteristics and the conventional identification of occupations and hobbies as masculine or feminine. Here I will be concerned with those factors that relate to the way science is taught and the view of science that is transmitted by these methods.

Real or supposed personality differences between scientists and non-scientists can be contrasted in general terms under the headings used by Head (1985) (Table 1).

Table 1 Personality differences between scientists and non-scientists

Scientists	Non-scientists
Emotionally reticent	Sensuous, passionate
Authoritarian	Opposed to rules, structures and authority
Intolerant of people who are very different from others	Tolerant of uncertainty, ambiguity and differences in others
Conservative	Radical
Diligent, hard-working	Value pleasure and diversion

Head's fascinating discussion of these qualities brings out the intricate web of possible causes and effects. For instance, perhaps the discipline and long hours of laboratory work required during the training of a scientist, as opposed to an arts student, both attract those of a certain type but also reinforce or even produce the typical characteristics. The point of relevance here is that, whatever the origin of the differences, they line up rather too well with the differences between males and females.

The research into differences between the sexes shows that, in general, differences occur in relation to the characteristics in Table 2. Head refers to psychological theories of parent–child relationships to explain these differences:

> In our society most children receive parental care from the mother, or another female acting as a mother substitute. That immediately poses different situations for the two sexes. The young girl is perceived as being almost an extension of her mother, being of the same sex, potentially sharing the same interests and problems. A close relationship often develops which gives the girl the benefit of relating closely to another person, with the sharing of ideas and awareness of another's perspectives. The boy is seen as being different, to be encouraged to achieve autonomy, taking some risks in the rough and tumble of play, learning to keep a stiff upper lip and not display emotion. A higher degree of independence and assertiveness is accepted in the boy.
>
> (Head 1985, p. 61)

Table 2 Gender-related characteristics

Males		Females
Less	Emotionality	More
Towards things	Orientation	Towards people
Not greatly discouraged	Reaction to failure	Discouraged
More	Objectivity	Less
More	Interest in abstractions	Less
Interest in ideas per se	Relevance of ideas	Interest in relating to the real world
More	Desire for control	Less
More	Independence	Less
More	Assertiveness	Less

The suggestion that the characteristics of non-scientists are closer to those typical of females than of males, throws into question the characteristics of *female* scientists. According to research reported by Head, women science students are highly extroverted but they tend to underrate themselves; however, they are more stable, tough and radical than girls studying arts subjects. The extroversion, it is suggested, facilities the choice of a subject that is unusual for girls, since extroverts tend to be less influenced by social conditioning. Thus the characteristics of scientists listed above are those of *male* scientists, while female scientists have a somewhat different personality profile. Both sexes are aware of the masculine image of science; one has chosen to conform to it and the other to deliberately go against it. Not surprisingly this means that girls who choose science are more committed and this shows in the very much lower proportional drop-out rate from science of girls compared with boys in the middle and late teens (Head 1987, p. 19).

The differences in the personality characteristics of males and females in our society (and we must remember that we are talking in generalities, not about particular individuals) leads to sex differentiation in interests, hobbies, occupations and careers, which are well researched and well documented. The differences appear early, in the primary school years (Johnson and Murphy 1986) and they are reinforced by the status quo. The situation is self-perpetuating; most scientists are men, thus the male-image of science is confirmed. However, there is evidence that the situation *can* be changed. There are countries where this sex differentiation is not evident, where as many women as men are doctors (and not just nurses), bus drivers, engineers, etc. The hope of breaking into the vicious circle in this society is supported by the evidence that it is the occupation of mothers, not fathers, which is associated with changes in girls' stereotyped views regarding scientific occupations.

Turning to the masculine image of science, the reality of this image is widespread and can easily be demonstrated; simply ask anyone to describe a scientist and you will find a high incidence of descriptions of the bespectacled, white-coated, solitary, unemotional, hard-working *male*. The science that these people are engaged upon so industriously is commonly seen as objective, concerned with facts and accuracy, impersonal and excluding emotions and feelings. Is this a correct and useful image of science? A growing number of science educators today would deny this. They point to evidence about the nature of perception and cognition, which leads us to acknowledge that preconceptions influence the way we observe and interpret the world around in a far from 'objective' way; pressures from social values also limit and introduce bias in developing ideas. Moreover, some interesting work by Gauld (1985) suggests that the myth of objectivity in the way scientists work comes from 'smoothing out differences' and looking at scientists as a group, not as individuals. When Gauld looked at individual scientists, he found quite a different picture of their work; the influence of preconceived ideas was very strong, there were glaring examples of 'fudging' the evidence to fit pet theories and often very little, apart from what could be called 'intuition', as a basis for hypotheses.

In reality, then, science has not been advanced by cold, calculated, logical analysis of evidence, but by using the human mind creatively, allowing imagination and feelings to play a part. Perhaps the perpetuation of the myth that has maintained it as a male preserve is more deliberate than accidental!

However, a less sinister answer to why science has been portrayed in the way it has, contrary to the evidence of what many scientists actually do, is to be found in the only encounter that the bulk of the population has with science, through the methods of teaching in schools. Most of us will have experienced science teaching, at our most formative adolescent stage, which constrained us to learn facts and principles, theories, theorems and laws in a way that left no doubt that these are 'true' and incontrovertible. In the very words used about who 'discovered' these things there is the suggestion that they were already there to be discovered. There was no indication that scientific knowledge might be tentative, controversial or open to disproof. Practical work was to confirm already known truths; everything there was to learn was there in the book. Until recently, very little has changed and, indeed, this change is only 'patchy'.

Few pupils actually enjoy learning like this and this accounts for the large drop-out rate in secondary schools. Those who persist often do so because of the value of the subjects for qualifications and for future occupations. It is certainly a very effective way to turn the vast majority of our future away from science and science-related technology. Clearly we must do better if we are hoping for a scientifically and technologically educated public.

SYNTHESIS

Bringing together the several threads in this argument, the hypothesis proposed is that process-based learning in science, as described earlier, is likely to project a more human view of science and to involve learning experiences that engage the thinking, imagination and interest of pupils as well as leading to an understanding of key concepts and principles. The aim of this approach is for pupils to learn with understanding, through development of their own ideas, which are taken seriously and not ignored in favour of the 'right answer'. This type of learning is more likely to appeal to all pupils and will open opportunities for them to develop ideas that are required for understanding and effectively contributing to the technological society. Thus a change towards teaching science in this way can make an important contribution to a scientifically literate public.

Process-based learning is not designed to appeal to girls and women but the argument has been advanced that it does so. Science taught as essentially a creation of human minds, always open to test and to change, acknowledging the role of social interaction in the generation of ideas, is much more likely to appeal to girls and women than conventional 'right answer' science. Thus there can be a double benefit: of more equal opportunity for both sexes to participate and for a wider interest and understanding in science. There is a third benefit, too, which is that science and technology itself may change as a result of the wider participation of women. The result may be science research that is more sensitive to feelings and human values (less exploitation of animals, for example) and applications that give priority to solving human problems (improvement of health rather than military capability, for example). Such a change is a long way off, but there is room for optimism that it is not impossible and that a start has been made.

A final point is that this process needs to begin early, as soon as children come into school, and the inclusion of science and technology as a basic subject at the primary level in the proposed national curriculum is perhaps the most welcome aspect of this new legislation in England and Wales.

REFERENCES

Asian Programme of Educational Innovation for Development (APEID) (1983) *Science for All: Report of a Regional Meeting, Bangkok, 1983,* UNESCO Regional Office for Education in Asia and the Pacific, Bangkok.

CIBA Foundation (1987) *Communicating Science to the Public* Wiley, Chichester.

Cohen, H. (1983) A comparison of the effects of two types of student behaviour with manipulatives on the development of projective spatial structures. *Journal of Research in Science Teaching,* Vol. 20, No. 9, pp. 875–83.

Comber, L. C. and Keeves, J. P. (1973) *Science Education in Nineteen Countries: An Empirical Study, International Studies in Evaluation I* Almqvist and Wiskell, Stockholm.

Department of Education and Science (DES) (1985) *Statistics of Education,* DES, London.

Faure, E., Herrera, F., Kaddoura, A-R., Lopes, H., Petrovsky, A. V., Rahmena, M. and Ward, F. C. (1972) *Learning to Be,* UNESCO, Paris and Harrap, London.

Gauld, C. (1985) Empirical evidence and conceptual change. In R. Osborne and J. Gilbert (eds.), *Some Issues of Theory in Science Education,* Science Education Research Unit, University of Waikato, New Zealand.

Gill, D. and Levidow, L. (eds.) (1987) *Anti-Racist Science Teaching,* Free Association Books, London.

Harlen, W. and Osborne, R. J. (1985) A model for learning and teaching applied to primary science. *Journal of Curriculum Studies,* Vol. 17, no. 2, pp. 133–146.

Head, J. O. (1985) *The Personal Response to Science,* Cambridge University Press, Cambridge.

Head, J. O. (1987) A model to link personality characteristics to a preference for science. In A. Kelly (ed.), *Science for Girls?,* Open University Press, Milton Keynes.

International Educational Achievement (IEA) (1988) *Science Achievement in 17 Countries: A Preliminary Report,* National Science Foundation, USA.

Johnson, S. and Murphy, P. (1986) *Girls and Physics*, Occasional Paper No. 4, DES.

Kelly, A. (ed.) (1981) *The Missing Half: Girls and Science Education*, Manchester University Press, Manchester.

Kelly, A. (ed.) (1987) *Science for Girls?* Open University Press, Milton Keynes.

Keys, W. (1987) *Aspects of Science Education in England*, Nelson/NFER, London.

Layton, D. (ed.) (1986) *Innovation in Science & Technology Education*, Vol. 1, UNESCO, Paris.

Maccoby, E. E. and Jacklin, C. N. (1975) *The Psychology of Sex Differences*, Stanford University Press.

Shortland, M. (ed.) (1987) *Scientific Literacy Papers: A Journal of Research in Science, Education and the Public*, Scientific Literacy Group, Department for External Studies, Oxford.

Secondary Science Curriculum Review (SSCR) (1987) *Better Science: Choosing the Content*, Curriculum Guide 2, Heinemann Education/ASE, London.

The Royal Society (1985) *The Public Understanding of Science*, The Royal Society, London.

The Royal Society (1986) *Science and Public Affairs*, No. 1, The Royal Society, London.

3.3

Analysing multicultural and antiracist science education

Reg Dennick

The consultation document for the Science National Curriculum, *Science for Ages 5–16*[1] and the Non-Statutory 'Guidance to the Science National Curriculum'[2] both contain recommendations for teaching science with a multicultural perspective. In addition the ASE has set up a Working Party which is attempting to guide and inform the Association in this area with the aim of producing a policy statement on 'Science and Multicultural Education'. In this respect the ASE Multicultural Education Working party has produced a discussion paper which was distributed at the 1990 Annual Meeting.[3] There have also been a number of recent articles in *School Science Review* concerned with the issue of multicultural science education.[4,5,6,7]

It is the purpose of this article to examine the underlying assumptions and concepts on which a multicultural science curriculum could be based. In order to do this it is necessary to briefly examine the debate between multicultural and antiracist education since there appears to be confusion concerning the meaning of these terms in the context of science education. Next the relationships between racism and the ideological distortions of scientific knowledge and methodology are examined. Finally curriculum initiatives in multicultural and antiracist science education are discussed.

MULTICULTURAL AND ANTIRACIST EDUCATION

Multicultural education can be seen as an attempt to provide a curriculum which allows children to explore other cultures as well as their own so that an ethical framework of respect and toleration is built up. In the context of science education this could involve looking at the scientific contributions made by other cultures or by undertaking some of the work suggested by the *Third World Science* project.[8] It is essentially a process of curriculum development and alteration designed to challenge and educate children out of their

From *School Science Review* (1992), Vol. 73, no. 264, pp. 79–88.

prejudices leading towards a state of 'social cohesion within cultural diversity'.[9] The 'problem' that multicultural education addresses is the conflict between different *cultures*.

Antiracist science education, on the other hand, starts from the assumption that the whole of the curriculum, the school institution, the teachers and the pupils, the Local Education Authority and society in general are influenced, either consciously or unconsciously, by a racist ideology which not only causes the overt activities of prejudice and discrimination but also subtly distorts the contents of the curriculum, views on the nature of the scientific enterprise and claims to the origins of scientific and technological knowledge itself. Antiracist education is specifically built on the premise that it is necessary to challenge and oppose racism in society and at school; tinkering with the curriculum does not solve the 'problem'; the 'problem' is racism.

Although this polarity between multicultural and antiracist education has created considerable conflict in the last decade, with the 'antiracists' accusing the 'multiculturalists' of being woolly-minded liberals trying to replace one racist curriculum with another, and the 'multiculturalists' seeing the 'antiracists' as hopelessly idealistic, radical revolutionaries, it is now clear that the two perspectives are inextricably linked. In order to discover the roots of racism in British culture, and the distorting influence that it has had on education and especially science education, it is necessary to analyse the history of the past few hundred years and in particular the period of British colonialism and imperialism.

RACISM AND THE IDEOLOGICAL JUSTIFICATION FOR SLAVERY

The origins and history of European slavery are well covered in the literature and there is not space to cover it here. However the three books produced by the Institute of Race Relations (*Roots of Racism, Patterns of Racism* and *How Racism Came to Britain*) are an ideal resource for dealing with this issue in the classroom.[10,11,12] Of more relevance to this article is the fact that the economics and practice of colonial exploitation and slavery clearly needed justification which was provided by the ideology of racism. Similarly there were more subtle ideological distortions of 'foreign' cultures which attempted to view them as 'primitive' and underdeveloped.

Although slavery has a long history and was the economic base of many ancient cultures including that of Egypt, Greece, and Rome, the 'Slave Trade' from the sixteenth to the nineteenth century reached new heights of inhumanity and barbarity possibly only surpassed by the purges of Stalin and the Jewish Holocaust in the twentieth century. The destruction of flourishing African cultures and the decimation of African populations weakened the infrastructure of many African societies laying them open to the final indignity of imperial conquest and exploitation in the nineteenth century. Such a massive process, which had an enormous impact on the economies of Western Europe and particularly Britain, had to be justified to the population as a whole and it is in this process that we can find the roots of modern racism.

The development of a racist ideology which legitimated slavery and colonial exploitation essentially revolved around a racial hierarchy with Whites at the top and 'Negroes' at the bottom. Thus a hierarchy of cultures coupled with the concept that white society had made the most 'progress' could be used to justify negative attitudes towards the history and achievements of foreign countries as well as ancient civilizations and constituted a pervasive cultural hegemony.

Religious ideology made a major contribution towards such attitudes and the 'white man's burden' was seen as an obligation to civilize and baptise primitive peoples and replace their culture with the 'White Anglo-Saxon Protestant work-ethic'. Similarly the knowledge that Sub-Saharan Africans had been enslaved since antiquity, coupled with the biblical story of God's curse on Ham, that he should be 'a servant of servants', provided ideal justification for treating blacks as slaves. It was with that peculiar evangelical fervour that characterizes the Christian religion that many missionaries took the 'Word of God' and the culture that went with it around the world. A systematic denigration and distortion of foreign cultures was assisted by the foreshortened historical perspective provided by the widely accepted chronology of Bishop Ussher, who, in 1650, put the origin of the Earth as 4004 BC. Such a lack of historical understanding over-emphasized the contribution made by Graeco–Roman civilization and ignored the contributions from the Near East, China, India and Africa. Africa was never considered to have had civilizations and despite Egyptian history and the history of many African cultures such as the Dogon, Songhay and the civilizations of Benin and Great Zimbabwe the contemporary historian Trevor-Roper stated that Africa did not have a history until it was subjected to imperial rule.[10] More recently Bernal in the controversial book *Black Athena*[14] has shown how scholars in the nineteenth century constructed a view of Greek Civilization which emphasized its white European origins and neglected its Egyptian and African roots.

THE EXPROPRIATION OF SCIENTIFIC DISCOVERIES

Throughout European history since the Renaissance there has been a tendency to disparage and downgrade the discoveries and achievements of other cultures and historians have been very prone to give credit where it is not due. Needham points out that possibly the three most important scientific and technological advances of the last millennium, namely paper and printing, gunpowder and the compass were not only discovered by the Chinese, in some cases a thousand years earlier than is commonly assumed, but were all popularly thought to have been discovered by Europeans.[15] Thus gunpowder is well documented in the ninth century AD in China although its discovery is often ascribed to Roger Bacon in 1269. The introduction of gunpowder into Europe in the thirteenth century had an enormous effect on the change from feudal fiefdoms to nation states and created the initial conditions for the formation of many of the modern European states. The spread of printing in Europe has always been seen as a necessary precursor to the Renaissance, the Reformation and the rise of Capitalism and its discovery is usually ascribed to Gutenberg in the fifteenth century. However, paper was developed in China in the second century AD and printing using blocks was known in 740 AD. The floating magnet was used as an aid to divination and geomancy in China for over two thousand years and was regularly used as a navigational aid by Chinese mariners in the eleventh century. However, many textbooks of physics state that William Gilbert discovered this use of the magnet in the sixteenth century. Again the impact that the compass had on navigation and subsequent voyages of exploration, exploitation and colonization was enormous.

Needham[15] cites literally hundreds of scientific discoveries and technological advances that were made by the Chinese during their long history and which inevitably filtered westwards over the millennia. But Chinese 'science' is often downgraded by historians to the status of 'technology' since in their judgement it did not display evidence of the hypothetico-deductive system coupled to mathematical generalizations characteristic of 'modern' science.[16]

To reduce Chinese science to 'merely technology' is to ignore the evidence of Sinological scholarship that has emerged in the last few decades, particularly that of Needham and his monumental work on *Science and Civilization in China*.[17] Technology, when used in this sense, has the connotation of 'trial and error' and 'chance' discoveries made without any underlying theoretical understanding. But all the evidence now available points towards the conclusion that what the Chinese carried was genuine 'science' with all the modern attributes of accurate and systematic observation, meticulous recording and communications, rigorous experimental technique, including the use of controls, in addition to the fact that it was based on theoretical structures, albeit different from our own, which underpinned their activities.

In addition it must be made clear that not only has Chinese science been devalued by historians of science and textbook writers but also Islamic, Indian, Egyptian and African science has frequently been reduced to the 'technological' level and their discoveries expropriated. The knowledge that eventually filtered back into European civilization through Moorish Spain after the so-called Dark Ages is sometimes seen merely as a collection of ancient texts that had been copied by Arab and Islamic scholars whereas what was passed on was a sophisticated Islamic Culture uniting art, religion and science in a profound world view which is still very much alive today.[18] Thus Sardar,[19] Ashrif[20] and Nasr[18] cite many discoveries made by Islamic scientists such as the pulmonary circulation of the blood, heliocentric theories of the solar system and important ideas in optics which are frequently ascribed to European traditions. Recent studies of African science have revealed the presence of steel making in Tanzania 1,500–2,000 years ago, evidence of an agricultural civilization in the Nile Valley 7,000 years before the Egyptians and many other astronomical, mathematical and medical discoveries produced by African scientists.[21]

Greek science on the other hand is frequently cited as the paradigm of scientific method because of its theoretical constructs which were, however, never tested empirically. The legacy of Greek philosophical speculation, despite its advances in logical and geometrical reasoning, led to the absurdities of Ptolemaic planetary astronomy, a universe made of immobile crystalline spheres and an overwhelming reliance on the writings of Aristotle and Plato which inhibited truly scientific investigation.

THE SCIENTIFIC METHOD

There is yet another important layer of ideological distortion which influences the thinking of teachers with respect to multicultural and antiracist science and that is the precise nature of the scientific method. That science is a human activity may appear to be stating the obvious, but to the public and children too often the image of science is that it is an impersonal process which avoids value judgements and which operates objectively and impartially.

However, in recent years there has been a debate in science education concerning the precise nature of the scientific method and its relationship to science teaching as ideas have shifted towards an emphasis on 'process science', and the ASE has been prominent in airing debates in this area. Some science schemes have been criticized for putting forward an inappropriate or 'philosophically inaccurate' view of the scientific method.[22,23,24] Modern formulations of the scientific method are essentially based on the 'hypothetico-deductive' model which emphasizes the role of subjective conjectures or hypotheses from which deductions can be made that are empirically testable.[25] It crucially stresses the creative role of the subject in the scientific process. The work of Kuhn[26] has furthermore shown that sociological factors are important in the progress of science, and that communities of scientists do not give up their cherished theories without a struggle even when there is overwhelming evidence that they are wrong. Science is anything but the coldly objective and rigid process that many people popularly believe and which science education fosters.

Such changes from the 'traditional' view of science as 'objective knowledge' to science as a human and social construction have influenced science education and have led to a greater emphasis on the processes rather than the 'facts' of science and to real investigational work being at the heart of science teaching. These changes have occurred in parallel with changes to the way that children are believed to learn scientific concepts, and which have led to different approaches to classroom learning.[27,28,29]

Such a view of the scientific method, coupled with a 'constructivist' approach to learning makes science a much more human and approachable subject. In addition this modern view of science throws open the whole debate concerning the difference between 'science' and 'technology' which some historians have used to belittle the type of science found in older civilizations. The difference between science and technology is merely one of degree and emphasis rather than a fundamental conceptual difference. Science and technology are both 'problem-solving' activities demanding the same intellectual rigour and using the same cognitive mechanisms.

It is now abundantly clear from Needham's work that what the Chinese practised was 'science' albeit with different theoretical structures and without the mathematical methods that characterized so-called 'modern science'. Similar arguments can be made for India, the Islamic world and Africa and once this is accepted the way is open for a fresh look at the scientific discoveries and ideas from these cultures, not as peripheral contributions to 'Western Science' but as scientific innovations in their own right. The different types of science developed in different cultures can then be seen in relation to the socio-economic conditions prevailing, and as responses to specific needs. As Needham points out:

> Science is one and indivisible. The differences are essentially sociological – what you do science for, whether for the benefit of the people as a whole, or for the development of fiendish forms of modern warfare; in a word, your motive. The differences will also be great according to whom you get to do it, whether you confine it to highly trained professionals, or whether you can use a mass of people with only minimal training . . . [130, p. 103]

THE UNIVERSALITY OF SCIENCE

The idea that scientific thinking is a normal human function has been put forward strongly by Robin Millar[31,24] who suggests that the scientific processes of observing, hypothesizing and inferring are general cognitive skills used routinely by everyone. Similarly Piaget suggested that the 'Logical Operation' stage of cognitive development was essentially characterized by the ability to perform scientific thinking. Chomsky[32] has speculated that all human beings possess an innate 'science-forming capacity' which lies at the core of the ability of human beings to develop scientific knowledge. Such ideas lead to the conclusion that 'scientific thinking' is a normal human cognitive function possessed by all people *at all times*, indeed that it is an innate capacity.

Science is not just an activity carried out by white men in white coats; it is an activity that all children from all cultural and ethnic backgrounds can participate in and 'own'. In addition if teachers do not see science as a worldwide and humanistic phenomenon they will continue to see the science and technology of other civilizations, both in the past and the present, in an ethnocentric and patronizing way, reinforcing racist stereotypes. But by recognizing the way in which ideological distortions deriving from racism have influenced the content and methodology of science education they can begin to undertake curriculum change.

CURRICULUM CHANGES IN MULTICULTURAL AND ANTIRACIST SCIENCE EDUCATION

A number of Local Education Authorities and their science advisers as well as University Education departments have been active in discussing, formulating, publishing and implementing science curricula for multicultural and antiracist education.[13,33,34,35,36,37,38,39,40,41]

Gill and Levidow[42] have edited a seminal book *Anti-racist Science Teaching* and there have been contributions to the literature on particular subject areas such as chemistry[43,44] and biology[43,45] whereas the following[4,5,6,7,37,40] have all discussed multicultural science teaching in general. However, possibly the largest contribution in terms of resource material, although in other respects controversial, is the Third World Science Project from the University of Bangor under the direction of Iolo Williams.[8] *Blacks in Science: Ancient and Modern* edited by van Sertima[21] and *Black Pioneers of Science and Invention* by Haber[46] have also been found useful in raising awareness of Black achievements.

There is not space to review these contributions in details but the Secondary Science Curriculum Review publication *Better Science: working for a multicultural society*[47], the consultation document for the Science National Curriculum, *Science for Ages 5–16*, the 'Non-statutory Guidance to the Science National Curriculum'[2] and the Association for Science Education and Multicultural Education Working Party Discussion Paper[3] are publications and initiatives drawing together most of the common threads and concerns from the above documents which have put antiracist multicultural science education high on the agenda and have raised and widened the debate on the nature of science education and the polarity between multicultural and antiracist education.

SCIENCE IN THE NATIONAL CURRICULUM

The main proposals of these documents which are relevant to this article concern the nature of science, the selection of appropriate science content, the method of teaching, equality of opportunity and challenging racism both in science and within the school. There seems to be a general consensus that there is a need to replace the image that science is culturally neutral and coldly objective with a more honest image of science as a human enterprise influenced by different cultures, religions, environments and economic and political formations. Thus the 'Non-Statutory Guidance to the Science National Curriculum' stresses that 'there are many scientific methods' and that there is an 'important place for imagination and for inspirational thinking'; that 'science is a human construction. We define its boundaries and decide what shall count as science'.[2,A4,3.2] It suggests that:

> Appreciating the powerful but provisional nature of scientific knowledge and explanation will bring pupils closer to the process by which scientific models are created, tested and modified. They will begin to see the uncertain nature of even the most established explanations of scientific evidence.[2,A5,4.5]

Although there is a recognition that the scientific method may be applied universally teachers and pupils must be sensitive to the way that scientific knowledge is interpreted in different cultures. The ASE suggests that:

Because science is a human activity, scientific ideas are developed in a cultural and a socio-political context and must be influenced by the values and institutions of that culture. Science and scientists are therefore not neutral . . . . It is important to recognize that different societies have viewed science in different ways . . . . It is important that science is taught in its human, social, cultural and environmental contexts, and there are related issues which cannot be ignored if science education is to be a positive force in tackling racism and raising children's awareness.[3;2]

Similarly the content of the science curriculum should reflect the fact that no one culture has a monopoly of scientific achievement and textbooks and work schemes should contain a variety of examples of people and processes from different parts of the world. The Non-Statutory Guidance to the Science National Curriculum is quite prescriptive in this respect:

People from all cultures are involved in scientific enterprise. The curriculum should reflect the contributions from different cultures, for example, the origins and growth of chemistry from ancient Egypt, Greece and Arabia to the later Byzantine and European cultures, and parallel developments in China and India. It is important that science books and other learning material should include examples of people from ethnic minority groups working alongside others and achieving success in scientific work. Pupils should come to realize the international nature of science and the potential it has for helping to overcome racial prejudice.[2;A10.7.8]

All of these documents suggest that particular attention should be paid to the language of science when dealing with ethnic minority students. Both the Non-Statutory Guidance and the ASE Multicultural Working Party recognize that specialized support teaching and, if necessary, bilingual materials should be made available.

The Science National Curriculum and its Non-Statutory Guidance, although outlining an ethnically sensitive curriculum which mentions 'the international nature of science and the potential it has for helping to overcome racial prejudice', nowhere discuss racism or the role that science teaching could play in its eradication. Its absence from suggested issues in Attainment Target 17, at the one point in the Science National Curriculum when it was most relevant, indicates that the National Curriculum Council does not see racism as an important issue in science education. The ASE, while welcoming the National Curriculum Council's recognition of the multicultural dimension of science are extremely critical of its lack of concern for challenging racism in science. Furthermore they feel that an opportunity was missed to introduce a global perspective into science teaching by ignoring the 'complex relationships and inequalities between and within nations' and 'the increasing interdependence between peoples in the world'.[2; 1.3]

THIRD WORLD SCIENCE AND 'GREEN SCIENCE'

This 'Global Perspective' links antiracist and multicultural science education into issues concerned with the Third World and 'Green Science' and provides an ideal opportunity to make cross-curricular links. *Third World Science*[8] is excellent resource material since it provides fascinating and relatively simple activities which are reasonably open-ended and can develop into extended studies and project work. Using *Third World Science* children and teachers can explore how people solve problems in different cultures with different resources.

However, used insensitively it could very well lead to a reinforcing of stereotypical views about 'primitive' and 'advanced' science and technology in the developing countries and the Western world. It is here that teaching strategy is important and the aim must be to demonstrate that science and technology throughout the world are 'problem-solving' activities, that all human beings and cultures possess this capacity but that it manifests itself in different ways depending on the historical and socio-economic conditions.

Scientific investigations based on Third World Science can branch out into geographical, environmental and economic issues. If problem solving is discussed within the context of 'limited resources' it seems legitimate to discuss the reasons for this which will inevitably involve looking at past colonial exploitation, cash cropping, deforestation, Third World debt and many other issues.

Similarly the types of technology found in the Third World are often on a more human scale and are frequently less environmentally damaging than some of the 'big' technologies of the developed world. Here very important issues concerning 'Green Science' and appropriate technology can be investigated and the scientific issue brought out. A recent paper by Turner and Turner[48] shows how the National Curriculum for Science can be used to provide an international perspective to science teaching.

THE ASSUMPTIONS OF ANTIRACIST SCIENCE – SCIENCE AS IDEOLOGY

The book *Anti-racist Science Education* by Gill and Levidow[42] was a milestone in this debate and brought together some powerful arguments for the primacy of antiracist science education. The agenda of antiracist science includes areas such as the refutation of 'race' as a valid biological category, the 'race' and IQ debate, biological determinism, the 'nature–nurture' debate, the claims of sociobiology, nutrition, hunger and poverty, Third World exploitation and debt, sickle cell anaemia in Black populations, and culture-fair forms of assessment. It is a very important development in science education since it challenges many fundamental views and at the same time expands our view of relationship between science, society and culture. While it is not possible to deal with all those issues here it should be mentioned that its fundamental assumptions are underpinned by a view of scientific knowledge as very much the reflection of the prevailing values of the culture in which it takes place and hence influenced by political, ideological and economic priorities. Thus Robert Young in *Anti-racist Science Teaching* declares:

Science is not something in the sky, not a set of eternal truths waiting for discovery. Science is practice. There is no other science than the science that gets done. The science that exists is the record of the questions that it has occurred to scientists to ask, the proposals that get funded, the paths that get pursued and the results which lead . . . scientific journals and textbooks to publicize the work . . .. Nature 'answers' only the questions that get asked and pursued long enough to lead to results that enter the public domain. Whether or not they get asked, how far they get pursued, are matters for a given society, its educational system, its patronage system and its funding bodies.[49;p.19]

Young suggests a culturally relative view of science and points to the way that different cultures have used science to develop different knowledge and belief systems and world views. He suggests that the antiracist curriculum should include a study of the Western capitalist approach to science which led to the separation of 'fact and value, matter and mind, mechanism and purpose'. When studying science all concepts and fact should be looked at in the context of, 'origins, assumptions, articulations, benefits, alternatives'. Young furthermore shows that the Sociology of Knowledge is capable of undermining the claims of science to value-free and objective knowledge and concludes that nothing, no matter how detailed, abstract or general, escapes the structuring of the social world, all is mediation.

But if all is 'mediation', what is it mediation *of*? Young moves his argument into the 'base-superstructure' debate of Marxism and discusses whether the development of science has its own internal dynamic resting on the history of ideas or if it is connected to the social and material means of production in the economic base of society. Young concludes that:

At the deepest level, world-views or philosophies of society are arguably historically constituted. Within a given mode of production different epochs call up different disciplines and topics, along with criteria for acceptable answers to the questions we put to nature. Within a given period different priorities and conceptual frameworks arise.[50;p.85]

The extreme view of the cultural relativism of science put forward by Young and the Marxist view that science is ideologically compromised in many areas seems to lead to a paradoxical situation since this concept of science is not only seen as a tool of the ruling capitalist class involved in furthering racist ideology, Third World exploitation, uncontrolled economic growth and pollution but at the same time, in terms of antiracist science education, it is the only legitimate method of countering and challenging this domination. Since, as Young argues, there is no such thing as a neutral, objective science and that all cultures and ideologies use science for their own purpose it is difficult to see how 'science' can be used to challenge such ideologies.

This problem is not addressed by Young or indeed any of the other authors contributing to *Anti-racist Science Teaching* but I think it is extremely important from a theoretical point of view to establish to what extent science can be used to challenge racism and the scientific distortions and ideologies which lead from it. It seems essential to try to find some ground on which antiracist scientists can stand when criticizing biological determinism, racism and other ideological distortions of science. Needham's assertion that 'science is one and indivisible' or the ideas of Piaget and Chomsky that scientific thinking is an innate, human attribute contradict Young's culturally relative view of science and provide a point of departure for a wider view of science in relation to culture.

It must be an ideologically untainted scientific method which can be used to refute racism and biological determinism and it is by challenging the way in which racists use their 'hypotheses', 'observations', 'theories' and 'evidence' from within the discourse of science that racist ideology can be 'scientifically' refuted. To accept Young's culturally relative view of science is to legitimize the ideology of racism as yet another 'valid' knowledge and belief system. Clearly this is not what Young or other antiracist scientists would want to do but by cutting the ground from underneath any possibility of an objective area within science they destroy any attempt to challenge racism scientifically.

Although there are areas of science that are clearly subordinate to ideology of one sort or another the fact that critics of racism and biological determinism can successfully refute such 'theories' from within the discourse of science implies that the scientific method can be used to fight the ideological penetration of science and that science can therefore remain 'liberating'.

CONCLUSIONS

It is hoped that all of the major assumptions that are relevant to multicultural and antiracist curriculum development have now been outlined. Most schools now accept that a multicultural curriculum must go hand in hand with an antiracist policy and the polarity between these views is gradually diminishing. Nevertheless, it is the recognition of racism and ethnocentrism in science that makes antiracist science education of fundamental importance. Not only should antiracist science teaching adequately challenge racist ideology in the classroom from a powerful scientific base but it should also make people aware of the global economic and ecological connections between different peoples on this planet. However, the conflicts generated in the educational profession within the discourse of multiculturalism and antiracism are as nothing in comparison to the real conflicts of racism, ethnocentrism, xenophobia, militant religious fundamentalism and nationalism which inflict the world daily and generate a constant stream of death, suffering, tragedy and political upheaval.

The resolution of these conflicts might be considered to be mankind's most pressing problem and although political and economic changes must be necessary precursors certainly one aspect of the solution must be in the area of education. Thus it is not too pretentious to suppose that antiracist multicultural science education can be at the forefront of educational attempts to reduce prejudice and conflict between individuals, ethnic minorities, cultures and nations. Science can be liberating when coupled to a strong humanistic, open-minded and truth seeking philosophy. It can cut the ground from beneath ideologies that would seek to keep human groups in a state of conflict, feeding on ignorance and irrational fear. It can lay bare the economic and material connections that link cultures and nations in relationships of dominance and servility. It can monitor and challenge attempts to destroy the global environment and the ecological networks on which all life depends.

REFERENCES

1. DES, *Science for Ages 5 to 16*. Proposals of the Secrertary of State for Education and Science and the Secretary of State for Wales, (HMSO, 1988).
2. DES, *Science in the National Curriculum*, (Non-statutory Guidance), (NCC 1989).
3. ASE, *ASE Multicultural Education Working Party Discussion Paper*, (ASE, 1989).
4. Antonouris, G., 'Multicultural science', *SSR*, 1989, 70(252), 97–100.
5. Chamberlain, P. J., 'Science education in multicultural Britain, *SSR*, 1986, 68(243), 343–8.
6. Pugh, S., 'Introducing multicultural science teaching to a secondary school', *SSR*, 1990, 71(256), 131–5.
7. Tunnicliffe, S. D., 'Teaching science to children from ethnic minority groups', *SSR*, 1986, 67(240), 607–11.
8. Williams, I. W., *Third World Science*, (Centre for World Development Education, 1983).
9. Lynch, J., *Multicultural Education Principles and Practice* (Routledge & Kegan, 1986).
10. IRR, *Roots of Racism*, (Institute of Race Relations, 1982).
11. IRR, *Patterns of Racism*, (Institute of Race Relations, 1982).
12. IRR, *How Racism Came to Britain*, (Institute of Race Relations, 1985).
13. Leicestershire, *Science Education for a Multicultural Society*, (Leicestershire Education Authority, 1985).
14. Bernal, M., *Black Athena – The Afroasiatic Roots of Classical Civilization*, (Free Asscociation Books, 1987).
15. Needham, J., *The Grand Titration*, (George Allen & Unwin, 1969).
16. Crombie, A. C., 'The significance of medieval discussions of scientific method for the scientific revolution', in Clagett, M. (ed.), *Critical Problems in the History of Science*, (Wisconsin, Madison, 1959).
17. Needham, J., *Science and Civilization in China*, (Cambridge University Press, 1954).
18. Nasr, S. H., *Science and Civilization in Islam*, (Cambridge, Mass., Harvard University Press, 1968).
19. Sardar, Z., 'Can science come back to Islam?' *New Scientist*, 23 October 1980, 212–16.

20. Ashrif, S., 'Eurocentrism and myopia in science teaching', *Multicultural Teaching*, 1986, 5, 28–30.
21. Van Sertima, I., *Blacks in Science: Ancient and Modern*, (New Brunswick, Transaction Books, 1983).
22. Hodson, D., 'Philosophy of science, science and science education', *Studies in Science Education*, 1985, 12, 25–57.
23. Hodson, D., 'Towards a philosophically more valid science curriculum', *Science Education*, 1988, 72, 19–40.
24. Millar, R. and Driver, R., 'Beyond processes', *Studies in Science Education*, 1987, 14, 33–62.
25. Chalmers, A. F., *What is this thing called Science?* (Open University Press, 1967).
26. Kuhn, T. S., *The Structure of Scientific Revolutions*, (Chicago: University of Chicago Press, 1964).
27. Driver, R., *The Pupil as Scientist*, (Open University Press, 1983).
28. Driver, R., Guesnes, E. and Tiberghien, A., *Children's Ideas of Science*, (Open University Press, 1985).
29. Osborne, R. and Freyberg, P., *Learning in Science: The Implications of Children's Science*, (Auckland: Heinemann, 1985).
30. Needham, J., 'History and human values: A Chinese perspective for World Science and Technology', in Rose, H. and Rose, R. (eds), *The Radicalisation of Science*, (Macmillan, 1976).
31. Millar, R., 'What is scientific method and can it be taught?', in Wellington J. J. (ed.), *Skills and Processes in Science Education*, (Routledge, 1989).
32. Chomsky, N., *Rules and Representation*, (Blackwell, 1980).
33. Brandt, G., Turner, S. and Turner, A., *Science Education in a Multicultural Society*. Report on a conference held at the University of London Institute of Education, 7 February 1985, (University of London Institute of Education).
34. Hollins, M. P., *Science Teaching in a Multiethnic Society 1*, (ILEA, 1984).
35. Hollins, M. P., *Science Teaching in a Multiethnic Society 2*, (ILEA, 1986).
36. Jones, I. (ed.), *Science and the Seeds of History*, (Manchester City Council Education Department, 1986).
37. Newnham, J. and Watts, S., 'Developing a multicultural science curriculum', in Straker-Welds, M. (ed.), *Education for a Multicultural Society*, (Bell & Hyman, 1984).
38. Turner, A.D., and Turner, S.A., *Report of a Meeting of LEA Science Advisers on Multicultural Science Education*, (University of London Institute of Education, 1988).
39. Turner, A. D. and Turner, S.A., *Science, the National Curriculum and Cultural Diversity*, (University of London Institute of Education, 1989).
40. Watts, S., 'Science education for a multicultural society', in Arora, R. K. and Duncan, C.G. (eds), *Multicultural Education*, (Routledge & Kegan Paul, 1986).
41. Watts, S., 'Approaches to curriculum development from both an anti-

racist and a multicultural perspective', in *Better Science: Working for a Multicultural Society*, (Harper & Row, 1984).
42. Gill, D. and Levidow, L., (eds.) *Anti-racist Science Teaching*, (Free Association Books, 1987).
43. Craft, A. and Klein, G., *Agenda for Multicultural Teaching*, (Longman, 1986).
44. Williams, I. W., 'Chemistry' in Craft, A. and Bardell, G. (eds), *Curriculum Opportunities in a Multicultural Society*, (Harper & Row, 1984).
45. Vance, M., 'Biology' in Craft, A. and Bardell, G. (eds), *Curriculum Opportunities in Multicultural Society*, (Harper & Row, 1984).
46. Haber, L., *Black Pioneers of Science and Invention*, (New York: Harcourt, Brace & World Inc 1970).
47. SSCR, *Better Science: Working for a Multicultural Society*, (Secondary Science Curriculum Review/Heinemann Educational Books, 1987).
48. Turner, S. A. and Turner, A.D., 'An international dimension to the teaching of science – opportunities in the National Curriculum', *Multicultural Teaching*, 1989, 8, 34–9.
49. Young, R. M., 'Racist society, Racist science', in Gill, D. and Levidow, L., (eds), *Anti-racist Science Teaching*, (Free Association Books, 1987).
50. Young, R. M., 'Interpreting the production of science', in Gill, D. and Levidov, L. (eds), *Anti-racist Science Teaching*, (Free Association Books, 1987).

3.4

Science teaching in areas of social deprivation

Joan Solomon

SOCIAL CLASS OR SOCIAL DEPRIVATION?

Teachers often comment to each other that they work in a 'rough' or a 'difficult' area. They are much less likely, in these times, to comment directly on the social 'class' of their pupils or on their 'poverty'.

Literature surveys of educational disadvantage, or equality of opportunity, show that much more has been written recently about issues of gender or race than about those of socio-economic class. This is a curious fact. The inequalities of education which attend on the pupils' gender or race are certainly a scandal, but the proportion who are disadvantaged through coming from a background which is socially deprived is far higher than the 4 per cent of ethnic minority or even 50 per cent females. There are locations – not necessarily in those areas of urban decay which spring so readily to mind – in which social deprivation is a huge majority effect. This major factor in educational disadvantage is so easily ignored that we need to begin by examining it, however briefly. What evidence is there that this disadvantage exists? What special factors are thought to contribute to it?

The distribution of affluence and opportunity has changed quite considerably since the 1930s or earlier. Indeed there was a famous study of Luton car-workers in the 1960s, *The Affluent Worker*, which sought to examine whether working-class attributes had actually disappeared. Prime Minister John Major came to power in 1991 on the ticket of a 'classless society'. Whether or not social class is a bridgeable divide, it is incontrovertible that poor social conditions of various types do diminish the capacity of pupils to profit from their schooling. Goldthorpe *et al.* (1968) have estimated that the children of manual workers still have only half the chance they would have of entering the professions if they had been given equality of opportunity. Such a bland statistic, however, omits all reference to other variables which are the concomitants of living and schooling in a depressed area. Fortunately there are several long-term studies which indicate all too clearly the size and nature of the disadvantages.

In 1973 Wedge and Prosser reported on a longitudinal study they had carried out on the health prospects of more than 10,000 children. They reported that those from disadvantaged backgrounds had the following health characteristics:

(1) a higher infant mortality and premature birth-rate, possibly due to a higher incidence of smoking during pregnancy;
(2) less likelihood of being immunized;
(3) more accidents in the home (possibly the result of overcrowding);
(4) a greater number of absences from school due to ill health and emotional disorders.

These findings are not confined to childhood. Large-scale general household surveys produced statistics for adults suffering from long-term disease. These too were strongly class related. There have also been longitudinal studies of cohorts of children from a variety of backgrounds which have highlighted two further points about home factors and educational disadvantage.

(1) A significantly higher percentage of boys who had achieved at a low level in school had also experienced parental divorce or separation before they were five. Girls were not included in this finding. (However, there is also substantial evidence that just the *stigma* of coming from a single-parent home accounts for a large part of the teachers' and psychologists' rating of such children as disturbed, as does the *stress* engendered by the actual divorce or separation.)
(2) Parental interest and encouragement, even at the youngest age tested (five years), was strongly associated with children's achievement up to and at school-leaving age (Hutchinson *et al.*, 1979).

This last finding, which is non-controversial in itself, may be interpreted in a number of ways. The large-scale investigation undertaken for the Plowden Committee – *Children and their Primary Schools* (Peaker, 1967) – used a sample of over 3,000 children and produced the following findings: differences both between schools (assessed by a reading task) and within school (assessed by teacher ratings) were largely accounted for by just three items of parental attitude:

(1) educational aspirations;
(2) literacy of the home;
(3) parental interest in school work.

There were also aspects of home circumstances which seemed to correlate with poor achievement, such as physical amenities, number of dependent children and father's job. (For more details of these and other research reports see Morrison and McIntyre, 1971.)

It did not escape comment that teacher rating was being used to assess the children. There was plenty of evidence to suggest that the teachers themselves might also be involved in building up the children's self-esteem, and that this had a profound effect upon the children's achievement. Research showed that teacher expectation was connected with, and possibly influenced by, the pupils' social origins. This seemed sinister. To many researchers in the 1960s and 1970s it was the stigma of lower social class which was influencing how the school and its teachers were treating these children. Teachers more often came from the middle class than did their pupils. Perhaps they simply made self-fulfilling predictions about the ability of those pupils whom they perceived as coming from a lower class. Such researchers repudiated any suggestion that working-class parents might want less for their children than did middle-class parents. Douglas *et al.* (1968) wrote simply in their influential book *All our Future*:

> Parents who have themselves enjoyed a high standard of education see the necessity of education for the future employment of their children while others, who have failed to get the education which they aimed at for themselves, try to ensure that the chances they missed would be taken up by their children.
>
> (Douglas *et al.*, 1968, p. 85)

If parental aspiration and encouragement, which had such a significant effect on their children's achievement, were totally unaffected by social origin or parental education, then it might simply be the teachers' perceptions which were responsible for the low achievement of working-class children.

Many classroom studies carried out during the time of selective education showed that pupils behaved and learned as they were expected to behave and learn – the Pygmalion effect (Rosenthal and Jacobsen, 1968). A large share of the blame for working-class children's lack of educational success was, for a time, placed firmly at the teachers' door. However, in the 1980s some researchers reconsidered their position. Perhaps the right way to interpret the evidence that working-class children achieved less than their middle-class peers, was to re-examine the culture and motivations of the pupils' families. This is how Willis (1983) wrote about it as he revisited an earlier work:

> the re-emphasis and promotion of a more complex, considered and moderate version of what I now want to call *cultural reproduction* – the process of meaning making, the alternative knowledges, the activity, creativity and social promise of subordinate groups . . . . These things are central; determined but also determining . . . the capacity of the working class to generate collective and cultural forms of knowledge [which are] not reducible back to bourgeois forms.
>
> (Willis, 1983, p. 108)

Willis recognized that the parents and families of working-class pupils might not all have the same middle-class aspirations for conventional educational success that had been suggested.

To summarize, the literature on low educational achievement related to social background – which is not in any way specially related to achievement in science – suggests that the following might well be important factors:

(1) poorer health and more emotional stress;
(2) violence and getting into trouble with the police (associated with single-parent families);
(3) teachers' low expectations;

(4) poor literacy in the home;
(5) physical amenities of the home;
(6) lack of parents' aspirations for their children's education (due, possibly, to an alternative subculture).

The rest of this article will give an account of a research project which explored how these factors brought about by social deprivation can affect science teaching. It is the first British study which is specific to science teaching.

THE RESEARCH SETTING

The study was carried out in what sociologists now called 'an area under stress'. This term includes a whole spiral of possible problems – family instability, poverty, poor prospects for employment, lack of adequate housing, vandalism, trouble with the police, etc. – all of which seem to come to a focus in particular localities. There was a general consensus, in the community and in the local teacher training institutions, that the quality of science teaching was high. The area was also thought to have a lower than average level of racial tension. Both these factors were valuable. The lack of racial tension removed one unwanted variable, and there was an initial level of researcher confidence that good practice was being explored which was essential and rose as the study proceeded.

Four schools participated: the 'Upper School' (13–18 years) in the region, the 'Middle School' (9–13 years) in the same situation, another Middle School ('Middle (2)') with a more socially mixed intake, and 'First School' (5–8 years) which drew its pupils almost exclusively from the area in question.

The large local estate in the region had been built in the late 1950s for workers in local industry. At one time almost 90 per cent of the residents would have been employed locally in 'the works'. By 1992 the number was less than 10 per cent. All the schools had a large number of 'free dinner' children and there was also a very high incidence of one-parent families. (In one Middle School class of 27 only four of the pupils had two parents at home.)

Upper School had recently completed a special-needs audit showing that in years 9 (age 13), 10 (age 14) and 11 (age 15), the total percentage of pupils noted in the return was a staggering 35 per cent. (Fewer than 1 per cent of these had purely physical handicaps, 28 per cent were in Warnock categories 2–5, and at least 29 per cent had been referred for professional social or psychological help at some time during their schooling.) Although there were no comparable figures for Middle or First School there is no reason to believe that they would be any different.

Teachers who taught science in all four schools, two technicians, a special-needs co-ordinator, and a school counsellor were all interviewed. The questions asked fell into three categories:

(1) learning problems and behaviour in science lessons which had been directly observed and could be compared with those experienced in other schools;

(2) inferences that the teachers made as to the causes of these behavioural problems;

(3) strategies adopted in teaching and management which seemed to improve science teaching.

Inevitably reflective and experienced science teachers were not satisfied with merely detailing their experiences of learning problems without speculating about their causes and offering suggestions for appropriate action. Indeed the fluency with which these teachers spoke, not only about difficulties, but also about their pupils' disadvantages and the unhappy effects of these on the pupils' schooling, suggested that the questions asked had already been the subject of informal discussion. There were some superficial contradictions. The laboratories and classrooms of all four schools were well decorated with the pupils' work and had a pleasant atmosphere. So did most of the lessons watched. The researcher commented in particular on the friendly attitude of the pupils in Middle School who greeted her and held doors open in a welcoming way. At times it was easy to forget the stressed and deprived nature of the areas which the schools served. However, almost all the teachers interviewed emphasized to us how extremely difficult their first year of teaching in this neighbourhood had been, and the shock of finding, even in First School, how very disruptive the pupils could be. One of the local teacher training institutes had stopped placing their science PGCE students in these schools because of the severe classroom behavioural difficulties.

DIFFICULTIES IN LEARNING SCIENCE

Every single one of the teachers interviewed spontaneously mentioned the pupils' lack of language skills. They reported that from the start their pupils have a language deficit which holds them back, not only in their learning, but in simple social exchanges with each other.

> They find it quite difficult to express themselves. Amongst each other you find there's a lot of one-word answers, a lot of body gestures rather than using language, not many adjectives, not many verbs, and a lot of confusion with the past tense.
>
> (First School)

In science, where so much of the work is concerned with describing observation, this lack of language becomes a special handicap. Difficulty in learning and retaining new words for science, and in expanding everyday vocabulary were common themes in the teachers' answers:

> it's really frustrating because language makes everything accessible to you. It makes ideas, understanding, and reading accessible. A lot of them find it difficult and it's frustrating for the kids.
>
> (science co-ordinator in Middle School)

> That's something that has been highlighted for the whole area's local schools, by the HMI report – that there is a deficiency, partly in the sophistication of

their language. In the SATs yesterday, quite a bright girl asked, 'What does the word *obtain*, mean?'

(Upper School)

Short attention span and poor concentration were the next factors mentioned at all three levels of schooling as being serious problems and commonly encountered.

They are unpredictable in their moods so you have to be ready to change what you are doing in order not to let them get off the roof! Their problem is that they get bored easily and they don't concentrate . . . and the whole thing is passive.

(Middle School)

Most of the teachers mentioned the children's low self-esteem and indicated that they thought this emanated from parents. The problem was more severe in Upper School, having been exacerbated, perhaps, by a longer history of lack of success.

A lot of what you are about is trying to build up confidence so that they feel they are achieving. That's a major obstacle because you'll even get some quite good children saying, 'My work's rubbish. I am no good at this, am I?' And they are scoring quite highly. They've got this rather low opinion of themselves.

(head of science, Upper School)

This poor self-esteem extends to the school and the whole estate in a self-defeating spiral of lack of pride, hope and ambition.

I think one thing the youngsters here don't have, which they did at [previous school], is a real pride in their institution. There is a tendency here, as a part of the general devaluing of themselves, to say, 'We're a dump school. We live on [the estate].'

(Upper School)

'Mucking about' with equipment was the only science-specific problem mentioned. The head of a special needs unit based at Middle School commented that, given the vulnerability of equipment, he could see why science teachers might 'argue a particular case' for back-up. A few of the teachers, and at least one laboratory technician, thought that both breakages and theft related to other social problems.

These children just grab what they can when they can. . . . It's not malicious – 'I'm going to break this test tube.' It's 'I must have it in case I don't get it.'

(Middle School)

It [lack of care with apparatus] seems to go with the whole attitude of being on the estate – the way the bus shelter is treated, that sort of thing . . .. There's this tendency for them to say, 'Look at this crummy old stuff that they've given us', where it isn't particularly. They assume they are going to get the crummy end of everything before they start.

(Upper School)

TEACHERS' INFERENCES ABOUT CAUSES

These teachers did not have any special psychological training. As they spoke about the reasons for their pupils' problems they were simply drawing on experience, their professional judgement, and local knowledge. Their inferences gathered conviction, however, when they were put together with data from the other schools and from the community knowledge of other workers.

The First School pupils were naive enough to speak more openly to their teachers about family problems and their own anxieties. Their teachers linked this with similar problems they had heard about from nursery teachers in the area. Middle (2) School gave especially valuable evidence about home influence because of its mixed intake. The absence of blame or criticism of parents was significant.

> You've got children with [supportive] parents who spend time with them
> . . . and then you've got children from appalling backgrounds . . . parents
> who don't give them time, parents who can't give them time . . . My God,
> they've got their own dreadful problems! If you've got a husband that's
> unemployed, and you're unemployed, you've got children around your
> knees, a little son who wanted to go to the library because he's got research
> to do for school . . .!
>
> (Middle (2) School)

Poor concentration, short attention span, and behavioural disturbance were put down to home stress by teachers in both First School and Middle School:

> I've found particularly that if there is turmoil within themselves and insec-
> urity, then those children find it very difficult to concentrate and need a lot
> of encouragement and need their self-esteem raised – long before you get to
> rating their intellectual learning.
>
> (First School)

The head of the special-needs unit made an interesting connection between emotional development and play which may well have a relevance for practical science:

> it is a fair assumption with a lot of our children that they haven't played,
> that they haven't developed emotionally. So if they can have the opportunity
> to learn to play and relax within themselves and get some pleasure, then they
> can perhaps begin the developmental process again.
>
> (head of special-needs unit)

In First School a 'shared reading' scheme was in operation where books were sent home to be read with parents. In view of the teachers' general concern with reading standards, this was of special interest:

> It's supposed to be a shared experience but it isn't half the time. I had about
> three parents tell me last year, quite openly, that they couldn't read very
> well. They actually want to help their children, but they can't. And that's
> aside from the ones that don't come forward. . . . The problem is that

parents have so many other pressing problems, and they don't value school – to a certain extent.

(First School)

A related factor in the children's poor literacy was the almost complete lack of books in many homes. It is hard to overestimate this factor. In a Year 8 class of twenty-three children in Middle School, the sum total of all the books in all the homes was only nine!

The final statement in the last quotation echoes a point made by about half the teachers – the lack of ambition of the parents for their children to go further than they had done themselves. Two of the teachers volunteered that they had grown up in working-class areas, and could recognize the parents' lack of educational aspirations as a working-class cultural effect (see the conclusions of Willis (1983) p. 5). The related attitude of 'we're stuck here and that's it!' would account, they said, for both the low self-esteem of these pupils and their passivity. In line with this parental attitude came problems relating to making money after school:

a lot of the kids are tired because they work late on earning money. As long as they get a job they don't mind what it is as long as it produces money. So one of the problems is trying to raise their horizons.

(head of science, Upper School)

Opinions about the effects of television varied. One Middle School science teacher simply referred to it as a useful knowledge source for the children in their book-deprived homes. But others saw parents as using television to keep their children quiet and under control. Clearly there was no way the teachers could substantiate this view: it was offered, usually by First School teachers, to explain the lack of image variety, and the intellectual passivity of the pupils.

What frightens me more than anything is that they're sat in front of television or whatever. So the imagination is not there. The imagination is more monsters and killing, and I'll make a gun, because that's what they've been used to seeing on television.

(Middle School)

In these socially uniform schools peer pressure was often blamed for a variety of ills: for watching television, playing computer games, watching blue videos, not answering in lessons, or even showing interest in science. This was more frequently mentioned in connection with older pupils. One of the Upper School science teachers admitted that many of the pupils bow to peer pressure, get by with as little work as they can, and continually underachieve. This social connivance in underachieving is another example of Willis's subcultural ethic.

APPROPRIATE TEACHING STRATEGIES

All the teachers emphasized that their first task was getting to know their pupils well. This was equally as true in an infants class as when trying to teach physics in Upper School:

When they're feeling insecure about something, if they feel they can't tackle it, their first reaction is to say it's boring. That's because within themselves they feel very insecure and they need to build up a relationship with you before they will respond. That's why students [PGCE] find it difficult, because it is so difficult to get this sort of rapport with the children – it takes time.

(First School)

Teachers can have only indirect ways of helping their pupils cope with stress and tension. One method was to avoid confrontation in class which might release the anger and insecurity which is often just below the surface. Even the most experienced teachers warned that in straight confrontations 'the teacher never wins': not only does the teacher lose face, but the pupils themselves do not learn from the incident:

mainly through experience you find out . . . you learn that you musn't place children in situations they can't escape from. It's a long-term process where kids gradually learn to trust what you're saying to them and they will respond. . . . I think the big thing is to give yourself a bit of time and space. . . . It is a very complicated relationship that not only are you helping yourself and [the pupil], but you are helping the whole class by preventing disruption. You get a lot of street cred out of it.

(science co-ordinator, Middle School)

All the schools took advantage of extra help – special needs helpers or the referral system – to calm the pupils' anger rather than to punish them. I would expect the day tutor would be aware of the youngster – aware of their problems. Broadly speaking every member of staff does some degree of counselling. The tutor deals with the average child in average difficulty, the senior tutor . . . with the average child in extraordinary circumstances . . . and I deal with the extraordinary child in extraordinary circumstances.

(counsellor, Upper School)

Science technicians also helped occasionally with calming down distraught children. Another effective strategy was giving extra time through the running of a science-related club, or just being on tap in the workshop, during lunch hours. This helped the teachers both to get to know the pupils better and to listen to their troubles.

The meticulous preparation of lessons would be a part of every good teachers' objectives, but in the case of these stressed and anxious children it was especially important for building up security. It was also important for dealing with their short attention span. A senior teacher in Upper School brought in the playing-with-apparatus problem: 'they play because they are not engaged with the task you've set'. It followed from that, he added, that 'the key is variety' in planning lesson activities.

The tendency to play around with equipment coupled with short attention span had implications for skills training, and safety in the laboratory:

Because they are emotionally distressed they find it very difficult to concentrate on the guidance you give them . . . so they need a lot more of what we

call over-learning, so you actually teach a skill again and again and again
. . . that's the biggest difference. They need a lot more reminding.

(First School)

Middle School teachers commented that behaviour in their science laboratory
was considerably better than it was in the classroom. The pupils seemed to
appreciate being allowed to work in the special place, a privilege which helped
to combat their feeling that, as one teacher put it, 'the world is against them'.

Because peer pressure was such a strong force amongst the older pupils,
Upper School teachers took special care in selecting groups for practical work.
This again needed deep understanding of the pupils' characters, as well as large
quantities of tact!

If they are in the right grouping they will help each other. Grouping them
right is down to knowing your kids. . . . If you've got someone that's cataly-
tic in the group then things can go quite well – the same if you've got a
catalyst in the other direction who causes disruption. So you've got to get
that right, that's why you extract some of them sometimes, take them on one
side and say, 'Look you're good! Why don't you turn round and show how
good you are?'

(head of science, Upper School)

Dealing with the ubiquitous language problems is a continual and wearing
struggle. For children with low self-esteem and poor language skills an emphasis on writing could almost be counterproductive. It shows up their weakness and asks for commitment where they least want to give it. However, all
the teachers said that they persevered with a policy of getting some writing
done in every science lesson.

In Upper School it is impossible to do good practical work without reading,
listening carefully to instructions, and writing reports. The teachers sometimes
reduced writing requirements to simple 'cloze' exercises with spaces for missing words to be filled in. Even then the pupils often asked for the word to be
given after only the minimum of thinking. Improving writing skills, lengthen-
ing attention span, and encouraging pride in doing good work, were all en-
tangled in a difficult and sometimes self-defeating way.

One partial solution might be to set more written work to be done at home.
This was under discussion in several schools but it was not always easy to
obtain parental support for homework. The nine to four working day is
thought by some parents to correspond to the school day. Once more a
cultural construct can be seen to be in conflict with educational aspirations:

We get parents coming up here and saying, 'You can't ask my kid to work
after four o'clock . . . he's got all these jobs to do when he gets home.'

(head of science, Upper School)

Several teachers also claimed that textbooks were not sent home because too
many were not returned; the school simply could not bear the cost of their
replacement.

CONCLUSIONS

In general, case-study research is valued for the richness of data it gives, rather than for its reproduceability. Science teachers reading this report may also give it personal credence to the extent that it matches their own experience. Because it reported on data from four different schools within the same industrial estate it may be considered a reliable picture of science teaching in the locality. It would have less validity for other estates where race or religious conflict was rife, where the physical condition of the school buildings was worse, the class size different, or the teachers less committed. Nor is it difficult to imagine other factors which might also diminish its validity for other situations.

There are two factors which tend to increase confidence in the internal validity of the data. The first is the general match between its findings and accounts of previous studies of education and social deprivation reported in the opening section of the paper. In particular the spontaneous references to parental attitudes is more in line with the thesis of cultural reproduction put forward by Willis (1983), than with the earlier perceptions of teachers' self-fulfilling hypotheses based on pupils' social origins. The chance of the science teachers being familiar with such social theories must be small.

Second, the three types of information given – about learning and behaviour problems, about the probable causes of these, and about effective teaching strategies – produced a large measure of correlation. Where teachers found most difficulty, as for example in language teaching, they could point to a number of social, learning, and deep emotional factors, already identi-fied, which contributed to and illuminated the difficulty they were experienc-ing. None of the teachers indicated that they wished to leave the area. On the contrary almost all gave cogent reasons for satisfaction with their present teaching posts. It seems very likely that their understanding of the nature of pupils' learning problems and the social causes which produced them, played a large part in making their own difficult work significant and fulfilling to them.

Acknowledgement is made to British Petroleum plc for the funding necess-ary to undertake this research, to the Association for Science Education for supporting it, to Alison Frost for her hard work and skill in carrying it out, and to the teachers who submitted patiently to at least two interviews, and allowed their lessons to be observed.

REFERENCES

Douglas, J., Ross, J. and Simpson, H. (1968) *All our Future*, London, Peter Davis.

Goldthorpe, J., Lockwood, D., Bechhofer, F. and Platt, J. (1968) *The Affluent Worker: Industrial Attitudes and Behaviour*, Cambridge University Press.

Hutchinson, D., Prosser, H. and Wedge, P. (1979) The prediction of educa-tional failure, *Educational Studies*, Vol. 5, pp. 73–82.

Morrison, A. and McIntyre, D. (1971) *Schools and Socialisation*, Harmonds-worth, Penguin, pp. 13–48.

Peaker, G. F. (1967) Regression analysis of the national survey, in *Children and their Primary Schools*. Report of the Central Advisory Council for England, HMSO.

Rosenthal, R. and Jacobsen, L. (1968) *Pygmalion in the Classroom: Teacher Expectations and Pupils' Intellectual Development*, New York, Holt, Rinehart & Winston.

Wedge, P. and Prosser, H. (1973) *Born to Fail?* London, Arrow Books.

Willis, P. (1983) Cultural production and theories of reproduction, in L. Barton and S. Walker (eds.), *Race, Class and Education*, London, Croom Helm.

3.5

Teaching science to children with special educational needs

Roy Purnell

INTRODUCTION

Everybody has difficulties with a facet of their education at some stage during their lives. Education is a personal affair and there is no panacea which is suitable for every individual.

There can be many barriers (both permanent and temporary) to learning, ranging through physical disabilities, family problems, learning difficulties to communication difficulties. The Warnock report (DES, 1978a), suggested that at least 20 per cent of children at some point in their school careers have learning difficulties which are deemed 'special', in fact about 1.3 per cent of the school population are now in special schools and units and this percentage will continue to reduce as more children are integrated into mainstream schools (although this is proceeding more slowly than expected due to pressures from the 1988 Education Act).

The term 'special education needs' (SEN) covers a wide variety of abilities, and is used to include those children who are said to be gifted (highly developed intellectually) as well as those who experience learning difficulties and those who are physically disabled. (Officially according to the 1981 Education Act, as incorporated into the 1992 Education Bill, 'gifted students' are excluded from the definitions of learning difficulty and special need.) As Fensham makes clear in article 3.1, 'Reflections on science for all', access to the science curriculum for the gifted pupil has not been a problem, so in the context of making science accessible to *all* children, this article will focus on those with learning difficulties and the physically disabled.

Under the 1988 Education Reform Act (DES, 1988) all children (in maintained schools) regardless of race, gender, disability or geographical location are entitled to receive a broad, balanced and well-differentiated curriculum. As a result of this Act, science is now considered a core subject in the school curriculum. But how has this affected SEN pupils?

Science has particular characteristics, which mean that pupils with special educational needs can still achieve success in science while experiencing difficulties in other areas of learning:

- [Learning science is] about firsthand experience.
- Knowledge and skills can be acquired in small steps through practical activity, so helping concentration.
- Scientific activities can capture the imagination and may help to reduce behavioural problems.

(NCC, 1992a, p. 2)

PRACTICAL SCIENCE

Experimental learning is fundamental to science. Science activities need practical skills and more often than not can be carried out without undue emphasis on reading and writing skills. This is important for SEN pupils as hands-on experience is both relevant and necessary. Children involved in worthwhile practical exercises will improve their knowledge, gain skills and, particularly importantly, gain in self-confidence and self-esteem.

Science activities can be devised to capture the imagination of disruptive pupils and so help to reduce behavioural problems to the benefit of themselves, their peers and the teacher. Involvement in learning, aided by the thoughtful design of experiments, is particularly relevant to those who have learning difficulties. In some circumstances group work can also be both helpful and necessary, as it encourages participation and communication. A purposeful activity solved by a team effort is both educationally rewarding and beneficial to pupils of all levels of ability.

Although the practical nature of science is essential, it can pose some difficulties. The range of appropriate apparatus, its availability and cost, and the access to specialized facilities are aspects which need careful consideration when planning activities. Often the control of apparatus and facilities is in the hands of teachers whose primary concerns are examination classes and who see apparatus and materials being more valuably put at the disposal of the more able children. Even though the cost of apparatus cannot be neglected, SEN children have equal rights and should have equal access. However, apparatus need not be complicated and expensive. In fact, everyday materials and appliances have many advantages as sometimes complicated apparatus can come between the child and the learning outcomes. Less sophisticated equipment gives pupils and teachers the opportunity to modify, adapt and improve – the very stuff of science.

Teachers must be aware of the safety demands of science experiments and activities. However, such considerations should not preclude the child who experiences difficulties with learning from engaging with the practical side of the subject. Where appropriate steps have been taken, the physically disadvantaged child is no more restricted by safety considerations than any other child. Safety can never be ignored at any level of activity and teachers should be fully aware of specific dangers but, if planned for, they need not become a barrier. Regular consultation with local advisers is essential. Reference to such publications as *Be Safe* (ASE, 1990) and *Safety in Science Laboratories* (DES, 1978b) must be made at all times.

HISTORICAL PERSPECTIVE ON SCIENCE TEACHING AND ITS RELATIONSHIP TO SEN PUPILS

As with any other institution or system, the educational machine has evolved through many changes to its present state. We are all shaped by the past experiences of ourselves and the society in which we live. Children with special educational needs and their education in science are no exception.

The Thomson Report (1918) and The Norwood Report (1943) pointed to the nation's poor performance in wartime as being due in part to a strong technological deficiency. A need for science as an essential factor in school education was highlighted.

By raising the school-leaving age, the Education Act of 1944 extended the emphasis on science education into the higher age range. As a consequence of this greater demand on science teaching, certain chronic weaknesses in the education system were highlighted. These included a shortage of competently trained teachers of science, laboratory technicians, laboratory accommodation, apparatus and materials, and finally inadequate financial support.

In 1955 a group of industrialists set up The Industrial Fund for the Advancement of Science Education in Schools. Some £3 million was collected and distributed to 200 schools to assist their science teaching. As a result the selected schools were able to build extra accommodation and purchase expensive apparatus. It was hoped that these schools would inspire other schools and LEAs to improve their facilities.

The General Certificate of Education (GCE), at what was termed Ordinary level, was introduced in 1951. The exam was designed for the top 20–25 per cent who followed the more academic grammar school curriculum. The Certificate of Secondary Ecucation (CSE) which followed in 1965 was designed for a further 40 per cent of the school population. The scope of exams was thus increased – recognition that a wider range of abilities should be examined and assessed.

CSE incorporated straightforward external exams and syllabuses (Mode 1), internal school syllabuses with external exams (Mode 2) and finally Mode 3 in which the syllabuses and exams were under the control of the teachers. Mode 3 was sometimes set at lower educational levels only. Exams were therefore no longer the sole domain of the more academically able. The two examinations (GCE and CSE), however, seemed to confirm and emphasize the academic/vocational divide.

The Association of Science Teachers was established in 1900 and from this the Science Masters Association evolved in 1909 and the Association of Women Science Teachers in 1912. In 1957 the two associations of male and female teachers of science began a comprehensive overhaul of science teaching syllabuses. The resulting reports and proposals created much attention and gained considerable support from both government and the profession. A team of gifted and enthusiastic teachers was freed from teaching and allowed to work and research in the field of science teaching. As a result, in 1962 the

Nuffield Science Project started work. The effects were wide-ranging, although the initial focus was mainly on the upper ability range in secondary school. This project was followed by the Nuffield Secondary Science Project, aimed at a lower ability level, and the Nuffield Junior Science Project. These appeared mainly as examples of good practice in a wide variety of schools, for example, rural or inner city. Thus it was beginning to be recognized that in science a wider spectrum of ability and age needed to be critically assessed and examined. In 1963 the two associations merged into the Association for Science Education (ASE) and since then the ASE has had a profound and major impact on all aspects of science teaching.

The Schools Council for Curriculum and Examinations was set up in 1964, which marked the beginning of deeper and tighter control of schools. In 1969 the Schools Council examined the feasibility of merging GCE and CSE (an idea which had been proposed by the NUT). As a result, a single system was recommended to the Labour Government via the Secretary of State for Education, Shirley Williams. (However, this merger did not happen until 1986.)

Around the mid-1970s a need was arising for more carefully designed and implemented alternatives to traditional 'grammar-type' curricula. Economic, technical and social changes were encouraging reforms of the curriculum. The rise in number and diversity of comprehensive schools created further pressures as the school curriculum and its control was becoming more and more political.

Up to the mid-1970s SEN children had followed, albeit at a distance, the science curriculum provided for the more able child. Possibly the first mention of the needs of pupils who have a wide spectrum of ability came from the Prime Minister, James Callaghan, in 1976. In his Ruskin College speech in October of that year he said: 'There seems to be a need for more technological bias in science teaching that will lead towards practical applications in industry rather than towards academic studies.' Shirley Williams, a year later, recognized that many problems regarding the teaching of science and technology lay in the primary schools and made it plain that the government intended to take more control of curriculum matters.

Despite the Ruskin speech, up to about 1979 little formal recognition had been made towards the teaching of science to pupils with learning difficulties. At most, such children were taught perhaps by a remedial teacher whose confidence in the subject was not that great. It was not uncommon to find the PE teacher also being asked to teach some science. Apparatus and laboratory use was severely limited, syllabuses were watered-down versions of those designed for the more able pupils, and textbooks were totally inappropriate. Brennan (1979) found that despite the advantage of being a practical subject science was rarely included effectively in the curriculum of SEN children. It was established that successful science work could only be found in 1 in 50 primary, 1 in 60 secondary and 1 in 9 special schools. (In a 1986 DES survey of science education (HMI, 1986) the existence of science for SEN pupils was shown to be thin and insubstantial even where provision *had* been made for science. These were the same schools that had a reputation for pupil achieve-ment in the subject.)

The Warnock report on meeting special educational needs stated that:

> The purpose of education for all children is the same, the goals are the same. But the help that individual children need in progressing towards them will be different. Whereas for some the road they have to travel towards the goals is smooth and easy, for others it is fraught with obstacles.
>
> (DES, 1978a, p. 5)

With the publication of the Warnock report it was officially recognized at last that there should be educational provision for SEN pupils.

This view was echoed by Wilson in *The Curriculum in Special Schools* (1981), in which it was suggested that the education of children in special schools should pay due heed to develop them 'socially', 'intellectually' and 'morally' in an equable fashion according to the general education of other children. However, she also states that 'Special Schools, since they provide for children with special difficulties, must necessarily have some special aims which pupils must realise on the way if they are ultimately to reach the goals which are the same for all pupils' (Wilson, 1981, p. 31).

In 1980 the Secretary of State for Education, Mark Carlisle, accepted com-mon 16+ examinations as desirable, and asked examination boards to draw up national criteria in every subject. In 1983 Sir Keith Joseph following the advice of SEC (the Schools Examination Council, which was beginning to replace the Schools Council) announced that a single system was to be implemented. GCSE courses then followed in September 1986 as a result of the national criteria. But this new offspring was to have a clouded future, as in 1989 orders were published for the new National Curriculum. At last, under the National Curriculum, SEN pupils were included in the provision made for all pupils. However, with this inclusion came the recognition that SEN children might require some amendments to this provision. The Education Reform Act (1988) contained statements such as:

> [teachers] may modify or disapply any or all of the requirements of the National Curriculum if they are inappropriate for an individual pupil.

> [a] statement of special educational needs may specify some modification in the range of levels appropriate at different key stages for the individual child.

> [guidelines] . . . will allow head teachers temporarily to disapply or modify the National Curriculum requirements for individual pupils.
>
> (DES, 1988, p. 12)

The permitted modification to the National Curriculum allowed SEN children to work at levels below the level specified for their age. Furthermore, state-mented children could have the National Curriculum suspended, modified or even disapplied. Recognition had at last arrived but there was still no real discussion, no solutions – the teacher in the classroom was still struggling without the necessary guidance, resources and governmental backing. So although the National Curriculum demanded that science must be in the curriculum of every child in maintained schools, delivery to pupils was another matter altogether.

The educators of children with learning difficulties therefore seemingly must aspire to the curriculum of other children. Yet according to the Warnock and Wilson reports, the curriculum must also be specific. Thus the teaching for pupils with special needs has to be flexible to allow for the ability of each child. The range in special schools and in classes of children with learning difficulties in mainstream schools is wide (Wilson, 1981).

CURRICULUM GUIDANCE

As indicated, exceptions to the National Curriculum requirements can be made, but these are fairly restrictive. Time limits are imposed and alternatives must be provided, as illustrated by the statement from Curriculum Guidance No. 1 (NCC, 1989a) which will allow headteachers temporarily to disapply or modify any part of the National Curriculum (for a limited period) provided a resolution is indicated. It was also accepted that not all SEN pupils would cover all the National Curriculum. Many SEN pupils will, at best, work only towards statements of attainment at level 1 and never beyond. Such sentiments are reinforced in Curriculum Guidance No. 2, A Curriculum for All (NCC, 1989b). However, all educators need to be aware that the government supports the premise that every pupil should have access to National Curriculum attainment targets and not be deprived on the grounds of disability (NCC, 1989c).

Similar views can also be applied to pupils with purely physical disabilities: '[pupils] . . . can learn to understand science concepts and can develop higher levels of reasoning skills, if afforded appropriate opportunity' (Jones, 1983, p. 13). As Jones also points out in a later section, access and achievement should in no way be limited by physical disabilities. A similar line is taken by many regarding other disabilities with the proviso that a range of science activities should be offered but that achievements in certain aspects may not be realizable.

As stated earlier, science has much to offer in the education of those with learning difficulties. Science 5–16 (DES, 1985) displays agreement regarding science and its benefits, such that SEN children should be educated to enable them to take part in, be accepted by and gain satisfaction from the society in which they live. Any study which encourages the learner to understand and appreciate his or her own environment must be beneficial. However, planning and appropriateness are vital. In some cases, material which is designed for a lower age range may profitably be used with older pupils. Science 5–16 (DES, 1985) recommends that work needs to be practical and SEN children may often be best served by curriculum material and methods similar in some ways to those developed for primary school use. However, pupils' sensibilities must not be ignored. If children see work as being designed for younger children, negative attitudes may follow.

More specific guidelines regarding the curriculum for those with learning difficulties is given in the Curriculum Guidance No. 9, *The National Curriculum and Pupils with Severe Learning Difficulties* (NCC, 1992a). This document recognizes that the implementation of the core subjects of the National Curriculum into the schools for the average child is one issue with its own set of problems and resource implications. It presents even greater problems for schools with pupils whose learning may be slower and less predictable. The guidelines set out detailed worked examples which help teachers to develop age-appropriate activities for pupils who are working predominantly at Key Stages outside those specified for their chronological age. It also gives indications of how the programmes of study can be extended and adapted to include pupils of all abilities.

Specific guidelines for science are given in Curriculum Guidance No. 10, *Teaching Science to Pupils with Special Educational Needs* (NCC, 1992b). It draws on current good practice and shows a variety of approaches to involve SEN pupils in science. Based on the philosophy of 'science for all', it includes plans for a whole-school policy, class schemes of work, and group and individual activities. The guidelines include examples related to the four attainment targets through the programmes of study, schemes of work, specific scientific activities, related attainment targets and statements of attainment.

INTERNATIONAL PERSPECTIVES

How do other countries approach the task of teaching science to children with special educational needs? Can we learn anything from their experience? In the USA, a scheme called SAVI/SELPH (Widlake, 1990) has been developed by the Lawrence Hall of Science at Berkeley, California. It covers a wide range of the SEN spectrum. (The term 'physically disabled' covers a much wider range in the USA than in Britain.) SAVI/SELPH is an interdisciplinary, multisensory science enrichment programme that has been used successfully with learners of all abilities.

Many different types of apparatus have been developed for the programme by adapting standard apparatus for use by sensory-deprived children, for example the SAVI thermometers in Braille, syringes modified with stops and Braille flexible metre rules.

The countries within the European Community also see integration of children with disabilities into mainstream schools as being of benefit to the education of such children. At a meeting of the ministers of education of the member states it was resolved that whenever possible full integration into mainstream schools should be a first option (Official Journal of the European Communities, 1990). The ministers see that the work of special schools should be viewed as complementary to the work of the ordinary education system. The integration could be facilitated by attending to the areas of teacher training, creation of new resources and innovations to the curriculum. The education officials see co-operation between the education services and other services such as health, social services, etc., as a method of promoting consistency within the integration programme and they see the use of new technology and individualized learning as a way forward towards integration.

DIFFERENTIATION AND ACCESS FOR SEN PUPILS

Differentiation and access are vital in the education of SEN pupils. They are interlinked so the neglect of either leads to frustration for both teacher and pupil.

Full access may lead to involvement whereas a lack of access may lead to disaffection. Furthermore, for pupils who see themselves as failures it is very important that the work is 'user friendly'. Immediate access is imperative, to enable the SEN pupil to start straight away, thus building up self-confidence. Obviously, access depends on the individual child and his or her needs. As an example, reading problems may be overcome by the use of pictorial clues, simpler language or even an oral presentation (reading or use of tapes with text).

Access for emotionally troubled pupils (including SEN pupils) can be aided by considering the following:

- Non-achievement is often due to emotional problems, and lack of confidence due to a previous lack of success.
- Misbehaviour is often learned in the classroom and at the social level. Poor behaviour is therefore preventable.
- The school provides the ideal environment for difficult behaviour to flourish and rules to be broken. However, all children have the potential for acting appropriately given the right atmosphere and conditions. Teachers should aim to achieve these conditions.
- If pupils are part of a regular, ordered and definite system within a group or class then they are less likely to misbehave.

There are a number of ways to improve access to the curriculum for all pupils:

- Non-essential changes should be kept to a minimum, especially language changes during a particular piece of work.
- Teacher attitudes towards misbehaviour must be consistent and firm.
- It should be made clear to the pupil what is considered unacceptable as well as acceptable behaviour.
- The work level should be matched to pupil ability.
- A secure, positive and constant classroom environment should be provided.

The distinction between differentiation and access for those with learning difficulties is not clear. In Curriculum Guidance No. 10 (NCC, 1992b), a list of methods is given to aid the difficult task of achieving successful differentiation. The list includes confidence building, multisensory approaches, simpler 'carrier' language (the language particular to the subject), matching demands to level of attainment, employing firsthand experiences, etc. As you can see, all these could be included in the factors necessary to ensure successful access.

Differentiation within the material used by the teacher is important. Successful differentiation enhances and encourages positive attitudes. It is particularly important for those with learning difficulties that failures are minimized and successes praised. The content, teaching methods, apparatus, aims and investigations should be tailored to allow for the range of experience and ability of the children. Differentiation and presentation lie at the basis of many problems in the teaching of children with learning difficulties (NCC, 1989d).

Teachers need to ensure that pupils feel secure, achieve success and sense that their work is worth while. The school, through the curriculum, has to satisfy two conditions. First, all children whatever their abilities need to achieve certain standards. Second, in order to allow for pupils with a range of abilities, individual characteristics and abilities need to be accommodated through well-differentiated work. The school and its curriculum must be sufficiently flexible to account for this two-way pull. Examples of good practice in this particular area are given in *Non-Statutory Guidelines in Science* (NCC, 1992c).

The importance of differentiation cannot be stressed too strongly. Successful integration of pupils with special needs in mainstream schools can only occur where there is an equality of opportunity and this in turn can only be attained by setting appropriate tasks and realistic targets. The outcome of unsatisfactory work in the past often resulted from poor differentiation being coupled to the provision of inadequate material.

Physical disability should be seen in the proper context. The pupil is a child with a physical disability, not a disabled child. It is important not to label the child as having a disadvantage simply because of a perceived physical disability. However, some physical disabilities can hinder learning and thus create a barrier. As Purnell says,

> The reverse is not necessarily the case, that is a disability automatically means that there is a gross learning barrier. It is therefore important not to hinder a pupil's learning by hanging a label around their neck, that of 'blind', 'visual impairment', 'moderate learning difficulties (MLD)', 'spina bifida', etc., as some people often assume the label automatically means inability to think or do practical tasks and that is not the case as there are as many variations of the degree of disability as there are levels of abilities. It is best to look at the abilities of the pupils rather than putting stress on the pupils' disabilities. Ability rules over disability.
> (Purnell, in Jones and Purnell, 1992, pp. 4–5)

An attitude change in society is once again a key element and this must be encouraged as the majority of physical disabilities are permanent and beyond cure. Some disabilities are also progressive. It is essential that other than making certain vital arrangements for the particular disability the child should be treated no differently to any other child with regard to expectation and standards of behaviour. Activities must be accessible with all necessary safety precautions taken into account. The contributions that a child with a physical disability can make must be enhanced. Peer co-operation should be positively encouraged. The child with the physical disability should, like any other child, receive science as a part of their curriculum, otherwise their education will be unbalanced.

PUBLISHED RESOURCES

Before the introduction of the National Curriculum both primary and secondary schools had the benefit of a large number of teaching resources for all pupils in science – worksheets, textbooks (advisory and pupil-based), videos, etc. – but in no way can these act as a replacement for the skilled teacher who can adapt, advise, add life and colour to a subject. However, there was a paucity of appropriate publications in science for children with learning difficulties. This was due in part to the perceived limited market. After the introduction of the National Curriculum, the number of published resources increased enormously, especially at the primary level. One possibility for the teacher of children with learning difficulties is to adapt and modify publications aimed at a lower age range. This approach can work well if factors outlined earlier are taken into account, for example pupil sensitivity, but it is an extra burden on already busy teachers.

What about the material which has been specifically designed for children with learning difficulties? Design and production of written work in science for SEN children is fraught with problems. Reid and Hodson (1987) found that in the first year of secondary schooling (Year 7) children spent only 9 per cent of their science lesson reading and this had only increased by 1 per cent by Year 9. Not only that but some 35 to 37 per cent of the reading was from the blackboard or an exercise book. Specially prepared worksheets written by teachers were found to be useful, particularly where teachers were able to set the language at the appropriate level. Unfortunately there is not a great deal of published material in worksheet form for those pupils with special needs – either the gifted or the less able. However, some worksheets have been published by Purnell (1989), and Jones and Purnell (1992). In these publications, aimed at Key Stages 3 and 4 and Key Stage 3 respectively, the concepts are limited to one per page, the instructions are clear and the stages of development are not too large. Diagrams and text are linked, clues are offered and pupils are given the opportunity to record directly on to their worksheets. The whole text is designed to assist and encourage the pupil.

A useful resource is *Science for Children with Learning Difficulties* (Kincaid *et al.*, 1984). This presents a variety of practical investigations for children in primary and middle schools. The book contains suggestions for teaching activities which are closely structured to enable those with learning difficulties to gain confidence. Another useful book, with a wider brief, is *Special Children's Handbook* (Widlake, 1990) which contains a series of articles describing methods, resources and systems providing teachers with many ideas.

ASSESSMENT

Formal assessment could be regarded as redundant in the case of children with learning difficulties. However, these children must aspire to improve, and teachers also need to gauge pupil progress. The School Examination and Assessment Council (SEAC) in *School Assessment Folder for Key Stage 3* (1992) states that their tests are designed to include those with special educational needs of all kinds. However, a very small number of statemented pupils may be disapplied from these.

Positive steps regarding assessment and examinations have been taken by the Welsh Joint Education Committee, who have for the last ten years been running examinations in science for children with special needs. The Certificate of Education (CoE) is aimed at low achievers, those who find GCSE inappropriate and even statemented children. The CoE is designed for the delivery and assessment of science within Levels 1 to 3 in the National Curriculum.

CoE provides syllabuses and resource materials, assessment techniques and reporting systems which emphasize the positive features of the pupils' work and raise pupils' self-esteem. Assessment is primarily through school-based continuous assessment, with minimal emphasis on end-of-term examinations. To alleviate difficulties oral questioning may be employed.

SUMMARY AND CONCLUSION

As a result of the 1988 Education Reform Act, every child in maintained schools has the legal entitlement to a broad and balanced curriculum. The National Curriculum appears to be accepted by nearly everybody as forming the cornerstone of the future curriculum for the great majority of children. A very high percentage of teachers of pupils with learning difficulties accept involvement in the National Curriculum as they see more opportunities for integration.

However, to attain integration within a class there must be appropriate differentiated activities and experiences for all children, especially for those with greatest need. The DES via the Inspectorate has recognized that this state of affairs has not always been achieved.

Science must answer the challenge created by SEN pupils and provide sufficiently and appropriately defined work. Equality of opportunity for SEN pupils can be provided in science, as the subject is practical, logical and uses everybody's experience.

To determine the success or otherwise of science being presented to children it is essential that pupils' responses be assessed. This assessment can only be valid when the material presented to the pupil is matched to ability. Thus the case for appropriate differentiation is further strengthened.

It has been accepted that the inclusion of science into the curriculum of children with learning difficulties imposes the logistical difficulties of providing sufficient numbers of teachers with suitable academic qualifications and a sympathetic understanding of the needs of children with learning difficulties. The problem arising from the lack of apparatus and suitable published material is another factor, but this could be solved by collaboration between the various agencies involved. Within every child, whatever their need, there is the potential to achieve success within the limits of their capabilities, and educators are duty bound to provide differentiated and accessible material to facilitate this. The maxim that 'ability conquers disability' is eminently true for science in the education of children with special educational needs.

REFERENCES

ASE (Association for Science Education) (1990) *Be Safe*, Hatfield, Association for Science Education.

Brennan, W. K. (1979) *Curriculum Needs of Slow Learners*, London, Schools Council.

DES (Department of Education and Science) (1978a) *Special Educational Needs*, Report of the Committee of Enquiry into the Education of Handicapped Children and Young People (Warnock Report), London, HMSO.

DES (Department of Education and Science) (1978b) *Safety in Science Laboratories* (DES Safety Series No. 2), London, HMSO.

DES (Department of Education and Science) (1985) *Science 5–16, A Statement of Policy*, London, HMSO.

DES (Department of Education and Science) (1988) *Education Reform Act*, London, HMSO.

HMI (Her Majesty's Inspectorate) (1986) *A Survey of Science Education*, London, HMSO.

Jones, A. V. (1983) *Science for Handicapped Children*, London, Souvenir Press.

Jones, A. V. and Purnell, R. F. (1992) *Science Specials*, Dunstable, Folens.

Kincaid, D., Rapson, H. and Richards, R. (1984) *Science for Children with Learning Difficulties*, London, MacDonald.

NCC (National Curriculum Council) (1989a) *Framework of the Primary Curriculum* (Curriculum Guidance No. 1), London, HMSO.

NCC (National Curriculum Council) (1989b) *A Curriculum for All* (Curriculum Guidance No. 2), London, HMSO.

NCC (National Curriculum Council) (1989c) *National Curriculum: A Teachers Guide*, London, HMSO.

NCC (National Curriculum Council) (1989d) *Implementing the National Curriculum* (Circular No. 5), London, HMSO.

NCC (National Curriculum Council) (1992a) *The National Curriculum and Pupils with Learning Difficulties* (Curriculum Guidance No. 9), London, HMSO.

NCC (National Curriculum Council) (1992b) *Teaching Science to Pupils with Special Educational Needs* (Curriculum Guidance No. 10), London, HMSO.

NCC (National Curriculum Council) (1992c) *Non-statutory Guidance in Science*, London, HMSO.

Norwood (1943) *House of Commons Parliamentary Debates/Curriculum and Examinations in Secondary Schools* (Norwood Report), Ministry of Education, HMSO, London.

Official Journal of the European Communities (1990) Participation by pupils with special educational needs, May.

Purnell, R. F. (1989) *Science Workout 1 and 2*, Cheltenham, Stanley Thornes.

Reid, D. J. and Hodson, D. (1987) *Special Needs in Ordinary Schools: Science for All*, London, Cassell.

SEAC (School Examination and Assessment Council) (1992) *School Assessment Folder for Key Stage 3*, London, HMSO.

Thomson, G. P. (1918) *House of Commons Parliamentary Debates*.

Widlake, P. (ed.) (1990) *Special Children's Handbook,* Cheltenham, Stanley Thornes.

Wilson, M. D. (1981) *The Curriculum in Special Schools*, London, Schools Council.

3.6

Science education through school, college and university

Roger Blin-Stoyle, FRS

CONCERNS

Many individuals and organizations, not least the Prime Minister's Advisory Council on Science and Technology (ACOST, 1991), are concerned that post-16 and higher education courses in science and technology are becoming less popular. This is shown in Table 1 for students taking science and mathematics A-level subjects from 1989 to 1992, although it must be recognized that more are taking science and technology BTEC courses. Table 2 shows how applications for science, technology engineering and mathematics university degree courses are similarly decreasing. Although the absolute numbers are not quite so bad, the trends do not augur well for the future when they are set against the high potential needs for trained scientific and technological personnel at all professional levels as we move into the twenty-first century (Pearson *et. al.*, 1989).

Table I Proportion of A-level students sitting science or mathematics subjects, 1989–92

	1989 (%)	1990 (%)	1991 (%)	1992 (%)	Percentage change 1989–92
Biology	6.55	6.75	6.67	6.57	+ 0.3
Chemistry	7.40	7.19	6.39	5.85	−20.9
Physics	6.98	6.47	6.24	5.65	−19.1
Mathematics	12.91	11.75	10.78	9.90	−23.3

There is clearly a lack of enthusiasm for science and technology on the part of an increasing proportion of students. There are, no doubt, various reasons for this. Not least are student perspectives on their future careers. For many, lucrative and high-status positions in finance, business, commerce and industry

This article was first presented as the Presidential Address to the Annual Meeting of the Association for Science Education in Loughborough in 1993. It is reprinted in *School Science Review*, Vol. 74, no. 269, June 1993.

Table 2   Proportion of students applying for university courses in science, mathematics, engineering and technology, 1989–91

	1989 (%)	1990 (%)	1991 (%)	Percentage change 1989–91
Biological sciences	6.73	6.45	6.26	− 7.0
Chemistry	2.11	2.00	1.82	−13.7
Physics	1.86	1.59	1.47	−21.0
Mathematical sciences	5.34	4.85	4.53	−15.2
Engineering and technology	9.80	9.08	8.72	−11.0

must seem very attractive. But, in the UK a good science and technology education is *not* seen as the best vehicle for achieving such positions. They are mostly filled by non-scientists. This is not, incidentally, the case in some other countries. A few weeks ago I heard Dr Heinz Riesenhuber, the Federal Minister for Research and Technology in Germany, speaking on this matter. In his country the heads of many industries are professional scientists, as is the Minister himself. This has, as he put it, clearly 'signalled' the benefits and standing of a science education to students who have responded accordingly. Germany, he said, does not have our problem. It is, therefore, imperative, and the ACOST report referred to earlier makes this point, that science and technology careers themselves be accorded higher status (and salaries) and be developed in such a way that they lead naturally to high management positions for those wishing to move along that path.

Compounding all this is the general lack of public understanding of science and technology and even, recently, the emergence of an anti-science lobby represented by such people as Bryan Appelyard and Fay Weldon. Things are not helped either by the level of public funding for research and development which does not always compare well with that in many other advanced countries (Royal Society, 1992). Organizations such as COPUS (Committee on the Public Understanding of Science), The Royal Society and the Save British Science Society, as well as many individuals, are trying, with some success, to do something about these problems. It is a formidable task and entails increasing awareness among all UK citizens, from the man or woman in the street through to the Cabinet, of the excitement and interest of science and technology, their cultural value, their potential and their importance for the future economic well-being of this country. Clearly the task begins with the teaching and learning of science within the education system. So let me now turn to this.

FACTORS

There are several important factors bearing on the provision of a successful science education which have to be taken into account at virtually all levels of education from school through to university.

First there is the wide ability range of pupils and students. Up to 16, except in selective schools, attendance is essentially 100 per cent. In the 16–19 age range it is now around 40–50 per cent for those in full-time education and increasing. And, in higher education it is heading for 30+ per cent. Now it is essential that science education is so structured at all levels that, whilst being a challenge and inspiration for the high-flyer, it is at the same time rewarding and not overwhelming for the less able. Inevitably, given the wide spread in ability at all levels, this requires a measure of differentiation both in delivery and assessment.

Second, science education must continually put the science being studied in the 'here and now' into the context of where it can lead to. This means explaining what is happening at the frontiers of science, discussing relevant technological developments, environmental and societal implications and, not least, career opportunities. Science must be seen for what it is, not a sterile body of established knowledge, but an area of study with many exciting uncertainties and possibilities at the frontiers and with profound implications, through associated technology, for the way in which life on this planet develops.

Third, science is a highly quantitative subject requiring, particularly in physics, considerable mathematical competence. It is vital that this aspect is not neglected. Frankly, my experience with incoming undergraduates over the last 40 years suggests that it is. I am also told that in vocational courses there is now less emphasis on mathematics. This is not so on the continent where mathematical competence has high priority in both academic and vocational courses. Here, I would stress the importance of a high level of co-ordination between science and mathematics courses and collaboration between course teachers, whether in school, college or university, so that each subject reinforces the other.

Fourth, and following on from my last comment, is the absolutely key role of teachers in science education (Woolnough, 1991). Success depends on their skills, confidence and enthusiasm. These, in turn, particularly at this time of rapid educational change, will be much enhanced if they are given appropriate support for their teaching activities. This means, as stressed in the ACOST report (1991) and also in the report *Only a Teacher . . . ?* (ASE, 1991) that appropriate finance for equipment, good teaching laboratories and generous technician support be provided. But, perhaps above all, is the need for time – time for preparation, learning, updating and reflection as well as for the increasing assessment and recording workload. My impression, from talking to science teachers, is that 'time' is in short supply as is, incidentally, the provision of supportive advice and in-service opportunities. Finally, and not least in this connection, more science teachers are needed, particularly to remove the current 'hidden' and 'suppressed' shortages of science teaching posts. For example, in 1992, nearly half the teachers appointed to teach physics did not have physics degrees.

NATIONAL CURRICULUM SCIENCE

Let me now move away from generalities and turn first to science in the National Curriculum. Science education provided from age 5 to 16 should satisfy a number of features. It should be balanced so that all the sciences are studied through to age 16. It should provide a sound basis for moving forward into post-16 education whether full- or part-time and whether or not in science or technology. It should be reinforced by and provide reinforcement for other parts of the curriculum, in particular mathematics and technology, and be seen to be relevant to the world outside. Above all, it should be motivating, enjoyable and stimulating.

I think that most would agree that science in the National Curriculum has the potential to fulfil all these requirements. However, aside from the general issues I touched on earlier, there are a number of more specific points that concern me.

At Key Stage 4, schools have the choice of delivering the science curriculum, with corresponding assessment through GCSE, as single science, double science or three separate sciences. Some schools require students to follow the double science course in line with the original philosophy of the National Curriculum. But many also provide the single science option, not only, for example, for the brilliant linguist or musician, as was originally intended, but also for any student who does not feel like taking the double course; or possibly, and I hate to say this, to help with a science teacher shortage. This means that once again what are, effectively, career decisions are frequently being taken in what is probably a cavalier fashion at the age of 13–14. This is highly regrettable.

At the other extreme there is the insistence of some schools, mostly in the independent sector, that the budding scientist takes the three separate sciences. I appreciate the reasons for this, namely that this provides a better preparation for A-level science courses and stretches the high-flyer more effectively. But it does introduce a regrettable 'status' issue into school science education. My own view is that this approach should not be necessary. As far as A-level is concerned then, since the bulk of potential scientists take double science, it is essential that A-level science courses, or whatever replaces A-level in due course (and I will come to this later), should join on smoothly to double-science GCSE. Turning next to high-flyers, it is, of course, immensely important that they should be stretched and here there are two developments which, I believe, could take place. First, GCSE will soon accommodate National Curriculum science up to Level 10. To achieve this level is a considerable challenge for any pupil and, of course, would require appropriately differentiated papers in GCSE. Second, there could be timetabled project work or advanced guided study either informally or through 'master classes' arranged in conjunction with local HE institutions. Here I should add that COPUS is taking steps to encourage HE and other scientific institutions to give much more help and support to local schools. But, if that is not enough, then I would be prepared to see supplementary GCSE papers taking pupils beyond Level 10. But my basic thesis is that double science, albeit differentiated, should be the standard currency for science education up to age 16.

That being said, I do have another concern about double science, namely about its mode of delivery. There are various modes, from the fully integrated through to co-ordinated teaching of the separate sciences. My concern is that when taught and learned in an integrated fashion, although there is considerable benefit in seeing science as a whole, the integrity and nature of the individual sciences may be lost. Here it must be recognized that, as Paul Black said in his Presidential address to the ASE in 1986, 'there do seem to be different ways of approaching problems and different styles of enquiry in chemistry, physics and biology'. Since, inevitably, the potential professional scientist will have to specialize in due course it seems to me essential that he or she is clearly aware, by the age of 16, of the natures and challenges of the different sciences. So, I would hope that when teaching integrated science, every effort is made to describe continually and clearly the areas of activity and approaches of the separate sciences so that their distinctiveness is manifest. It can also be argued that GCSE grading of double science, as well as referring to overall performance, should also give information about performance in the separate sciences.

Of course, two questions must now be asked. First, how effective is double science in encouraging pupils to take up science A-level courses and, second, how do they fare once on these courses? It is early days yet to expect definitive answers, but some work has been done which I would like to mention. There is the May 1992 report by John Sears (1992) on the uptake of A-level science which was commissioned by the ASE and which among other things notes that the change to double-award science has coincided with a numerically improved uptake of A-level science. Then there is the September 1992 report by Eric Macfarlane (1992), commissioned by The Royal Society and the Department of Employment, which compares success at A-level science of students who have taken double-science GCSE courses with those who have taken separate science courses. He concludes that the double-science students performed at least as well as those who had taken separate sciences. Both reports are limited in their samples, but they are encouraging and do hold out hope for the future.

Finally, I would like to emphasize again the absolutely key role of teachers in motivating pupils' interest in science and its potential from the earliest age. It has to be recognized that some young children, particularly girls, come into primary school already conditioned against things scientific and technological. On the other hand, most children at primary level are receptive, enthusiastic and thirsting for knowledge. So, those teaching science in the primary sector have a heavy responsibility and it is good that the ASE is doing so much to support them. Primary science teaching is immensely important because, once pupils are 'turned off' science it is a hard job to turn them 'on'.

By and large, however, as I said earlier, National Curriculum science at the double-award level has the potential to provide not only a comprehensive grounding in science as part of a broad, general education but also a sound basis for moving on into more advanced, specialist science and technology courses at the post-16 level.

SCIENCE AND TECHNOLOGY 16–19

After GCSE at age 16 a pupil continuing in full-time education has critical decisions to make. In general the stark choice is between academic courses embodied in A- and AS-levels or vocational courses such as BTEC which in due course are to be absorbed into the GNVQ. Occasionally it is possible to take the international baccalaureate. The situation as it stands is unsatisfactory for a number of reasons.

First, the separation both in organization and in status of academic and vocational courses introduces a regrettable inflexibility into the system. It also introduces a counterproductive distinction between courses which, to a large extent, is not reflected in the real world. Many so-called academic courses are highly vocational. For example, I heard David Pascall, the Chairman of the National Curriculum Council, emphasize that his first degree in chemical engineering was a vocational qualification. Much academic knowledge is a vital input to vocational activity and the sooner the current emotive usage of the academic/vocational labels is dropped from educational discussion the better.

Second, the traditional approach to this phase of education is to impose, explicitly or implicitly, a high degree of specialization. In particular, the dropping of any form of science education post-16 by very many students is reprehensible. Among them, for example, will be many who, in due course, will be responsible for running industry, commerce or even the country, for whom some continuing contact with science and technology would be of considerable benefit. Then, at this time of Europeanization, modern languages should surely continue to feature as part of 16–19 education. Many key employers, and research and professional organizations have stated quite unequivocally that they would wish to see much more balance in this phase of education than at present. Of course, it is possible to achieve some balance using, for example, conventional A- and AS-levels and more students are doing this. There is also the intention to introduce various core skills into A/AS-level courses. But all of this does not go far enough because there is still no externally imposed *requirement* for balance and many students follow extremely narrow courses.

Third, there is currently a perceived, if not actual, discontinuity in style and content between GCSE science courses and A-level courses. The latter are seen as 'passive', requiring the acquisition of parcels of received and frequently dull knowledge. There is little opportunity for discussion and argument or to continue with the more investigative style which has been introduced into National Curriculum science. These perceptions certainly discourage some students from embarking on A-level science courses.

Fourth and finally, the system is highly inflexible. Consider a student starting an A-level science course. He or she is faced with two years' hard work with a

20–25 per cent probability of failing at the end; much higher in physics if A-level mathematics is not taken. And yet these students are high in the ability range. The problem is that, once on an A-level tramline-type course, there is virtually no opportunity to transfer to another course along the way or to get out with credit, say after one year. The system has little, if any, flexibility and suffers greatly from this. Students are aware of the situation and the 'all or nothing' nature of science courses and the 1:4 odds on failure must be very discouraging.

Major change is needed if 16–19 science and technology education is to be more attractive than it is at present. To this end it should be much more flexible, provide for a wide range of abilities, accommodate the continually changing aspirations and interests of students on courses and should not have rigid boundaries between vocational and academic studies. To achieve flexibility and to ensure some balance requires a *single integrated system* including both academic and vocational elements. Such a scheme was recommended strongly by The Royal Society in its report *Beyond GCSE* (The Royal Society, 1991) and its main features are as follows:

- The system should join smoothly on to the pre-16 curriculum, its more active styles of teaching and learning and its assessment processes.
- There should be a requirement that all students preserve a measure of balance in their studies. This could be done by requiring some minimal study in each of three broad domains:
  (1) social, economic and industrial;
  (2) scientific, mathematical and technological;
  (3) creative, language-related and aesthetic.
- The system should provide for a relatively wide range of abilities. Here, the use of differentiated assessment would be important so that, whilst providing a challenge for the most able, weaker students will be able to show, and have assessed, their positive achievements.
- Flexibility and ease of transfer between courses is essential so that the tramline effect already mentioned is removed or, at least, minimized. This can be achieved most easily by using a modular system including both academic and vocational modules at foundation and advanced levels. This has the advantage of introducing short-term targets and is the approach being adopted in higher education. Students will also be able to taste and hopefully enjoy more advanced science without the massive commitment currently required. Further, it readily allows the study of cross-curriculum and integrated themes. Modules to be taken should not, of course, be chosen on a supermarket basis but should be negotiated following appropriate counselling and guidance so that courses are sensibly coherent.
- The system should ensure the development of important core skills such as communication, problem solving and study skills. The latter are still frequently deficient in students entering higher education.

- Teaching and learning, as well as using the more passive didactic approach, should make much more use of active learning such as supported self-study, flexible learning packages, open-ended investigative work and learning in context including, if possible, the workplace. The latter can be very beneficial but needs to be of high quality.
- Assessment should be varied involving end-of-module and end-of-course examinations together with the course work and projects. Reporting on assessment should be primarily in the form of National Records of Achievement stating clearly what has been achieved. This will be much more valuable than the current single grade. Finally, using credit accumulation, certification after one year (Certificate of Advanced Education) as well as two years (Diploma of Advanced Education) should be available.

I believe a structure such as this would seem much more attractive to a 16-year-old, particularly because of its flexibility, the use of short-term targets, its recognition of positive achievement and its active learning approach. As far as the different sciences are concerned, they would be studied through various modules such that the content covered nationally agreed common cores. Their treatment should continue to have the features already discussed for pre-16 science education, including applications, relevance to the world of work and the environment. In particular, each science should be seen as a whole and the relationship of individual modules to this whole should be continually emphasized. The basic thrust should be for confident understanding rather than maximal rote learning of facts.

Such an approach to 16–19 education is widely supported by virtually all educational, industrial, technological and engineering professional organizations. Many of its features are already incorporated into baccalaureate schemes, most recently the proposed arrangements for the ScotBac and Scot-Cert. Some of the proposals that have come from government such as GNVQs, the Advanced Diploma and the introduction of BTEC courses into schools, are small hesitant steps in this direction. According to recent publicity, GNVQs at Level 3 equate to A-level. So why not bring them under the same umbrella so that they do literally, in the words of the advertisement, carry the same respect as A-levels? In this connection, I was encouraged to read in the press a few weeks ago that a ministerial think-tank under the chairmanship of Gillian Shephard is looking into the idea of an English baccalaureate.

One frequently raised emotional argument against proposals of this kind is that, if adopted, the gold standard of A-levels would be lost for ever. I have two comments here. First, to be meaningful the word *standard* in this context has to be defined. If it refers to learned factual content, then maybe. If it refers to understanding, to problem-solving ability, to a spirit of enquiry, then I beg to differ. Even on factual content, given the use of differentiated modules, there is no reason at all why the content level should not be maintained or even enhanced. The scheme proposed can raise students to very high standards as well as accommodate in a rewarding way more 'run of the mill' performances. Of course we cannot change things overnight, but the main aims of an approach such as this should be continually in the public eye so that the piece-meal changes being introduced now can be judged against the needs of this longer-term perspective which, I firmly believe, will be in place before too long.

SCIENCE AND TECHNOLOGY IN HIGHER EDUCATION

The educational changes already under way in schools and colleges, never mind those that are likely to take place in the next few years if 16–19 education is rationalized, have profound implications for higher education. For the first time in educational history we have a bottom-up situation in which higher education in the UK is responding to developments in school and college education rather than the reverse. Science and engineering degree courses now have to be matched to the very varied needs and wide ability spread of the incoming students. The courses will increasingly have many purposes; not only to provide an education for potential professional scientists and engineers at all levels, but also the provision of background scientific understanding of value in many other types of career and, not least, to contribute to general intellectual development.

As I said at the outset, the ability range in higher education is increasing rapidly and will soon be around three times greater than it was twenty years ago. Further, incoming students have followed courses with different syllabuses, additionally complicated by varied syllabus emphasis in different schools. They are also increasingly being joined by mature students with very different backgrounds. In general, for science and technology courses, this has meant a decrease in the average level of factual knowledge and mathematical competence of incoming students. And changes in 16–19 education along the lines I have been advocating will somewhat enhance this trend. On the other hand, these students should have better understanding of what they do know, better capability and study skills and altogether be better prepared for the learning needs of higher education.

As far as selection for higher education is concerned, this is still mainly based on predicted and actual A-level results, although BTEC courses are rapidly becoming more important as a basis for entry. A-level predictions have recently been shown to be highly inaccurate (Polytechnics Central Admissions System, 1992) and although there is some correlation between degree performance and actual A-level results (Smithers and Robinson, 1989), it is not that strong. It is therefore important that other factors are taken into account such as motivation, general capability and perceived potential. Records of Achievement could play an important role, as should interviews and, possibly, psychometric tests such as are widely used in the USA.

Once science and technology students have been selected, it is vital that their transition to university work should be rewarding and appropriate for their very varied needs. In some cases preliminary or access courses will be necessary. These could vary from pre-entry short crash courses aimed at dealing with specific knowledge gaps through to one-year foundation courses for the generally ill-prepared student. The latter courses, which are already happening in some places, could either be in the universities themselves or be franchised out to further education colleges. They should be geared to the needs of young students with an inappropriate 16–19 educational experience for embarking directly on a science degree course and also to the needs of mature students.

In starting the degree course proper, no longer can departments get by simply with standard didactic lecture courses linked with classes and tutorials. The spectrum of abilities, knowledge and understanding is too broad for this. Aside from flexible group and individual tuition, departments will need to make much more use of self-learning approaches and, inevitably, computer-assisted learning and interactive video will become of increasing importance.

The thrust of all this is to introduce a flexibility into the transition arrangements for students of all ages entering the university system. And it is vital that this flexibility continues. This is best achieved using a modular course structure. In fact, many science and technology degree courses are already modular in nature if not in name. But, in any case, most universities are moving formally to a modular structure for all their courses. As with the arrangements advocated for 16–19 education, it is essential that approved degree course modular packages are coherent with clear specification of prerequisite modules. With a modular approach it is then possible to develop a credit accumulation system enabling transfer between courses as well as between institutions. At the same time it facilitates the provision of part-time courses and intermission.

The foregoing remarks apply essentially to all degree courses. So let me now turn specifically to the nature of science and technology courses. Here a great deal of rethinking about their structure is under way and, in science, this is best exemplified by the changes which are happening to physics courses. The changes were initiated by a report on *The Future Pattern of Higher Education in Physics* (IOP, 1990) produced by the heads of physics departments in universities and the then polytechnics in conjunction with the Institute of Physics. The findings and recommendations in this report were based on the recognition that, quite apart from the changing preparation in physics and mathematics of incoming students, physics degree courses have become increasingly overloaded because of the rapid developments that have taken place in the subject. As a result, although high-flyers have continued to fly through the courses, many students have learnt a lot, often parrot-wise, but have understood much less. Most have had little time to reflect on or consolidate their understanding; neither have they developed important capability skills, such as communication, vital for any professional career.

In the light of this the report recommended that the content of physics degree courses should be reduced by approximately one-third so as to give time for the development of much fuller and more confident understanding of the subject as well as capability skills. It also recommended that courses should introduce students to topical issues and to physics-related developments in civil science and industry; in other words, develop their professional awareness. Such courses would differ from current courses but should be no less intellectually demanding and would lead to the usual honours degree. They would be a good basis for moving forward into most relevant areas of employment.

But, beyond this, the report recognized that further training is needed for those who are to go on to work in research or development (up to about 25 per cent) and advocates the establishment of a more advanced qualification – an extended and enhanced first degree to be known as the MPhys or MSci. This qualification would have the advantage of being in line with European qualifications such as the German *Diplom*, an important factor as the single European market comes into operation.

The proposals were widely supported, not least by ACOST (1991), and the physics community was delighted in the summer of 1991 when the Department of Education approved the four-year course for mandatory awards. Similar arrangements already exist for engineering courses (leading to the degree of MEng); the mathematicians wish to go down this path and I have no doubts that in due course so will the other sciences.

There are two further developments in higher education that I would like to see take place. First, in the interests of flexibility, I would like to see the availability of what I call honourable exit points at intermediate stages in a degree course. At present it is usually three years or nothing. There should be the possibility of leaving after one year, or after satisfactory completion of a given number of modules, with a record of what has been achieved and, if of a sufficiently high standard, with, say, a Certificate of Higher Education. Similarly, after two years, or its equivalent, a Diploma of Higher Education could be awarded as already happens in some institutions. Such students could move into some other form of training, to which the award could be credited, or into employment.

Second, as well as, or preferably instead of, summarizing degree-course performance in terms of the usual degree classification, a course record should be provided. No longer should it be possible to have said, as I heard at an interview of a physicist with a distinguished research record, that you could see his third shining through.

CONCLUSION

So, in summary, what I am advocating is an education and assessment system in science and technology at all levels which is more flexible than at present; a system which is appropriate to the needs of those of moderate ability whilst, at the same time, being a challenge to the high-flyers; and a system in which credit is given for positive achievement. As is said in the ACOST report (1991) referred to earlier, we need 'to shift the emphasis from processes that dissuade, sift out and exclude to those that attract, encourage and support'. Science courses must engender interest and enthusiasm by relating to other studies, to research frontiers, to the world outside, to technology, to the environment and to career possibilities.

Within such a system we need inspirational teachers at all levels; teachers who are well supported in every sense, who are happy and confident in their profession so that the excitement of science and its awesome potential are enthusiastically communicated.

More pupils and students will then, I believe, be inclined to follow courses, and eventually professional careers, in science and technology. And, further, the general public understanding of science and the appreciation of its vital importance will be significantly increased.

REFERENCES

ACOST (Advisory Council on Science and Technology) (1991) *Science and Technology: Education and Employment*, London, HMSO.

ASE (The Association for Science Education, with The British Association and The Royal Society) (1991) *Only a Teacher . . . ?*, London, ASE.

IOP (The Institute of Physics, with The Standing Conference of Physics Professors and The Committee of Heads of Physics in Polytechnics) (1990) *The Future Pattern of Higher Education in Physics*, London, The Institute of Physics.

Macfarlane, E. J. (1992) *Double Award GCSE Balanced Science: Its Contribution to A-level Success*. A project undertaken for The Royal Society and the Department of Employment. Further copies can be obtained from South East Information Network, TVEI Centre, Canterbury College, New Dover Road, Canterbury.

Pearson, R., Pike, G., Gordon, A. and Weyman, C. (1989) *How Many Graduates in the 21st Century? – The Choice is Yours, Report No. 177* Institute of Manpower Studies, Brighton.

Polytechnics Central Admissions System (1992) Unpublished report.

The Royal Society (1991) *Beyond GCSE*, London, The Royal Society.

The Royal Society (1992) *The Future of the Science Base*, London, The Royal Society.

Sears, J. (1992) *Research into A-level Science Uptake*. A report commissioned by the Association for Science Education sponsored by BP and ICI, Hatfield, Association for Science Education.

Smithers, A. and Robinson, P. (1989) *Increasing Participation in Higher Education*, London, BP Educational Service.

Woolnough, B. E. (1991) *The Making of Engineers and Scientists*, The Institute of Physics, The Institution of Electrical Engineers and National Power, Oxford University Department of Educational Studies.

3.7

Science for all: a case study of the science foundation course at The Open University

Eileen Scanlon, Dee Edwards and Elizabeth Whitelegg, with Alison Ashby and Elaine Brown

INTRODUCTION

This article describes how The Open University, through the science foundation course, makes a contribution to 'science for all'.

The Open University in Great Britain was given its charter in 1969 to provide university education for adults from all walks of life. The first science foundation course (coded S100) was presented in 1971 and is currently in its third version (coded S102). In this case study we describe the design decisions taken to invent a methodology suitable for the distance teaching of science subjects which led to the unique blend of multimedia teaching that is associated with Open University study, the experience that students of varied backgrounds have of using the course material and the improvements that have been made to the course material over the past twenty years. By comparing the success rates of differently qualified students, we will examine the challenges facing The Open University (OU) in its attempts to deliver science for all.

We focus on The Open University experience of presenting a course in science to adults who have not necessarily had any experience of studying science beyond a minimum general education provided by their early schooling. (For some students, this may have been twenty or more years earlier.) This course aims to prepare students for further study of science at a level equivalent to those of traditional universities.

The previous articles in this book have looked at 'science for all' in a general sense and also in specific areas of disadvantage. Neither of these were the case in the development of the OU course. The intention was to produce a course that would give all adults a chance at higher education in science but there was no policy to encourage specifically students who fell into other categories of disadvantage – those from ethnic minority backgrounds or women, for example. The importance of a sound grounding in science for all adults has been well established by the previous articles, yet as Fensham states in article 3.1 of this book, 'We have not yet achieved an effective science education in schools for the 80 per cent or so who most probably will not continue with any formal education in science after they leave school'.

The OU science foundation course provides a 'second chance' for those who might have come to regret their lack of opportunity or motivation to study science the first time around. It must also be attractive to those 'turned-off' by earlier encounters with science.

DISTANCE TEACHING AND LEARNING

Distance teaching and learning as a way to deliver science for all

The mode of distance learning adopted by The Open University moves away from heavily teacher-centred methods to foster active participative learning. Within a weekly package of work, students can set their own pace of study and plan this around other commitments, for example their jobs, homes or children. The materials for foundation courses such as S102 allow for different entry levels, so those students with some knowledge in certain areas can design their study accordingly. Students are also in control when it comes to exposing their own misconceptions. They may choose to share them with others in a tutorial or seek help from a tutor privately, by telephone if they wish. OU study provides the opportunity for, but does not require, regular attendance at a local study centre. Students are encouraged to attend the regular evening or weekend tutorials (typically once a fortnight) that accompany the foundation courses. Those students who do not or cannot attend these sessions are of particular concern to tutors who should take the initiative in contacting the student to ensure all is well.

These are some of the features that make distance teaching and learning of the kind offered by the OU appropriate for those who are the focus of any 'science for all' policy. Not surprisingly students studying with the OU include those who care for the elderly or the sick; those with children who are restricted in the amount of time they can leave their homes to attend regular lectures at a local higher education institution; disabled people who have problems of access to public buildings; Muslim women who cannot go outside their community for cultural reasons; people in full-time employment wishing to improve their knowledge and qualifications. For these people, and others, the OU's distance teaching methods make the study of science a real possibility.

With each version of the course, concern to reach the widest audience is influential. If study of science is to be available to as many of the population as possible then other issues that open up the curriculum and are not just the preserve of distance learning, must be addressed. Some of these are discussed elsewhere in this book, for example: a gender-inclusive science curriculum (Fensham, 1993); a multicultural and antiracist approach to science teaching (Dennick, 1992); and differentiated access for students who experience difficulties in learning (Purnell, 1993).

The OU, like its contemporaries elsewhere in conventional higher education institutions, is only now seeking to address issues of this kind.

The Open University: the 'Heineken'[1] of higher education

Registration for OU courses is restricted to those who are aged 21 years or over (the median age is about 33) although there are special schemes that break the pattern. The students study part time, using the specially designed, multimedia packages of materials sent from the OU centre at Milton Keynes to their homes, so there are students from the Shetlands to the Isles of Scilly. There are no formal entry qualifications; students need only basic literacy and numeracy and a little general knowledge. The open-entry policy of the OU science foundation course is a vital element in its aim to provide a basic science education for all. Students do, however, need a great deal of motivation and persistence and at least twelve hours per week to set aside for study.

Typically, each undergraduate student begins with a foundation course in one of the five Faculties (arts, social sciences, mathematics, science or technology) before moving on to higher level courses, called second and third levels, offered by any of the above Faculties or the School of Education (there is no foundation course in education). A system of continuous assessment based on assignments and an end-of-course examination is used to award course credits.

Currently and historically the OU operates a modular 'course credit' system, and to obtain a BA degree a student needs six credits (eight for the BA Hons), which may be taken at up to a maximum of two credits per year. (With the introduction of credit transfer schemes (CATS), this will change to a points system in the mid-1990s.) The structure was based on the Scottish model of full-time undergraduates studying four-year honours degree courses. (Walter Perry, the founding Vice-Chancellor had been Vice-Principal of Edinburgh University.) Now, twenty years since the first OU courses were designed, amendments are necessary to this structure to keep the OU up to date with national and international changes in higher education.

At present (1993) there are around 80,000 registered undergraduate students, with a further 11,000 associate students (that is students taking single courses but not registering for a degree); there are also 20,000 students on short courses, 5,500 taking diplomas, 6,700 taught masters and 750 postgraduate research students. Around 74,000 other packs of learning materials have been sold. As an illustration of the size of the operation, in 1991 the University processed 68,109 applications, resulting in 19,000 new undergraduate students. Around 6,500 students graduate each year, adding to the total of 122,552 graduates and 23,398 honours graduates of the University. This makes The Open University one of the largest single contributors to higher education in the UK.

Added to this, many students are not registered for the BA degree but take only one or two courses, as a degree is not their aim; the production of graduates is therefore an underestimate of student participation.

Teaching and learning science at a distance

In 1974 Kaye and Pentz wrote about the multimedia teaching of science at a distance at the OU, from their respective positions of educational technologist and first Dean of the OU's Science Faculty involved in the production of the first science foundation course. They regarded the pressure to develop distance teaching science systems as stemming from a number of socio-economic factors and rapid developments in educational technology. For example, techniques for analysing teaching materials, especially those stressing individualized instruction, led to the adoption of an approach using a variety of media, closely integrated. They outlined the specific problems posed by teaching science at a distance, for example language, structure, quantification and precision, practical work, and the hierarchies of concepts and processes embedded in learning science. We touch on each of these in the following paragraphs.

Briggs (1970) suggested that a valuable function of the different media in a multimedia system is to provide some redundancy by presenting the teaching material on the same topic in different ways. The course designers at the OU took the efficacy of the combination of media as a planning assumption. From the beginning, OU science courses were designed to include printed text, television and radio broadcasts, home experiments and assignments. The role of each is outlined below.

The television components are often used to show the student the practical (experimental) work necessary for a thorough grasp of the course material. This is especially useful when practical work is too complicated or expensive to do by means of an experiment kit (see below). Television broadcasts can help students to visualize dynamic processes, or provide vicarious experience of field work. Radio programmes were often used to provide an informal tutorial around the topic of the printed material, or to guide the student through a mathematical exercise. By 1980 radio had been largely replaced by audiocassettes. These are used in a similar way to radio but have the great advantage that they can be designed for partial and/or repeat usage, adding another dimension to the student's control. Practical work can have various functions. It can help students to understand the concepts being taught, help to develop scientific skills in handling equipment and experimental data, and, at its most developed, can give students the experience of being a real scientist.

Science teaching is recognized to be difficult for some of the reasons referred to by Johnstone (1991) in the companion volume of this book (Edwards, Scanlon and West, 1993). Students need to be comfortable in talking about science and to be able, for example, to answer the question, 'How do you pronounce glycolysis?' And this 'comfort' is often achieved by presenting course work through more than one medium.

The language of science is a mixture of ordinary language, technical terms, diagrams, equations and special notations and this can make science texts difficult for some students to understand. Teaching students of widely varying backgrounds makes the assumption of a 'shared context' difficult, and just grasping the meaning of a text can depend on creation of this shared context. Problems exist both at the level of individual words, and extended pieces of argument. Even the names of things can cause a problem that can be accentuated by students studying in isolation. In face-to-face teaching, when a lecturer uses an alternative name for a concept, the blank incomprehension of the audience usually signifies a term having no meaning and different words must be used. In distance teaching this reaction must be anticipated. This is easier in some areas than others. In the settled subject areas of science, such as basic mechanics, a glossary is helpful, but in an area where the meaning of terms is still shifting, even the construction of a glossary of agreed terms may not suffice. Presenting information in different ways using a range of media can help overcome misunderstanding and achieve a shared understanding.

Whatever one's view of the psychology of learning science, it is clear that science at university level depends on the prior learning of a set of lower-level concepts, upon which further building can take place.

In OU courses, the main tool for solving many of these problems is the teaching text. Much of the success of the OU science foundation course has stemmed from the accessibility of the printed material, especially the science texts, called 'course units'.

When The Open University was founded and the first courses were planned it was felt that much of the teaching could be done through guided study of existing texts or 'set books'. This was found to be unsatisfactory, particularly for 'foundation' students just starting their studies. As a result, the OU's model has been to develop and publish specially prepared teaching texts. The requirements to be fulfilled by these texts, taking unqualified students to degree level, gives them a central role. They are colloquially referred to as 'units' and could be described as the 'tutorials in print'. This draws attention to the fact that the OU text has to reproduce many of the functions of the conventional tutorial in traditional university education. It is used not just to carry information about the subject under study but also to stimulate discussion and to organize other aspects of the course such as practical work or projects. To function successfully as teaching texts, the units must allow the reader to be active, engaging with the activities and questions that are an integral part of the body of the text.

Two further concerns particular to the study of science are emphasized by the distance teaching mode of study and by the choice of content for a course that purports to be suitable for all comers. These are the mathematics background of the student and the arrangements for practical work.

Mathematics background

For students in conventional institutions, many assumptions are made about the development of their mathematical skills. These cannot be made for OU students and a significant effort is put into the production of special preparatory material in mathematics for students intending to study the OU foundation course in science. This aspect of the course is under continual review and development as the type of difficulty encountered by students evolves with the changing student characteristics.

Practical work

When the first foundation courses were developed, the difficulties surrounding practical work were felt by many contemporary commentators to be the biggest stumbling block to developing the distance teaching of science. Students on conventional science courses spend a large amount of their time doing practical work and OU science students needed an equivalent experience. Three complementary approaches evolved: the first was to provide practical experience through the development of experiment kits (packages of equipment on loan to students); the second was to have a residential component in the course so students could use laboratory facilities at other institutions; the third was to use television.

In the next section we discuss the specific features of the current science foundation course (S102).

S102: A SCIENCE FOUNDATION COURSE

A course unit for the science foundation course is equivalent to one week of study. It typically contains the printed course text specially written by OU academic staff, notes to accompany associated broadcast programmes or audiocassettes, and details of assignments and instructions for any practical work to be completed using the student's experiment kit. After finishing their study of the unit, students complete an assessment, which may be marked by the student's locally based tutor if it is a tutor-marked assignment (TMA) or the OU computer if it is a computer-marked assignment (CMA). The multiple-choice CMAs are particularly useful in checking students' coverage of the course. The course is studied over 32 weeks (February to October). It is multidisciplinary and to some degree interdisciplinary, covering general science, physics, Earth sciences, chemistry, and biology as can be seen from the list of course units given in Appendix 1.

The course components

Course texts or 'unit'

The printed course texts, often called 'units' are the main study vehicle, and students expect to spend around eight to ten hours per week studying a unit (assignments, broadcasts, etc., take the overall study time up to twelve to fourteen hours).

The course unit texts differ from conventional textbooks, in that student goals, aims and objectives are highly specified and the material is highly interactive. This helps to maintain interest and to enable students to check their own progress regularly. A number of devices are used: ITQs (in-text questions that develop the argument), SAQs (self-assessment questions at the end of sections), activities (such as the integrated practical work) and assignments. There is frequent reinforcement through the answers and explanations provided for the ITQs, SAQs and activities. Students are also provided with an *Introduction and Guide to the Course,* and each unit has its own study guide which serves as an 'advance organizer' (Ausubel and Robinson, 1969).

The extensive planning and development which go into OU courses help to ensure that the package presented to students is designed to have a clear structure and overall coherence. It is not surprising that OU course texts are widely used by students and tutors in other educational institutions (Moss and Brew, 1981) and for other purposes such as in-service training for teachers with little background in science.

Television and audio

Television, radio and audiocassettes were innovative features of OU courses when they began in the 1970s. Television, in particular, is regarded as an essential part of the teaching strategy. In addition to the important contribution that programmes make through practical demonstrations, there is the possibility of 'taking' students to locations that they could not otherwise visit (such as the particle accelerator at CERN near Geneva to study physics, and Iceland to study geology). Through television OU students can 'see' many locations that are denied to conventional students and can observe scientists at work as the programmes demonstrate the essential exploratory nature of science. (This approach has been developed in the context of 'science for all' criteria outlined by Fensham (1993)). Television is also used to explain difficult sections of the texts such as the derivation and use of a particular equation (for example Newton's laws of motion). Like the teaching texts, these programmes are known to be widely used in other contexts (Moss and Brew, 1981).

In the early years, television programmes also performed an important pacing function, helping students to keep up with the course. Although this function has been undermined by home video recorders, allowing students to record the programmes and watch at times of their own choosing, the stop and replay facilities on videos have enhanced the potential contribution that programmes can make to student study. Students on the course may also borrow copies of the television programmes on videotape.

Audiocassettes, too, have the advantage of play and replay. As these are mailed to students as part of the course materials, they are designed for more direct teaching than was usually possible with radio broadcasts. Audiotaped sequences are used to help students with practical work or difficult parts of the course, for example help with chemical equations in molecular biochemistry or the mathematics needed to understand a particular scientific topic.

Experiment kit

A package of equipment (such as glassware, chemicals, rock and mineral specimens) is supplied to students, so that they can complete some experiments and practical work at home. This equipment is called an experiment kit. The instructions for when and how to do the practical work are contained within the course text. Obviously, the practical work is designed to be done at the point in the learning process that matches the science theory being studied, as it illustrates this science content. This model has proved successful and is a good example of the learning of practical and intellectual skills and processes flowing naturally from the nature of the science topics rather than being a primary focus of the learning. This fits well with the framework advocated by Fensham, in article 3.1 in this book.

Care has to be taken to design experiments that can be done outside a conventional laboratory, with a minimum of equipment. For example students measure the distance between the Earth and the Moon, using a broom handle and a couple of discs to eclipse the Moon. Repetitive experimentation is avoided.

Opportunity for a different range of practical work is provided by the residential school (see below).

Preparatory materials

In the mid-1970s the Science Faculty realized that many students had difficulty coping with the mathematical content of the science foundation course, although this had been kept to a minimum. As a result a preparatory package called *Mathematics for the Foundation Course in Science* (MAFS) was prepared and sent to students before they began the foundation course. A book of more general study skills, *Preparing for the Science Foundation Course*, was also sent. Further evaluation during the 1980s highlighted that students with poor mathematics background found MAFS rather difficult, too. On a pilot basis, new preparatory materials called *Into Science* have been written and trialled during 1990–92. This package consists of integrated 'maths plus study skills' and is presented as twelve modules, building from an initial module designed to take two to three hours, up to a full-length unit (eight to ten hours) at the end. The context of the teaching is to use everyday objects and situations (such as the slope of a roof) or those of contemporary concern, such as fossil fuel burning or the quality of drinking water, as the vehicles for elementary science content, calculations and mathematical skills development. By recognizing students' existing knowledge (or lack of it) and working from examples that stem from the familiar it is hoped that these *Into Science* materials will prepare as many students as possible for successful study of the course. The preparatory work also provides a gentle introduction to study with the OU, removing the large first step that some students feel they encounter when beginning S102.

Residential school

All foundation courses at the OU have a one-week residential school, held during the summer. The Science Faculty regards this period of intensive practical work, in laboratories and in the field, as an essential part of the course, one that aims to provide an experience with equipment or material that could not be provided by the student's experimental kit. Thus students can work with expensive or bulky apparatus, for example spectrophotometers in chemistry, spectrometers in physics, and microscopes in biology and Earth sciences. In the words of the first Dean of Science, 'We developed a course *in* science, not *about* science', and the residential school is a linchpin of this differentiation.

For some students, it also provides the *only* opportunity for face-to-face tutorial support. For many students the 'summer school' is the high point of the course, when many concepts come together and are clarified through hours of conversations with other students and staff.

Course development

The course package is put together by a team of academics, together with editors, support staff, designers, television producers and consultants. This team is known as the Course Team and is collectively held responsible for the course components. Extensive discussions are held, sometimes weekly or fortnightly over the three-year production phase, to review and comment on every stage of the course. It is the Course Team process of drafting, redrafting and acting on colleagues' comments and suggestions that makes OU units, good teaching material. Most staff acknowledge that their draft units have been greatly improved by critical colleagues working through the texts, presenting requests for change with the certainty that 'If I can't understand this clearly, how will a student cope?' External assessors are appointed to read and comment on the course texts; these are academics selected for their knowledge and expertise in the subject area of the course, and for their strong teaching background.

Tutorial support

The materials generated centrally by the Course Team are sent to all students of the course. There is also a student support system based on thirteen regional centres and about 300 local study centres (often institutes of further or higher education).

Foundation students are allocated a tutor-counsellor, who helps and advises on all aspects of students' study including study skills and future course choice. Formal arrangements are made for students to meet their tutor-counsellors, and other students studying the course, approximately once a week. The science foundation course students also have specialist tutors who assist them with the academic content of the course. As a result students may have contact with up to four tutors, though frequently the tutor-counsellor is also tutor for at least one of the science disciplines. (The science foundation course is different from other OU courses, where students have only one tutor-counsellor for all their contact.) Continuity is provided by the tutor-counsellor who will try to ensure that students benefit from contact with several staff with their different perceptions and skills.

The tutorial and counselling sessions, and any other study centre activities are optional, and indeed it is recognized that some students are unable to attend, for example because of travel difficulties or personal circumstances.

However, all students receive individual written feedback from the tutor who marks their TMAs, and a computer-generated feedback letter on their mistakes on the CMAs. The teaching function provided by this feedback is regarded as at least as important as the grading function of the TMAs and CMAs.

The tutorial and counselling staff are recruited and supervised by staff tutors, faculty academic staff who work from the thirteen regional centres. Staff tutors can also arrange special sessions, for example for particularly isolated students or those disadvantaged in other ways.

Study patterns

During the year students have considerable freedom of choice over the place of their study. Although some students are able to study during the day, most students study in the evenings, at weekends and in any spare moments. The University has photographs of taxi and bus drivers studying between journeys; business people and those in the armed services study overseas, as do EC staff in Brussels. OU staff on holidays have seen their texts being read on campsites in France and Spain – even on boats in Turkey!

Constraints are put on a student's study schedule by assignments that must be submitted at regular intervals. Procedures exist to prevent habitual late submission of TMAs by students and delays in marking by their tutors. The OU computer rejects CMAs received after the published 'cut-off date', as feedback on the answers is by then in circulation to students.

Special features of S102

The OU science foundation course differs from degree-level courses offered by conventional institutions in several ways. These can be grouped under the following headings:

- course design and content;
- student study;
- feedback to students.

Course design and content

The main distinctive features are:

- Assumed knowledge for the OU science foundation course is basic literacy and numeracy skills, and some general knowledge; no formal qualifications are required. This was a revolutionary idea when the OU started in 1970, when traditional universities demanded at least two A-levels. Now, in the 1990s more students without formal entry qualifications are being encouraged to enter higher education elsewhere, through 'access' courses of various kinds, but we consider that the OU is still a leader in this field.
- OU courses are generally studied by individuals separated in time and space from the development of the course, rather than through group

study contiguous with the teaching. As a result the course materials must be free-standing. Expected reactions from students must be anticipated and this helps to ensure that the Course Team has identified and explained aspects of a topic which might be taken for granted in a more traditional exposition.

- Students are usually working towards a non-vocational qualification. This means the course is not based on an assumption of the need for 'benchmanship' or a 'craft apprenticeship' in the laboratory or the field that are often included as aims of conventional science degrees.
- The deliberate decision was made by the academic members of the OU Science Faculty that the course should concentrate on teaching 'principles' rather than details.

An underlying, unproved contention is that a general science education may produce a more adaptable, flexible, and academically 'broadminded' individual and that these traits are at a premium in a society where technology is changing so fast that one of the only certainties is change. A course based on broad principles should enable connections to be made easily and this is a valuable skill. In addition, the approach is justified by the belief that it promotes understanding of science in ways that rote learning does not.

The course is a course *in* science, not *about* science. Although the science content of a *distance* learning course cannot take into account all students' experiences and needs, the foundation course attempts to teach science through everyday contexts wherever possible, through television programmes (for example the use of skaters at an ice rink to demonstrate Newton's laws of motion) and practical work (for example examining the spectra of street lighting).

Student study

When considering the underlying structure of the course, there arises the question of exactly how much learning actually takes place in group situations compared to work done individually. The fact is that many students spend much of their time studying in isolation, in their own rooms, the laboratory or library. An advantage of the OU system is that the situation of the 'lone learner' is acknowledged and decisions are taken as to what science can be learned independently, with kits at home, and what is best learned in a group situation, through tutorials, day schools or residential schools.

At the design stage of any course, the Course Team gives much thought to how best, through the various media, students can be helped to become independent learners, and to develop the skills upon which their success as 'long-distance' students depends. The nature of the course text, designed for independent learning, helps this process. Students are helped throughout to check their understanding of the topics and concepts. The very fact that course texts are available for public scrutiny and are worked through very thoroughly by thousands of students each year means that mistakes or misconceptions are brought to the attention of the Course Team, directly by student letter, or from tutors.

Where the conventional student does have a distinct advantage is that once a problem is encountered – academic, administrative or personal – staff and students are close at hand to supply help. A sense of isolation when in trouble is probably one of the worst problems for Open University students and it is here that the tutorial and counselling system in the regions can provide support.

Feedback to students

The Open University has developed formal mechanisms for ensuring that students receive feedback and reinforcement through the assignment marking and monitoring systems. It is difficult to make direct comparisons with conventional courses, where the lectures, laboratory work and seminars tend to be less integrated and may provide only intermittent formal feedback. For CMAs, students receive answers and comments on incorrect alternatives. Tutors write extensive comments on students' written assignments (TMAs), as it is recognized that this commenting function is the only individual attention that the university can guarantee that all students will receive, so great stress is placed on it.

Does S102 provide 'science for all'?

Fensham has argued for four conditions that need to be met by courses aiming to provide 'science for all' – the two of these that we address here are organizational support and selection of content. The description of the science foundation course provides clear evidence that an enormous amount of effort has gone into the structural and organizational implications of teaching science at a distance. The practical problems associated with providing a means of studying university-level science for adults without traditional university entrance qualifications, or for those unable to study outside the home, have been addressed. In Article 3.2 in this book Harlen quotes two sets of criteria for choosing content. The criteria selected by the Secondary Science Curriculum Review (SSCR) include the following:

- [The curriculum] must be able to be taught to, and owned by, all pupils; [. . .]
- science content must be consistent with a broad and balanced science curriculum;
- the necessary teaching strategies and resources must exist to teach it;
- it must provide a basis for further study;

(Harlen, 1989, p. 129)

Content in the science foundation course has been selected to appeal to adult learners, but also to serve the needs of future science courses that students may take. Fensham considers that fact to be the dilemma surrounding the selection and preparation of students for a science training in higher education and how preparation leads to selection. It would seem that the 'open-type' universities, such as the OU, clarify this dilemma by not demanding any preparation and by having no selection criteria. Fensham raises questions about entry levels of the 'novices' to science and their eligibility for entry into professions. In the following section we re-examine the previous qualifications of the 'novices' in order to provide some evidence to assess the foundation course in Fensham and Harlen's terms.

For inexperienced students learning at a distance, such as those studying S102, The Open University has demonstrated that the design of the course, its intentional pattern of conceptual development and the regularity of feedback play a crucial part in the psychological well-being of the students. It also seems that the course is relatively successful in helping students from a wide variety of backgrounds to study science. This is shown by the drop-out rates which are far lower than those for an introductory course in many other distance education institutions (Woodley and Parlett, 1983).

The success of the OU's science foundation course may lie in the selection of content and organizational support provided. Certainly the practical problems associated with providing a means by which adults, without traditional university entrance qualifications, or unable to study outside the home can study university-level science have been addressed. By not demanding any preparation and having no selection criteria for those enrolling to study the course the OU is forced to design a course that makes studying science a possibility for all students.

LOOKING AT OUTCOMES

Quantitative evidence of success

Measuring success in providing 'science for all' can be viewed in several ways. The number of students who have taken the OU science foundation course provides statistical evidence, for example, in terms of the number of students with varying educational backgrounds who have been successful on the course and those who have not, or in terms of the proportion of women studying the course. Given the great variety of students who enrol, these statistics do seem to be one valid way of measuring success. In particular, the degree to which we can retain students with low prior educational qualifications is a key indicator of our success in claiming to address 'science for all'.

It is important for this detailed look at the outcomes to define the measures that we will use. Since 1971 the Survey Research Department (now the Student Research Centre) of the Institute of Educational Technology at the Open University has collected and analysed student characteristics at milestones during each OU course. These milestones are the decision to take the course (initial registration), the decision to continue with the course after a few weeks of study (final registration, which we take as our baseline), and the decision to take the examination. At each stage the number of students still studying is noted, and this number is often expressed as a percentage of the number who finally registered for the course. Students who successfully complete continuous assessment and the final examination are awarded a credit. Categories under which these results are analysed include: year of entry to OU, region, sex, age at which full-time education ended, present occupation, occupation on entry to the OU, intended occupation, current

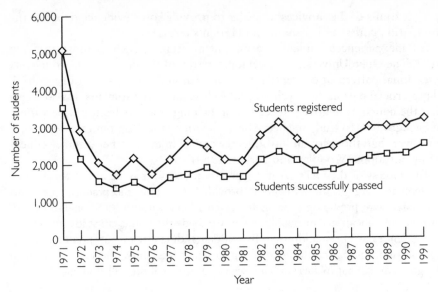

Figure 1   Numbers of new students registered for and successful in the foundation course in science

highest educational qualification, and highest educational qualification on entry to The Open University.

Numbers taking the course

One measure of 'success' is to look at the number of students that have studied the course and the proportion that were successful in gaining a course credit. Figure 1 shows the numbers of *new* students that have registered for the course during the period 1971–91. (It does not include information for students, around 1000 per year, who chose the science foundation course at a later stage in their studies with the OU.) The lower line shows the number of students who were successful in each year.

DES statistics (DES, 1991) show that, in the UK in 1990, around 93,000 undergraduates were studying science subjects full-time. (These figures include medicine and paramedical subjects, but exclude engineering.) If one were to assume that 40 per cent of the total were in their first year (30 per cent each in Years 2 and 3) then around 37,000 new undergraduates begin science each year in the UK. So, a number equal to 10 per cent of the full-time science students begin science with the OU.

In sheer numbers, therefore, a total of 53,000 adults have been given skills and knowledge of science through study of the OU foundation course in science over the twenty years that the course has been running.

Retention of students through the course

Each year, around 16 per cent of all registered foundation course students in the OU are studying the science foundation course and on average, about 75–80 per cent of those who (finally) register turn up to take the end-of-course examination. Of these around 93 per cent gain a course credit. These statistics compare well with the OU maths and technology foundation courses, but not quite so well with the figures for the arts and social science foundation courses. Although it is known that these retention rates are much better than non-OU correspondence courses, where, on average, fewer than half the initial student numbers finish the course, directly comparable statistics from other institutions are difficult to find. Judgements concerning the OU's success in providing 'science for all' therefore, have to be based on the comparative statistics available, for example achievements by gender or previous qualifications, and qualitative evidence amassed over a number of years.

Reasons for the 20 per cent who choose to 'drop out' through the year are extremely varied but can include minor or major personal difficulties; while for some studying the course for personal development was sufficient and they did not feel the need to pass the examination and gain the certificate. Other course-related factors have been described by Woodley and Parlett (1983).

Numbers and achievement by gender

Figure 2 shows that after a period in the 1970s to mid-1980s when the proportion of male to female students registered for the science foundation course stayed at 70:30, the proportion of females has begun to rise, since the presentation of the most recent version of the course in 1988.

In most years a slightly higher proportion of women end up with a course credit. This is usually attributable to a lower drop-out rate, that is a higher retention rate, as exam performance is about the same for both sexes.

It is worth noting that this high percentage of female students gaining credits is consistently maintained beyond the foundation course in science. Of the

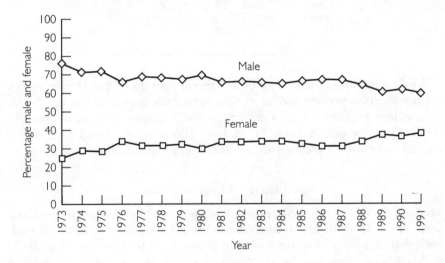

Figure 2 Proportion of the finally registered foundation course students that are male/female, 1973–91

female students finally registered for post-foundation science courses 70–72 per cent gain credit as against only 60–61 per cent of males.

Previous educational qualifications

One important feature to consider in trying to assess the outcome of the OU's attempt to teach science to all is pass rates. However, simple pass rates do not give the whole picture. Our success depends not just on how many students pass but how well students with poorer previous educational qualifications fare in comparison with their better qualified colleagues. The OU collects data on students' highest educational qualifications on entry to the OU, according to ten categories. These categories can be combined into three groups: 'low' for students who would not qualify for entry in other higher educational establishments, 'high' for those with some previous higher educational qualification, and 'middle' for those in between.

Mike Pentz, first Dean of the Science Faculty (1988), has used this information to compare the performance of high and low groups and calculate an educational discrimination factor (EDF) for the science foundation course as the ratio of the pass rate of the high group to that of the low group. Table 1 shows information for the predecessors of the current course (S100 in 1971 and S101 in 1981).

Table I Educational discrimination factor for the science foundation course

	Pass rate/%	
Group	1971	1981
Low	57	65
Middle	69	75
High	80	85
EDF	1.4	1.3

We do have encouraging signs in that recent figures (1990–91) have shown improvements in performance on the current science foundation course (S102) with an increase from 74 to 78 per cent of finally registered students who gain credit. Over the period 1988–91 we have also noticed a trend towards increased success for students with low and medium qualifications.

Qualitative evidence of success

Many of the OU's tutorial staff teach science courses in other institutions and some of our students are themselves teachers. We know from informal feedback that many use or recommend our course texts to their own students as background reading and that the structure and content of the course have an influence on their own teaching. Although the OU does not deliberately seek external approval beyond that of formally appointed assessors and examiners, the widespread use of OU texts and other course components in other institutions speaks for itself.

Many students start the foundation course apprehensive and not very confident. Many find the course difficult, but interesting, stimulating and a worthwhile intellectual exercise; at the end of the course their self-confidence and self-esteem are higher. For some students this experience is enough – they never intended to study science further and their aims have been achieved; for others, the aim is a science degree and so they move on, to higher-level courses. During the evaluation of the course we solicit comments on students' experiences; inevitably grumbles are voiced but these are outnumbered by positive comments.

The following comment is from a student who had completed S102:

> Generally it was a very stimulating course. I thoroughly enjoyed it. I feel a better person for having done it. I can now appreciate how things happen around me better. With a view to nuclear power I found it most enlightening to a point where I am now amazed by people's ignorance of the demands of this technology on the environment. Congratulations to the Course Team.

A student who had also completed the technology foundation course, T101, made the useful comment that S102 was 'Twice as hard a course as T101 both in depth of understanding required and amount of work we covered.' Of course, 'hardness' is relative, but evidence like this provides useful feedback to the Course Team on perceived student workload.

Student feedback of all kinds is important to the Course Team and often influences the discussions with the course tutors and residential school tutors in ways that heighten awareness of particular aspects of the course and the ways that they are received by different types of students.

Opening up access for students with disabilities

The OU can claim major success in the number of students with disabilities that it has attracted: in 1991, 3529 (4 per cent) of OU students were categorized as having a disability. This success may be due to the considerable framework of support structures that has been developed to facilitate study for these students. Examples of these aids are:

- audiocassette tape versions of printed course materials;
- transcripts of radio and television programmes, and audio and video materials;
- subtitled course videos for the foundation course television programmes;
- examination papers in large-print format, on audiocassette or in Braille;
- use of an amanuensis or a typewriter/word processor for examinations;
- schemes whereby the University will lend various items of equipment (for example, radio microphones, programmable calculators, speech pitch reducers for audiocassettes played at high speed), or enabling hardware and software (for example, a specially adapted personal computer with synthetic speech output for the visually impaired).

Special provision is also made at residential schools and, whenever possible, students with disabilities are encouraged to attend by the provision of special facilities to help them take part. The Science Faculty is particularly anxious to make students aware of all the special facilities that can be made available at the S102 residential summer school. Such facilities include:

- a personal helper for each disabled student;
- lower laboratory benches for those in wheelchairs;
- enlarged diagrams via video screens;
- microscope/video camera links;
- 'hearing support teams' to act as sign-language intepreters, lip-readers and VDU equipment operators;
- extra demonstrator to provide alternative sessions for groups of students who are unable to go on field trips;
- helper for students with a disability, to assist in general accommodation and living arrangements.

Judging success

How successful is the enterprise of science teaching and learning for all at the OU? We will attempt to answer this question by looking at four areas: success at attracting students to study science; the extent to which students with different backgrounds are successful in studying science; the use to which students have put science courses; and the influence of OU material on other institutions.

Success at attracting students to study science

The numbers of students taking OU science courses, some of which are quoted above, give an indication of the scale of the enterprise. Since 1971 applicants for the science foundation courses have totalled around 170,000, resulting in around 53,000 successful completions. On second-level science courses there have been around 62,000 successful students, 22,000 at third (honours) level, and 5,000 have graduated. These figures are quoted in the report on science for 16–19-year-olds prepared for The Royal Society (1991, p. 18).

The extent to which students with different backgrounds are successful in studying science

Some figures for the science foundation course are given (Table 1). These may be inconclusive but attempts are being made through initiatives such as the *Into Science* preparatory material (see above) to improve further the success rate in this area. Continued improvements are also planned with respect to other groups, for example students with disabilities, women and ethnic minorities.

The use to which students have put science courses

Reasonable questions to ask of an OU science student are: 'What use has your degree been to you?' and 'What did you think of it?' These questions have been addressed to some OU physics graduates by Ross and Scanlon (1991). They asked 448 graduates their opinion of the courses they had studied. It was overwhelmingly favourable: 98.9 per cent said they had found the courses enjoyable and relevant. Many had also found their degrees useful: 56 per cent had changed their job since registering for OU study and, for 82 per cent of these, OU qualifications had been useful in making the job move. Three-quarters had moved to a higher-level job. For others the OU had been a passport into the world of work. To quote one respondent: 'I started [under-graduate studies] as a full-time housewife; my OU degree was my entrance ticket into IBM for whom I now work' (Ross and Scanlon, 1991, p. 7).

Swift (1978, 1979) has shown that using criteria such as determination and tenacity, many employers value the traits that success on OU courses implies.

The influence of OU material on other institutions

Leslie Wagner (former lecturer at the OU, now Vice-Chancellor of the University of North London) in an address at the OU in 1992, paid tribute to the enormous influence of the OU on the staff of other higher education institutions, particularly the new universities. The OU had acted as a large in-service training enterprise for staff in the sector. In this he echoed some earlier findings (Moss and Brew, 1981) that a lot of OU teaching material was finding its way into conventional universities.

Other distance teaching universities have included less science in their course profiles. For example, Guri-Rozenblit (1990) writes of the small numbers taking natural science courses at The Open University of Israel, and the high drop-out rate they record (46 per cent).

So the OU's science teaching has had some degree of success. Students study with us and succeed. Yates (1986) quotes Onushkin and Zubkov (1982) on the performance of the 2.3 million evening or correspondence students in the then Soviet Union, many of whom in 1978–9 were studying science or technology at one of the conventional universities. Onushkin and Zubkov reported that first-year science courses had a high drop-out rate (for example 67 per cent of students following mechanics courses dropped out). However, for those who complete the six to eight years of courses, the success rate is high. Compared with this general assessment of part-time study, the success rate of the OU science foundation course is very good. Nevertheless, we would like to improve our performance. In this section, we give Pentz the last word:

> They said back in 1969 it can't be done, you can't teach university-level science at a distance to part-time students. The evidence shows it has been done up to a point. Under the circumstances, I think we did pretty well and I would endorse an assessment of science teaching at the OU that said something like 'good – but we could do much better'.
>
> (Pentz, 1988, p. 45)

REVIEW AND LOOKING TO THE FUTURE

The latest version of the science foundation course, S102, is due to be replaced by a new course, S103, in 1997. It is fair to say that S101 and S102 were based heavily on S100; both new courses were only partial remakes, reusing existing text and television programmes quite heavily. Much work was done on evaluating the different versions of the course and refining the teaching. A great deal of feedback was collected from tutorial staff and students, on conceptual difficulty, workload and interest. These data guided decisions on, for example, successively reducing the student workload at each remake. It is true to say that we have had varying success with the teaching of different sections of the course. One of our concerns is that perhaps the courses failed to open science up enough through the content of its curriculum, judged against 'science for all' criteria.

Will S103 be an evolution, or a revolution? At the time of writing, many feel that S100, S101 and S102 were courses for their days and that a course looking forward to the twenty-first century needs to make new assumptions about students, their entry behaviour, ambitions and needs, to reflect the changes in science, technology, employment and the national educational scene. A radical rethink is going on within the Science Faculty at the OU, and working groups are developing proposals. For example, thought is being given in one of these groups to providing teaching materials using personal computers, which could be used to provide animations, spreadsheets and 'what-if' calculations, besides data analysis and word-processing skills.

Computer-aided learning could provide endless reinforcement for very weak students, while providing 'fast-track' pathways for the more able, whereas at present course units have to be aimed at the level of a 'typical' student. One of the questions being addressed is whether anyone could call themselves a scientist, or scientifically literate, in 2001 without basic computer skills. Against this are arguments that requiring use of a personal computer would make the course inaccessible for some groups of students, for example the unemployed, women and other disadvantaged groups. If so, perhaps this should be a separate parallel course, not an integral part of the new foundation course.

One thing is certain: that the lessons learned during the continual evaluation of the course mean that the authors of the replacement course in 1997 need to take account of the weak backgrounds of many students, both in study skills and mathematics, if all potential students are to have equal access to the new science foundation course.

CONCLUSION

In this article we have described The Open University's science foundation course and examined it in the context of some 'science for all' criteria. Fensham, elsewhere in this volume, has argued that content in science courses needs to be influenced in various ways. Content in the science foundation course has been selected to appeal to adult learners, but the main achievement of the course has been in tackling the practical problems associated with providing a means by which adults without traditional university entrance qualifications, or unable to study outside the home, can come to study university-level science. Through the evidence that has been presented above, it can be seen that the OU science foundation course does offer an effective basic science course to novices. The OU can claim some considerable success in what Fensham (1993) calls structural or organizational support. The challenge for the future will be to provide more support for students with weak backgrounds, both in study skills and maths, in order to ensure that they are not disadvantaged when it comes to learning science. The assertion, suggested by Fensham, is that the key to 'science for all' is through changes to the content of the curriculum. The challenge for The Open University is to attract students from all walks of life to its foundation course in science and make the experience of learning science positive and successful so that they can gain the confidence and the ability to continue their studies.

We would like to thank Alan Woodley of the Student Research Centre, Institute of Education Technology, OU, for additional advice on the statistics included above, and Mike Pentz, the first Dean of Science, for providing the inspiration.

NOTE

1. 'Heineken' is a brand of lager which used the advertising slogan '. . . refreshes the parts other beers don't reach.'

REFERENCES

Ausubel, D. P. and Robinson, F. G. (1969) *School Learning: An Introduction to Educational Psychology*, New York, Holt, Rinehart & Winston.

Briggs, L. J. (1970, 1981 edition) *Handbook of Procedures for the Design of Instruction*. First edition 1970, Pittsburgh, Pennsylvania, American Institute for Research, second edition 1981, Educational Technology Publications.

Dennick, R. (1992) Analysing multiracial and antiracist science education, *School Science Review*, Vol. 73, no. 264, pp. 79–88. Reprinted as Article 3.3 in Whitelegg, E., Thomas, J. and Tresman, S. (eds.) (1993) *Challenges and Opportunities for Science Education*, London, Paul Chapman.

DES (Department of Education and Science) (1991) Education statistics, London, HMSO.

Edwards, D., Scanlon, E. and West, D. (eds.) (1993) *Teaching, Learning and Assessment in Science Education*, London, Paul Chapman.

Fensham, P. (1993) Reflections on science for all, in Whitelegg, E., Thomas, J. and Tresman, S. (eds.) *Challenges and Opportunities for Science Education*, London, Paul Chapman. Adapted from Fensham, P. (1985) Science for all: a reflective essay, *Journal of Curriculum Studies*, Vol. 17, no. 4, pp. 415–35.

Guri-Rozenblit, S. (1990) Assessing perseverance in studies at the Open University of Israel, *Assessment and Evaluation in Higher Education*, Vol. 15, no. 2, pp. 105–14.

Harlen, W. (1989) Education for equal opportunities in a scientifically literate society, *International Journal of Science Education*, Vol. 11, no. 2. Reprinted as Article 3.2 in Whitelegg, E., Thomas, J. and Tresman, S. (eds.) (1993) *Challenges and Opportunities for Science Education*, London, Paul Chapman.

Johnstone, A. (1991) Why is science difficult to learn? Things are seldom what they seem, *Journal of Computer Assisted Learning*, Vol. 7, pp. 75–83. Reprinted in Edwards, C., Scanlon, E. and West, D. (eds.) (1993) *Teaching, Learning and Assessment in Science Education*, London, Paul Chapman.

Kaye, A. and Pentz, M. (1974) Integrating multi-media systems for science education which achieve a wide territorial coverage, in *New Trends in the Utilisation of Educational Technology for Science Education*, Paris, UNESCO.

Moss, G. D. and Brew, A. (1981) The contribution of the Open University to innovation in higher education, *Higher Education*, Vol. 10, pp. 141–51.

Onushkin, V. G. and Zubkov, V. (1982) *Making Higher Education Accessible to Young Workers and Peasants: the Soviet Experience*, Paris, UNESCO.

Pentz, M. (1988) It can't be done! A personal view and critical appraisal of science teaching at The Open University. The second Ritchie Calder Memorial Lecture delivered at the Royal Institution, London.

Purnell, R. (1993) Teaching science to children with special educational needs. Article 3.5 in Whitelegg, E., Thomas, J. and Tresman, S. (eds.) (1993) *Challenges and Opportunities for Science Education*, London, Paul Chapman.

Ross, S. and Scanlon, E. (1991) Physicists all: are Open University graduates different?, *Open Learning*, Vol. 6, no. 2, pp. 3–11.

Swift, B. (1978) Most Open University graduates want to continue their studies, *Outlook*, Vol. 2 (graduate magazine), Milton Keynes, The Open University Press.

Swift, B. (1979) Satisfied, expanded, happier and maybe promoted as well, *Outlook*, Vol. 4 (graduate magazine), Milton Keynes, The Open University Press.

The Royal Society (1991) *Beyond GCSE*, London, Royal Society.

Wagner, L. (1992) Lecture to Council, Open University, September (1992).

Whitelegg, E., Thomas, J. and Tresman, S. (eds.) (1993) *Challenges and Opportunities for Science Education*, London, Paul Chapman.

Woodley, A. and Parlett, M. (1983) Student drop-out, *Teaching at a Distance*, Vol. 24, pp. 2–23.

Yates, C. (1986) The teaching of science at a distance. Unpublished MA thesis, University of London.

Appendix I   List of course units

Unit	S102 Unit titles
I	Science and the planet Earth
2	Measuring the solar system
3	Motion under gravity: a scientific theory
4	Practical work in science
5 and 6	Into the Earth: earthquakes, seismology and the Earth's magnetism
7 and 8	Plate tectonics: a revolution in the Earth sciences
9	Energy
10	Modelling the behaviour of light
I I and 12	Atomic structure
13 and 14	Chemical reactions and the periodic table
15	Chemical equilibrium
16	Chemical energetics
17 and 18	The chemistry of carbon compounds
19	Life and evolution
20	Inheritance and cell division
21	Genes and evolution
22	Biochemistry
23	Physiology
24	DNA: molecular aspects of genetics
25	Ecology
26	Biology reviewed
27	Earth materials and processes
28 and 29	Geological time and Earth history
30	Quantum mechanics: an introduction
31	Quantum mechanics: atoms and nucleii
32	The search for fundamental particles

Part 4: Images and Understanding

Introduction

Jeff Thomas

The articles in Part 4 of this Reader consider the way in which science is perceived and understood by non-practitioners, and they also question the purposes of science education. Two themes predominate, each of which impinges upon 'why' and 'how' science is taught.

The first is that the image of science held by the public has changed greatly over the past fifty years or so, generally for 'the worse'. In the euphoric aftermath of the Second World War, there was a naive belief that the progress of science was synonymous with promotion of the public good. Nuclear bomb testing and the ill-effects of early pesticides, notably DDT, were two examples that prompted disillusionment; these seemed to hold more sway than the positive transformations in daily lives that science had engineered, increasing both comfort and convenience.

The first article chronicles this change of heart. It is taken from Marcel C. La Follette's book *Making Science Our Own: Public Images of Science 1910–1955*. She has analysed science coverage in popular American magazines of the era and shows how the images of science conveyed an unreal impression of the 'scientist as hero' and falsely raised hopes of what science can realistically deliver. The new promised era of atomic energy did not materialize, neither did the promised 'cure for cancer'. The world looked more gloomy; science seemed more culprit than victim.

Why should the jaundiced perceptions of science evident in the modern era matter to educationalists? The answer to this question constitutes our second major theme, or rather it involves returning to a familiar theme – what is science education for, what is it meant to achieve? Is the aim to ensure some wide-scale 'scientific literacy' in the public, with the unstated intention of generating more widespread support and consequently more generous funding? Is the aim more defensive, that of countering an anti-science culture? Edgar Jenkins' article entitled 'Scientific literacy and school science education' identifies the key questions in the debate very clearly.

The paper by Robin Millar and Brian Wynne – 'Public understanding of science: from contents to processes' – helps to define the type of scientific understanding that might best achieve 'scientific literacy'. Rather than define a 'body of knowledge', of uncertain volume and density, the authors identify a need for greater understanding of the *processes* of science.

In the UK science now occupies a dominant though not unassailable place in the school curriculum. Bryan Chapman's article, 'The overselling of science education in the eighties', questions this pre-eminence. It asks whether there is a genuine need for greater scientific understanding. The virtue of his power-fully argued case is that it encourages those more inclined to defend science's case to think more deeply about *means* and *purpose*.

Inspirational vision and the enthusiasm of individual teachers have key roles in all forms of teaching, as the final article reminds us. Al Baez was just such an inspirational teacher, as is evident in his paper, 'Curiosity, creativity, compet-ence and compassion – guidelines for science education in the year 2000'. It provides reasons for optimism about the future. Those who share his belief in the benevolence of science have to ensure that the future application of science to human needs will be more intelligent and considerate than it has often been hitherto.

The end of progress: promises and expectations
Marcel C. La Follette

Opposition has raised its head in vain. 'Make way for science and for light!' has cleared obstruction from every path. If there have been doubters they have been branded as foes to progress . . .

(The editors of *Cosmopolitan,* 1910)

When science's cheerleaders cried 'Make way for science and for light!' they employed a metaphor common throughout twentieth-century popular science. Science sought to shed light on 'the never-to-be-accepted darkness' of ignorance. The scientific imagination incorporated a series of visions that 'flashed before the mind' of a researcher. Scientists' eyes were 'windows of intelligence', enhanced by such instruments as telescopes and microscopes. Popularizers even accused science's critics of proposing to return society to the 'dark ages' when there was no science.

To these writers – and probably to most readers of the popular magazines – the light of science and its incessant search for new knowledge seemed unequivocally positive. As part of this assessment, popularizers tied the metaphor of light to the equally powerful metaphor of progress. To shade or to dim the light of science risked inhibiting progress and endangering the flow of benefits. If scientists were to illuminate the forests of ignorance, then they must work without restraints. Writers did not question science's authority as a body of knowledge, as a social system, or as a method; instead there was 'a general tendency to regard the scientific man as the one trustworthy authority'.

These images of enlightenment and authority enhanced the effect when scientists repeatedly promised benefits from research. Because scientists possessed intelligence and stamina, they seemed able to do almost anything. Early in this century, the popular press effused a stream of promises that science's extraordinary success would never stop, as long as scientists were free to do their work. Even today, scientists' writings and public speeches, and the official

From La Follette, M. C. (1990) *Making Science our Own: Public Images of Science 1910–1955,* University of Chicago Press.

reports of scientific advisory committees routinely promote research benefits but they rarely question the inevitability of such benefits.

Attention to science's 'report card' is not, of course, necessarily bad. Many other groups and professions spend considerable money and time promoting their own accomplishments. For scientists, however, the exploitation of science's products created an unreasonable level of public expectation of cures and technical solutions and, over the course of this century, contributed to a politically volatile tug-of-war between control and freedom of research.[1]

The power of those promises derived in part from the popular images that surrounded them [. . .] each article on science reiterated traditional images – in metaphors, descriptions, and tone – of scientists as hardworking and intelligent, scientific methods as reliable, and scientific knowledge as authority. The effect of the roll-call of promised benefits must be measured therefore against the background of such stereotyped attributes, none more complex than the allocation of social authority.

SCIENCE: THE TRUE AUTHORITY

From one perspective, it could seem that, in this century, science received much of its praise by mistake. As engineers, managers, and industrialists did their work, the stack of benefits attributed to science grew in the popular press. Even when a new product – automobiles, radio, electrical appliances, vaccines, synthetic materials – was correctly assigned to a clever designer or inventor, there was at least a nod to its scientific foundations. The praise for science's contribution to modern technology was often quite sweeping. One *Century* author asserted in 1924 that 'most of the new ideas of the last two decades have been in some way or other scientific in character. Anything that goes under the aegis of science gains a special claim to consideration.'

In part, this contradiction in the allocation of credit stemmed from science's unusual social prestige. The ordinary person, one writer observed, 'speaks mistily about the men working in science as "THEY" ' and gives to scientists the place of authority once reserved for political or ecclesiastical rulers. This authority is more dangerous, he added, because it is unquestioning, and because the scientists are so remote. The ordinary citizen 'does not even know the names of these intellectual leaders, and probably has never come into contact with one of them', even though he speaks 'hopefully about the way in which "They" are sure to master the secrets of Nature'.

Such confusion of science and technology (and their combined record of success) formed a litany repeated endlessly in the magazines, a theme that reinforced science as an unquestionable authority. To doubt scientists' recommendations or promises betrayed a lack of faith in science, popularizers accused; they dismissed scepticism as not only inappropriate but possibly dangerous. The scientists' 'boasted power to foretell and control upon the basis of [their] hypotheses has been too often vindicated to permit a skepticism . . .'

Scientific authority also rested [. . .] on the acceptance of research methods as the only legitimate routes 'for the discovery of truth and for its explanation and description'. Reflection in tranquility might not guarantee understanding of the human mind, but the experiments of psychology definitely would. Some critics blamed scientists for deliberately promoting such an image, for deluding society 'into believing that the only proof worthy of the name, adequate and true, is proof set up in scientific formulae', but such accusations were rare in the popular magazines. *Science*, for most writers, represented 'a prestige word of great potency'; when attached to a topic, a method, or a programme, the term awarded an 'honorific significance'. Expressing attitudes widespread at the time, sociologist Robert K. Merton observed in a 1937 speech that there existed 'an increasing gap between the scientist and the laity. The layman must take on faith the publicized statements about relativity or quanta or other such esoteric subjects.' As a result, Merton continued, 'science and esoteric terminology become indissolubly linked' and thus when 'apparently scientific jargon' clothes mysticisms or political ideology, the layperson cannot judge its authenticity. 'The borrowed authority of science', Merton noted, 'becomes a powerful prestige symbol . . .'[2]

The dangers inherent in allocating unquestioned authority to every scientific pronouncement concerned many observers. J. W. N. Sullivan, the great British science writer, speculated that in the absence of more specialized information, nonscientists initially assessed scientific theories by the degree to which those theories 'squared with common sense' (that is, by whether the theories agreed with what they already knew). As theoretical constructs moved farther from everyday experience, he noted, readers easily developed an 'uncritical credulity' towards science. As instruments became more complicated, the objects of scrutiny smaller, and the theories more abstract, nonscientists willingly gave 'a measure of credence to almost anything that professe[d] to be scientific', and thereby intensified the influence of pseudoscience labelled as science. Even if an idea was far-fetched, Sullivan wrote, simply labelling it as *scientific* would ensure its acceptance; most laypersons would not risk dismissing a scientific theory 'merely because it sounds ridiculous'. A few journalists retained some 'shallow' scepticism in the face of such pressure, but most presented science as 'the one key to knowledge, the one source of truth, in the modern world'.

When scientists spoke authoritatively on topics outside their field of expertise, they relied on these and related popular beliefs for acceptance. Writing in 1921, entomologist Vernon Kellogg asserted, for example, that there were many areas of human life in which, although the biologist might be inexperienced, he might nevertheless 'believe he has at least as much right as anyone else to venture'. By the late 1920s, some scientists seemed inclined to become self-appointed experts on almost everything. The practice attracted considerable criticism but continued nonetheless. Magazinists warned their readers against assuming that 'the specialist in any particular science is ipso facto also well qualified to speak with equal authority on religion and philosophy'. As one journalist wrote, in such a climate there appeared to be little difference between 'a scientist adrift in religion and a Methodist bishop floundering in Geology'.

The overreaching scientific expert became even more of a political problem in the 1940s. Both the scientists lobbying for *and* those lobbying against federal policy on atomic weapons used their scientific reputations to attract public support for their political views, although many of their colleagues found such practices inappropriate. In 1945, sociologist George Lundberg, for example, attacked scientists who knowingly used their scientific reputations to gain a public hearing:

> Both scientists and the public have frequently assumed that when scientists engage in ordinary pressure group activity, that activity somehow becomes science or scientific activity. It is not surprising, perhaps, that the public should be confused on this point, because it may not always be clear when a scientist is expressing a scientific conclusion and when he is expressing a personal preference.[3]

Lundberg argued that it was 'unpardonable' of scientists to confuse statements based on what they knew as scientists with statements based on their personal beliefs about religion, morals, or politics. 'To pose as distinguished scientists announcing scientific conclusions when in fact they are merely expressing personal or group preferences is simple fraud.' No one argued that scientists should make no public statements about science-related political issues; rather, commentators pointed out that scientists had a responsibility in such situations to acknowledge the social or political nature of the issue and to clarify that they spoke as citizens, but not necessarily as experts.

Other scientists agreed more with the view, espoused by chemist Harold C. Urey in the 1940s, that although scientists should indeed speak as citizens on certain public issues, their citizenship carried special privileges and responsibilities. Urey unfortunately demonstrated in his writings some of the same narrow-minded attitudes that he condemned. 'Most scientists', he wrote, 'prefer to view their present interest as "social awareness" ':

> It is as if a bacteriologist had discovered a dread disease which might lead to a disastrous epidemic. He would not be a 'politician' if he asked that the city health commission take measures to deal with a plague. He would merely be demonstrating common decency and social awareness of what his discovery meant to human lives.[4]

To readers in 1946, that analogy probably seemed farfetched: surely the bacteriologists would know best about epidemics and public health decisions. Today, after such episodes as the swine flu vaccination programme (in which epidemiologists' advice influenced a premature and inadvertently harmful programme of mass inoculations), we have ample evidence that even the most well-intentioned scientific announcements can sometimes provoke unforeseen and terrible political and social consequences, and can even result in loss of life.[5] Urey's suggestion that it would be both advisable and responsible for scientists to use their authority as scientists to stimulate political action represented attitudes prevalent in the scientific community at the time and helps to explain why even sceptical journalists allocated such unwarranted universal authority to scientists.

PROMISES

The chain of authority linking the legitimacy of scientific methods and the authenticity of scientific knowledge to the personal opinions of scientists also tied together the promises of science and the public's expectations. The popular magazines record an extraordinary message communicated throughout this century, a litany of promises that science would cure every disease, fix every problem, and brush away every tear – if only research was kept free of undue restraint. This 'song of science', when viewed en masse in the texts of thousands of magazines, showed a public image of science that was not only inconsistent with reality but also politically unstable.

It is easy to understand why so many journalists inadvertently treated the scientists as able to predict the outcome of all their research: as anthropologist and science writer Loren Eiseley has written, people 'have an insatiable demand for soothsayers and oracles to assure them and comfort them about the insubstantial road they tread'. Whether portrayed as hero, wizard, or expert, the magazine scientist was a man in motion, ever seeking the news. Even when standing still, he stretched to peer over the next horizon. He thus became both prophet and producer.

Sensitive to the dangers of inflated public expectations, a few scientists tempered their remarks with qualifications. In 1912, astronomer Edward Arthur Fath wrote that the possibilities of his research were 'endless, but, in view of the fact that our actual knowledge is practically nil, such speculation is largely fruitless'. Similarly, a biologist commented in 1921 that naturalists could claim only that they know 'a part of the order of nature'. But far more articles painted a different picture, and both journalists and scientists participated in developing those expectations. Journalists in fact often seemed to lean forward and encourage scientists to make predictions. Each time a scientist complied, it reinforced the journalists' expectations of such behaviour.

If scientists had limited those responses to cautious and qualified predictions, science's real achievements would in fact have afforded ample prestige: but, as hundreds of articles show, they rarely did so. Contrary to what some historians have argued, most scientists participated extensively (and apparently willingly) in the cycle of promises. Perhaps out of enthusiasm for their work, perhaps out of some naive desire to please the journalists who were interviewing them, or perhaps out of a spirit of self-confidence, the scientists promised benefits from all they did. In article after article, they abandoned the usual tentative language of their scientific papers and adopted the popular rhetoric of 'the sure thing'.

Several years ago, in commenting on the evolution of public attitudes to science, Charles Spencer divided the 1970s 'rebellion against science' into two separate influences: one he identified as the counterculture's 'humanistic view'; the other as changes in 'what people believe science can do for them or for society'.[6] The 1970s disillusionment, he believed, derived from the combination of images of science as 'the key to utopia' and the realization that utopia was no longer within reach. Spencer suggested that to study the roots of this attitude, one might review systematically 'what science promised society'. In fact, by analysing the texts of articles in twentieth-century popular magazines, it was possible to do just that.

The magazine's promises ranged from the modest ('You'll be able to walk through a downpour after the war without losing the crease in your pants') to the fantastic ('Out of the test tube comes a thrilling age of magic, in which you will melt your unwashed dishes down the drain, buy fifty new suits of clothes and throw them away unlaundered'). In 1910, readers were told that 'every hour is pregnant with promise of other discoveries'; in 1920, they were reminded of 'the unlimited possibilities of future scientific productivity'; and in 1946 they were assured that if a solution existed to any problem, then scientists would eventually find it. A physicist was quoted in 1950 as saying that he thought 'scientific research is the answer to every material problem now facing us'. Even J. D. Bernal, the British crystallographer and Marxist critic, predicted that 'we may judge from the history of science that even greater possibilities lie in new discoveries of which at present we have no idea'. The promises involved about every conceivable solution to human problems or fulfillment of human desires. A *Cosmopolitan* article in 1912 outlined scientists' utlimate promise – 'the conquest of death itself' – as it described their attempts to provide 'immortality' for all people.

Promises sometimes involved the use of new technologies. Articles in the 1910s and 1920s hinted at the social changes that radio would bring, for example. Although some of those predictions represented plausible ideas, others represented magnificent fantasies. Radio 'both fitted into and extended Americans' notions of how the future would be made better, maybe even perfect, through technology', one historian observes, by helping to deliver society 'from a troubled present to a utopian future'. In 1924, Waldemar Kaempffert described 'To-Morrow's Wireless' thus:

> As a wine-glass vibrates with sound when its rim is rubbed, so the earth will vibrate electrically when it is subjected to the action of millions of impulses correctly timed. And those impulses will be imparted by gigantic induction-coils incorporated in immense towering steel cages. . . . In every large city, you will see such a steel frame, projecting far up into the sky, overtopping houses and buildings.[7]

Kaempffert reported that Nicholas Tesla, inventor of the induction coil, imagined that his device would enable the world to unite in a 'community of interest' for a 'harmonious existence' in the future, a promise repeated in another article which predicted that radio would bring 'education and happiness and democracy' as well as cultural, social, and political unification.

One of the most prominent 'boosters' of science and engineering in the 1920s, Floyd W. Parsons, believed that people could not be 'sheltered from the effects of scientific advance', for science was 'revolutionizing' industry and 'transforming business from a routine grind into a romantic adventure'. He was certain that the scientific advances of the next decades would 'represent more progress than had previously been made in all recorded history'. His articles mixed impossible or implausible examples with some that now we take for granted. Parsons predicted that 'surface cars' would 'go out of business'; there would be 'power transmission without wires'; airplanes would sell for $150; accurate earthquake and flood predictions would minimize damage; sidewalks would be 'arcaded under the buildings'; there would be colour motion pictures; and there would be radios on all trains.

Promises regarding the production or processing of food were common. Articles predicted that science would 'so increase productivity' that starvation would be eliminated and that synthetic food would soon become a reality. In the 1940s and 1950s, Collier's authors predicted such wonders as 'new bread from the sea', a sea algae that would provide 'an inexhaustible supply of food'. In another Collier's article, the staff writer advocated a 'Manhattan Project' to meet international food needs: with such a crash research effort, he argued, Western society could 'win the stakes' in the 'food race' and grow 'enough food for the millions today and those to come'.

Some promises were linked to ongoing research. In describing weather forecasting, authors declared that 'physicists are brewing sample patches of the weather we'll enjoy tomorrow' and that scientists could already 'produce rain or snow virtually at will'. Once the space programme was underway, authors made many promises about its success. 'The Army Air Force has announced that research underway might produce a rocket to the moon within the next eighteen months,' Eugene H. Kone wrote in 1946.

Postwar debates over two scientific issues – atomic energy research and cancer research – exemplified how promises that continued from decade to decade throughout this century could build a foundation of essentially unfulfillable public expectations.

The promises of atomic energy

Long before Alamogordo gave proof of atomic energy's terrible potential, journalists had publicized the promises inherent in the research (see Figure 1). In 1933, Charles F. Kettering wrote, 'Suppose that, within twelve months, scientists, using the tools already in their hands, begin to blow atoms to pieces.' A 1934 Harper's article explained the newest 'Discoveries within the Atom' and promised many new uses. And Collier's editors described in 1940 'the new and fascinating way of life that lies within the immediate grasp of man through utilization of Uranium-235, the long-sought, parochial source of atomic power'. 'War itself will become obsolete,' the author of that article predicted: 'Although engineers would apply this new power,

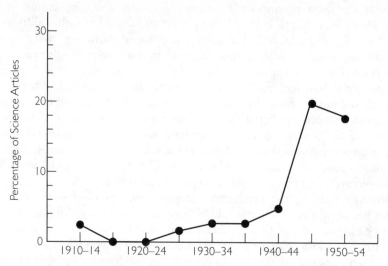

Figure I   Articles on atomic energy, 1910–54. The proportion of all articles which discussed atomic physics research or research related to atomic energy (*n*=45). Data are taken from a sample of eleven US mass-circulation magazines and are given as a percentage of all science articles published in those magazines during each five-year period

some of the glory must be reserved for the physicist,' he insisted with unforeseen irony.

In the *Post* in 1940, William L. Laurence told breathlessly how the atom had already given up its secrets; he described the newest work of Otto Hahn, Lise Meitner, Enrico Fermi, Niels Bohr, and other physicists, and then outlined what their research could mean for society. [. . .] Although Laurence and other journalists knew of suggestions that atomic energy would have considerable military usefulness, they optimistically emphasized the domestic uses of atomic physics. In *Harper's*, John J. O'Neill wrote that, after weighing the possible benefits and the dangers of atomic energy, 'the net results appear to be an indication that the discovery of the Uranium 235 process for the release of atomic energy promises the dawn of a new era for mankind'. In the early 1940s, most popular commentators regarded the 'new era' as one to be welcomed, not feared.

After the American public learned about the terrible destruction at Hiroshima and Nagasaki, they could not ignore the other side of this gift from the scientists. Even the most optimistic booster of science could see what the new dawn had revealed; in the magazines, themes of destruction and death increased. And, as historian Paul Boyer describes in *By the Bomb's Early Light*, this tone of fear pervaded all of American culture. Although magazines continued to praise scientists for having helped to win the war in the Pacific, the cheers had a hollow ring.

Some of this change resulted from scientists' own public statements about government programmes for atomic energy research and from their participation in the debate over military control. Manhattan Project scientists had soon realized that they could not pack the moral and political implications of atomic weapons away with the uniforms and campaign ribbons, and some of them began nationwide lobbying efforts to inform public decision making. Because they knew that research on ever more destructive weapons was moving forward, physicists sensed the urgency of affecting political plans to expand the research and to restrict international cooperation.

Public concern, as reflected in the tone of magazine coverage, developed slowly, however, perhaps because the initial expectations had been so high. The boosters of atomic power also continued to exaggerate its potential. Even after the war, optimistic outlines of the peaceful uses of atomic energy continued. When sociologist Steven Del Sesto analysed postwar reaction to atomic power, he found that the idea of 'unlimited power' captured the imagination of all sorts of writers – politicians, political scientists, and scientists – who promoted it as, among other things, potentially reducing manual labour, propelling automobiles and ocean liners, and assuring world peace.

Within a year or so, positive expressions gave way to mixed messages of expectation and fear, as more and more articles described the lingering physiological effects of radiation, the 'deplorable' state of current civil defence, and the implications of the new 'nuclear politics'. Some of this change coincided with deteriorating relations between the United States and the Soviet Union and the consequent demands of the Cold War. In 1957, lawyer and science writer James R. Newman reconstructed the process then taking place within the scientific community. The scientists, he said, 'were certain that the use of fissionable and radioactive materials would lead to further significant discoveries in basic science, which in time would produce innumerable and unpredictable technological devices', but that they believed such benefits were far away. In the near term, he said, there were 'limited' medical applications and possibly some [in] domestic energy production. Newman then identified the issue that still lies at the heart of public attitudes to nuclear energy: the unpredictability of its use. Something about this product of science seemed different, its ambiguity unmistakable. Biologists had made startling and uncomfortable discoveries; chemists had developed chemicals of alarming toxicity; but any of these results seemed more controllable than the new atomic physics. The atomic and hydrogen bombs made suspect all previous generalizations about research applications and about whether researchers could control their science. Newman attributed public disillusionment to the scientists' apparent inability to predict what research would bring. The same people who demonstrated startling insight 'into the heart of the atom', he wrote, 'can only guess at the scope of the application of the power they have won; and they profess no confidence at all in predicting the social, economic, and political consequences of their discovery'.

In fact, uncontrollability, not technical unpredictability, raised the level of fear. Scientists could predict accurately the technical limits of their work (e.g., the range of a bomb's destruction, its so-called killing power) but they could not predict the social and political aspects of its use, such as whether, when, how, or by whom it might be used.

Such descriptions as Newman's portrayed scientists as failed magicians. Some scientists might continue to predict that some day 'wholesale blessings will flow from the atom,' and others might call atomic energy 'a gift richer by far than the gift of Promethean fire that started man on his slow march from the cave on the road to the stars'; but, face to face with their own discovery, the scientists appeared powerless to live up to their own promises.

The ambiguity apparent in magazine discussion of atomic and nuclear power through the 1950s persists today. As recorded in many social surveys, a majority of Americans can identify some benefits from the production of nuclear energy, but most also see possible harmful consequences from the work. In the mid-1980s, Americans were almost equally divided on whether the benefits outweighed the harms or vice versa.[8]

Cures for cancer

The promises of atomic energy encompassed the fate of the whole world; biology, on the other hand, promised results of concern to each individual reader.[9] In 1954 *Collier's* observed that

> A little more than a decade ago scientists unravelled the mystery of the atom and began the atomic age. Today an equally basic mystery is being solved – that is the living cell, indeed the secret of life itself. As a result, we may be on the threshold of a hopeful new era in which cancer, mental illness, and, in fact, nearly all diseases now regarded as incurable will cease to torment man.[10]

Postwar biology in fact provided science with some of its most notable successes and its longest unfulfilled promise. In the 1940s and 1950s, descriptions of discoveries that might cure some disease or relieve some painful condition filled the magazines. Many promises proved correct, although not always in the time predicted:

1941   In a few more years . . . chemotherapy – will give us a cure for tuberculosis.

1944   The magic which will eradicate leprosy and tuberculosis may be just around the corner.

1949   In the four years since its discovery, streptomycin has become recognized as the best of all known drugs for combating tuberculosis. . . . Its promise is staggering.

1950   We are also apparently on the verge of discovering a vaccine for polio.

On occasion, a journalist might emphasize that a researcher was reluctant to say anything 'which might arouse false hopes in the ill'; in interviews, some scientists carefully stressed the 'serious shortcomings' of their work or warned that it might not live up to its early promise. Neither journalists nor readers could ignore the impressive advances that medical research had already made,

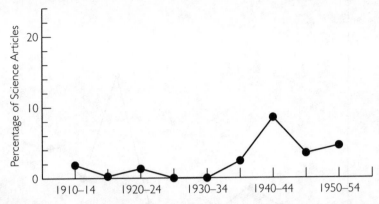

Figure 2 Articles on cancer research, 1910–54. The proportion of all articles which discussed research on cancer (*n*=14). Data are taken from a sample of eleven US mass-circulation magazines and are given as a percentage of all science articles published in those magazines during each five-year period

however, and it always seemed that even better things were to come. No matter how cautiously they phrased the first part of an article, few writers seemed able to resist adding stirring, hope-filled conclusions. 'They no longer apply the word "hopeless" to any disease,' one journalist wrote in 1950:

> During the last few years they have made greater discoveries than during all the long history of medicine. They are now digging deeper into the unknown than ever before. They still have a long way to go before they discover remedies for all our ills, but they are marching steadily toward that goal.[11]

In the midst of all this optimism, one longtime promise of medical research remained conspicuously unfulfilled: a cure for cancer. Few science topics were covered by the magazines with such consistency throughout the period studied. Each of the eleven magazines [surveyed] published many articles on the treatment and cure of cancer (see Figures 2 and 3). From 'Conquest of Cancer' (*Cosmopolitan*, August 1912) to 'Chemicals for Cancer' (*Atlantic*, March 1954), journalists and scientists alike recounted 'the latest and most authoritative statements on the subject'. They told readers about 'the recent gains . . . and the further moves necessary' and described how 'the great ring of science [was] slowly surrounding the greatest disease killer of the present day'.

Early in the century, writers routinely repeated inflated promises made by scientists. In the 1920s, one author remonstrated, 'I am happy to assure my readers that cancer is curable, *provided* the advice of those who have been in constant contact with this terrible disease is sought and followed.' Even in 1954, the head of a major research group boasted that, despite the inadequacy of current research methods, the development of a cure was inevitable: 'The basic advances which have been made foretell the future development of more effective treatment as certainly as the day follows the night.' Later in the same article, he used more cautious language, but such reticence did not dampen

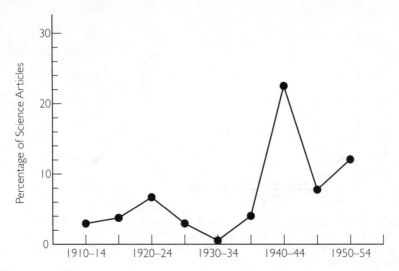

Figure 3   Articles on medical research, 1910–54. The proportion of articles which discussed research on all types of diseases or medical conditions, including cancer (n-34). Data are taken from a sample of eleven US mass-circulation magazines and are given as a percentage of all science articles published in those magazines during each five-year period

public expectations, fuelled by decades of medical progress. The Gallup Poll for December 1949 reported that 88% of Americans believed that 'a cure for cancer' would be found within the next fifty years. In the late 1940s, writers even linked the promises of peaceful atomic energy with cancer research: 'No scientist now would dare predict just where or when in the struggle against cancer the final break will come. We can be sure, however, that atomic energy in its various forms will contribute heavily to the final victory.'

After decades of promises about a cure for cancer, the tone of discourse slowly changed. A note of caution – slight but perceptible – had appeared in the magazines by the 1950s. Journalists still cheerfully assured readers that cures would be found, but they also appraised with a more jaundiced eye the time and effort required to achieve such cures. Fewer and fewer articles trumpeted the small steps forward. The level of promise and excitement remained high (compared to discussions of other research fields), but writers were more cautious about predicting universal cures. The tone changed noticeably from nervous impatience to wary appraisal.

Perhaps improvements in the quality of medical reporting overall influenced this change. Perhaps the writers simply had a better idea of the realistic potential of the research. By then, the researchers themselves were also acknowledging how complicated the scientific questions were; their statements to journalists may have reflected their own reassessments of whether a cure was possible. More likely, better reporting and the scientists' caution combined with shifting public attitudes toward science in general to produce a more tempered perspective on the research potential in this field.

This interpretation is consistent with data from social surveys conducted in the 1950s, which showed public confidence in all types of research to be relatively strong. A 1957 survey by the National Association of Science Writers, for example, concluded that the public 'believed that science and technology had won the war, created "miracle" drugs, and would continue to produce a cornucopia of benefits to American society'.[12] Most people thought that science made their lives 'healthier, easier, and more comfortable.[13]

Similar continuity may be seen in public estimates that are neither Polly-annaish nor thoroughly supportive of the success of cancer research. The 1985 National Science Foundation survey found that 55% of the public thought it 'very likely' that researchers would discover a cure for common forms of cancer in the next twenty-five years or so, down slightly from optimism of previous years but still high; 37% thought it 'possible'; and 6% thought it not likely at all.[14] Even though estimates of the likelihood of a cure are now more realistic (and therefore more pessimistic) than fifty years ago, the general image of medical research has not changed all that much and still translates into a poignant hope for the cure of all sorts of diseases and conditions. A mood of yearning optimism, now tempered with pragmatic caution, remains the principal metaphor, probably because the researchers themselves consistently endorsed this image.[15]

DEVELOPING EXPECTATIONS

No dramatic sea change took place in the public presentation of science from the 1910s through the 1950s; it did not shift abruptly from positive to negative (or vice versa). Clusters of images all fit together to create a portrait of something called *science* conducted by some people called *scientists*.

Nevertheless, one common message echoed throughout these magazine articles. It was elusive (and unmeasurable in any quantitative sense) but persistent. There was an unmistakable tone of expectation – not anticipation of any one benefit, or fear of any specific harm, but a shared expectation that science would not be passive, and that scientific research would produce a better world. Americans surely did not believe that scientists would solve all problems. They did not really believe that science could wash away hunger, poverty, and disease, or that it could be 'the very death of death'. They did, however, appear to expect that *something* would happen and that in most cases the benefit would be large.

Several distinct characteristics of the popular presentation of science contributed to this tone of expectation. First, repeated descriptions of research success and a constant, unquestioning emphasis on the reliability and accuracy of scientific methods (Salomon's *science as technique*) reinforced an image of science's strong cultural authority. Second, each time they failed to question a scientist's claim to universal expertise, journalists inadvertently strengthened the social prestige of all scientists. Third, when popularizers' emphasized science as power, by listing its products and describing the productivity of scientists, they boosted expectations of its potential usefulness. Fourth, describing the scientists as different, as simultaneously apart from and superior to the rest of society, made them appear to be subject to different rules. Fifth, the repeated assertion that scientists were motivated only by altruism or intellectual curiosity made them appear to be trustworthy and reliable in all their promises. And, sixth, the omnipresence of science in all parts of popular culture, not only through specific descriptions, but also through multiple references to science or scientific methods in discussions of most other topics, increased its seeming importance.

The authority, power, prestige, complexity, and bounty of science so overwhelmed nonscientists that even naturally inquisitive journalists, as well as unsympathetic social commentators and critics of science, accepted without question most of what scientists said. The scepticism inherent in political reporting was rarely applied to science, at least in the first part of the century. Muckraking magazines like *Cosmopolitan* and *Collier's*, which excoriated corrupt politicians in almost every issue early in the century, let scientists appear to be without fault.

Perhaps this tendency represented a human predisposition to choose the rosy promise rather than admit the gloomy possibility. The magazine scientists seemed optimistic and well-meaning; they looked toward the future, not the past, and worked with confidence and boundless energy. Perhaps both the journalists and their audiences wanted to believe in the scientists' best intentions and, even though they knew that it was impossible, also wanted to believe that science might eventually dispel all evils. The optimism inherent in every act of research undoubtedly fuelled the hope – especially in the years before and after the great wars – that science would rescue society from the morass of difficulties facing the world. Science would do what politicians seemed unable to do: provide sufficient food, make war obsolete, prevent natural disasters, and eliminate disease. Journalists and scientists alike endorsed research as the universal panacea.

This concurrence of promise and potential also helped to maintain the public's faith in science through the 1950s and 1960s, even though many promises went unfulfilled, and unpredicted side effects seemed to threaten human life and well-being. Cancer research had yet to find a cure; Rachel Carson showed that chemical pesticides harmed more than insects; but the public's expectations and enthusiasm remained unabated.

Loren Eiseley has argued that unfocused waiting (i.e., waiting for nothing in particular) is symptomatic of this century's confusion and despair, and that confusion over what society wants comes from its failure to control its own institutions. Certainly this seems true for science. Americans allowed scientists both to predict what bounty they would produce and to choose which research areas they would pursue. Convinced that science was incomprehensible and that scientists were the only ones who should control science, society could only watch and wait. As critic Roy Kenneth Hack wrote in an *Atlantic* short story in 1916, 'The modern world has persuaded itself that all it has to do is to hand over its fortune to science. Science has accepted the trust.' Until mid-century, few journalists or politicians questioned the wisdom of that trust. The tone of anticipation observed in the magazines thus represented the failure of both the journalists *and* their audiences to question science and scientists. All too often, they both accepted science's promises at face value.

REFERENCES

1. House Committee on Science and Technology (1986) *The Regulatory Environment for Science*, Science Policy Study Background Report No. 10, 99th Congress, Washington, Government Printing Office, December 1986.
2. Merton, R. K. (1937) 'Science and the Social Order' reprinted in Merton, R. K., *Social Theory and Social Structure*, revised and enlarged edition, Glencoe, The Free Press, 1957, p. 546.
3. Lundberg, G. (1945) *Can Science Save Us?*, p. 529.
4. Harold, C. Urey, as told to Michael Amrine, 'I'm a frightened man', *Collier's*, 5 January 1946, p. 19.
5. Neustadt, R. E. and Fineberg, H. V. (1978) *The Swine Flu Affair: Decision-Making on a Slippery Disease*, Washington, U.S. Department of Health, Education and Welfare.
6. Spencer, C. D. (1973) 'Commentary', *Newsletter of the Program on Public Conceptions of Science*, No. 3, April 1973, p. 10.
7. Kaempffert, W. (1924) *To-Morrow's Wireless*, p. 516.
8. National Science Board (1987) *Science and Engineering Indicators – 1987*, Washington, National Science Foundation, Table 8–21, p. 162.
9. Patterson, J. T. (1987) *The Dread Disease: Cancer and Modern American Culture*, Cambridge, Harvard University Press.
10. Davidson, B. (1954) Probing the secret of life, *Collier's*, 14 May 1954, p. 78.
11. Woodbury, C. (1950) The race against pain, *The American Magazine*, January 1950, p. 130.
12. House Committee on Science and Technology, *The Regulatory Environment*, p. 148. Data from a contractor's report written for the study by Miller, J. D.
13. *Ibid.*
14. National Science Board, *Science and Engineering Indicators*, Table 8–9, p. 150.
15. Rettig, R. (1978) Testimony given in hearings on nutrition and cancer, held by the Senate Subcommitte on Nutrition, Committee on Agriculture (12 June 1978).

[In its original version this article contained a substantial number of references to popular magazines. These references have been removed but they refer to articles from: *Harper's Monthly, The Atlantic Monthly, The Century Illustrated Monthly, Everybody's Magazine, Collier's, The American Magazine, The Saturday Evening Post, Imagining Tomorrow, The World's Work, The American Mercury, Scribner's Magazine*, and *Reader's Digest*.]

4.2

Scientific literacy and school science education

Edgar Jenkins

INTRODUCTION

In a recent review of the 'motives, meanings and implications' of 'science for all', Hodson and Reid suggested[1] that the principal aim of school science education should be the *scientific literacy* of all pupils, irrespective of their different interests, experiences and abilities. However, while the review acknowledged the difficulty and ambiguity of 'science for all', the notion of scientific literacy escaped close scrutiny, perhaps because, like such other persuasive terms as 'balanced science', 'relevance' or 'human rights', scientific literacy seems to have an entirely benign, even honorific flavour.

This article offers a brief historical perspective on scientific literacy and indicates the variety of interpetations evident in some of the recent literature. More significantly, it suggests that if scientific literacy involves the empowerment of future adults in relation to some of their eventual concerns as citizens, then its adoption as an educational objective entails consequences for the content, organization and pedagogy of school science education that are both profound and radical.

THE SEPARATION OF SCIENCE FROM GENERAL CULTURE

One of the noble features of the development of science during the early nineteenth century is the extent to which scientific knowledge appealed to, and was eagerly sought by, a wide range of individuals and groups. The breadth of this interest stemmed from the fact that scientific knowledge was useful in serving a variety of purposes. An understanding of science offered possibilities 'as polite knowledge, as theological instruction, as professional occupation, as technological agent, as value-transcendent pursuit, and as an intellectual ratifier of a new world order.'[2] Scientific knowledge was disseminated in a number of ways. These included the activities of the Mechanics' Institutes and the Literary and Philosophical Societies, the demonstrations conducted by

From *School Science Review* (1990) Vol. 71, no. 256, pp. 43–51.

itinerant lecturers, and a remarkable variety of books, journals, tracts, pamphlets and magazines, many of which would be categorized today as 'teach yourself' publications. Although it is difficult to assess with any precision the scale of the demand for scientific knowledge in early nineteenth-century England, it seems likely that scientific knowledge and an interest in matters scientific were not only 'very much a part of early Victorian high culture'[3] but also quite widely diffused among other classes in society.

By the beginning of the twentieth century, this situation no longer prevailed. Sir William Huggins, President of The Royal Society from 1900 to 1905, was by no means alone in lamenting 'the quality of the national mind in relation to the importance of natural knowledge'.[4] This transformation of the position of science in society has been studied by a number of scholars among whom Shapin and Thackray have concluded that 'it was in the years from 1870 to 1900 – that the divorce was effected between natural knowledge and the general culture'.[5] Shen, writing from a different perspective, reaches the same conclusion, commenting that 'Between the 1870s and World War I . . . the increasing professionalization of scientists . . . finally induced them to take on a new attitude towards the lay public . . . the explaining of science to the layman [came to be regarded] as something not entirely worthy of the professional'.[6] The timing of this 'divorce between natural knowledge and culture' is significant since it coincides with the growing involvement of the state in the provision of scientific education. The resolution of the apparent paradox lies in the tacit social contract struck between science and society in the nineteenth century and, more particularly, in the consequences of that contract for the schooling of science. The essential features of the contract represented science as an objective, neutral, value-free and an increasingly professional activity to be pursued *for its own sake*. The scientific community was to be free to determine its own priorities in scientific research in return for a promise to generate economic and material benefits for society, but only on the understanding that these benefits were long-term, unspecified and, at least often as not, unpredictable.

The terms of this accommodation of science within the society of which it formed an increasingly important part had several consequences. As far as science education is concerned, the dominant values of the scientific community were incorporated within the curricular of emergent educational institutions and formed an integral part of the processes whereby the ideology of science, delineated by the social contract referred to above, came to be consolidated and burnished. Such consolidation was at the expense of the diversity of purpose and procedure that had marked scientific education in early Victorian England when scientific knowledge was widely sought by literate adults precisely because of its utility. Reinforced by Armstrong's emphasis on the teaching of scientific method as an educational objective and encouraged by Morant's *Regulations* of 1904, the developing secondary schools of the early twentieth century accommodated and endorsed the professional function of secondary school science education that had been so carefully nurtured from the 1860s onwards. As with science itself, this pre-professional scientific education was marked by an emphasis on abstraction rather than utility, disengagement from potentially contentious personal, social, political, or economic issues, and attention to the concerns of science itself rather than to those of the wider community of pupils or adults.

Over three quarters of a century later, the introduction of comprehensive schools and the much more recent advent of the GCSE seem to have done little to challenge the pre-eminence of this pre-professional function, and all that it implies, in secondary school science education. Earlier attempts to 'bring science into the homes of the people' and scientific knowledge 'to bear upon the environment and avocations of human life' have met 'with limited success'[7] and contemporary official policy maintains that 'the essential characteristic' of school science is that it introduces pupils to the 'methods of science'. Such a policy is obviously open to the charge that it is simply a means of preserving pre-professional 'grammar school science' within a comprehensive system of education. More significantly in the present context, it raises the question of the relationship between an ability to 'bring a scientific approach to bear on the practical, social, economic and political issues of modern life'[8] and the 'universal scientific literacy' which Hodson and Reid regard as central to the achievement of 'greater social justice' and which, more generally, might be expected to command widespread support as an educational objective.

THE CASE FOR SCIENTIFIC LITERACY

In 1985, The Royal Society claimed that 'Improving the public understanding of science is an investment in the future, not a luxury to be indulged in if and when resources allow.' The Society justified its claim by arguing that such improvement 'can be a major element in promoting national prosperity, in raising the quality of public and private decision making and in enriching the life of the individual'.[9]

The more general case has been well-summarized by Thomas and Durant.[10] Reviewing an 'extensive and diverse' literature, they identified nine arguments for the promotion of the public understanding of science. These arguments are distinguished by reference to the benefits associated with them, namely, benefits 'to science itself, to national prosperity, national power and influence, democratic government, society as a whole, intellectual life, aesthetic appreciation and morality'. Clearly, some of these arguments overlap, e.g. benefits to individuals may advantage society at large in a variety of ways, and, as Thomas and Durant also recognize, the classification is almost certainly not exhaustive. In addition, each of the arguments has more than one focus. Thus, 'the benefits to science' may be of different types. An extreme view might be that of Asimov who has asserted that 'Without an informed public, scientists will not only be no longer supported financially, they will be actively persecuted.'[11] A less dramatic position and perhaps one more readily recognized by the majority of practising scientists, is that public scientific literacy underpins the political support required both for the successful prosecution of science in a modern, industrialized democracy and for the ability of the scientific community to counter opposition, e.g. from religious fundamentalists or animal rights groups. The achievements of science and technology and the dominance of 'scientific rationality' as an approach to the solution of a wide range of problems suggest another way in which science itself might benefit from a more scientifically literate population. This is that greater scientific literacy may act as a counter to the unreasonable and unrealistic expectations encouraged by past triumphs, i.e. a greater understanding of science and, more particularly, of its limitations, might diminish the risk of widespread disenchantment with, or even hostility towards, science, the rudiments of which are perhaps already in evidence.

Arguments for scientific literacy that relate to the benefits to individuals may likewise rest on a variety of grounds. For example, scientifically literate citizens may have access to a greater range of employment opportunities and feel more confident in responding to the demands made by new technologies. They may be better able to evaluate 'scientific' evidence used in advertising or better equipped to take decisions about matters that affect their personal or economic well-being, e.g. diet, medication, safety, energy usage. In addition, they may achieve intellectual or aesthetic satisfaction from an appreciation of the elegance, beauty and power of the scientific conception of the universe.

Some of the arguments for scientific literacy reviewed by Thomas and Durant have a long ancestry. Those, like Rapoport[12] who see in the scientific endeavour ethical standards and modes of conduct and discourse that might be applied with benefit to social affairs in general share common ground with those Enlightenment thinkers who held that the development of scientific understanding led not only to knowledge but also to moral improvement. Similarly, Paul Weiss's claim, made in 1959, that science offers 'a basis for responsible and judicious self-direction as a design for living'[13] shares a common moral dimension with Richard Gregory's assertion in 1916 that science should be taught because it provides 'an intellectual outlook, a standard of truth and a gospel of light'.[14]

The case made for greater scientific literacy depends markedly upon time and social context and, more particularly, upon the primary purpose for which a given argument is advanced. Today, the integration of science within the economies of industrial societies and its association with, for example, the technologies of war and of pollution have made any contemporary appeal to the ethical virtues of the scientific enterprise seem not merely inappropriate but, for some, dishonest. In contrast, arguments about the importance of scientific literacy to national economic prosperity or security inevitably have become more prominent as economic growth or defence issues have risen on the political agenda and as the scientific community has sought to defend itself against its critics.

It is also important to acknowledge that arguments for scientific literacy are value-laden and that, as such, they may not easily cross national or cultural boundaries. Thus, the potential of science to inform and empower decision-making by individuals, community activists or groups is unlikely to be encouraged within a totalitarian society or, for that matter, welcomed by a multinational corporation anxious to prevent scientific scrutiny of some aspects of its operations. Similarly, in a truly Islamic society, the furtherance of scientific literacy can be justified only by reference to the same values that support science itself within that society, i.e. it increases the understandings of the signs of God and hence brings the *ummah*, the worldwide Muslim community, closer to the Creator.[15]

SOME NOTIONS OF SCIENTIFIC LITERACY

It is evident that the arguments referred to above rest upon, or entail, a number of different conceptions of scientific literacy. Arons has described[16] twelve abilities which, in his view, characterize a person who is 'scientifically literate'. Miller has reviewed[17] attempts to measure scientific literacy along the 'three constitutive dimensions' of:

(1) the norms and methods of science;
(2) cognitive science knowledge;
(3) attitudes towards organized science.

These dimensions are evident in the investigation by the National Science Foundation of scientific literacy among adults in the USA in 1979. This combined an understanding of the scientific approach, of basic scientific constructs and of science policy issues into a single measure of public understanding of science. In 1987, Thomas and Durant concluded[18] that much of the existing literature, which is substantial, identifies some or all of the following eight characteristics of scientific literacy:

(1) an appreciation of the nature, aims and general limitations of science; a grasp of the 'scientific approach' (rational arguments, the ability to generalize, systematize and extrapolate) the roles of theory and observation;
(2) an appreciation of the nature, aims and limitations of technology, and of how these differ from those of science;
(3) a knowledge of the way in which science and technology actually work, including the funding of research, the conventions of scientific practices and the relationship between research and development;
(4) an appreciation of the inter-relationships between science, technology and society, including the role of scientists and technicians as experts in society and the structure of relevant decision-making processes;
(5) a general grounding in the language and some of the key constructs of science;
(6) a basic grasp of how to interpret numerical data, especially relating to probability and statistics;
(7) the ability to assimilate and use technical information and the products of

technology; 'user-competence' in relation to technologically-advanced products;

(8) some idea of where and from whom to seek information and advice about matters relating to science and technology.

More recently, Hodson and Reid's outline curriculum 'capable of ensuring scientific literacy' embraced scientific knowledge and its applications, the skills and tactics of science, the interaction of science with technology, the history and development of science and technology, and a study of the 'philosophical and sociological concerns centring on scientific methods, the role and status of scientific theory and the activities of the community of scientists.[19]

SOME MEASURES OF SCIENTIFIC LITERACY

Many studies of scientific literacy among adults have been concerned with attitudes towards, rather than knowledge of, science. Reviewing work undertaken by 1985, The Royal Society observed that 'public attitudes to science appear to be similar in the USA and the United Kingdom' and concluded that the general public 'is interested in science and would like to know more about it; tends to over-estimate the ability of science to solve what are essentially social problems; gives higher funding priority to applied than to fundamental research (though some areas . . . such as astronomy and cosmology, generate great public interest); and, generally, is guardedly supportive of science while being wary of its applications'.

Measures of scientific literacy based upon or incorporating the scientific knowledge possessed by adults have produced results generally regarded as disappointing. In 1979, Miller used a minimally acceptable score on the 'three constitutive dimensions' referred to above as a determinant of scientific literacy among a sample of 1635 adults in the USA. He concluded that 'the overwhelming majority of the American adult population is scientifically *il*literate'.[20] A subsequent American survey revealed that only 19 per cent of a sample of 1992 householders had a 'clear understanding' of how a telephone works and 24 and 31 per cent had a similar degree of understanding of computer software and radiation respectively.[21] In the United Kingdom, a pilot study of 'science and the adult student' in 1986 included questions about the degree of understanding among 259 adults of such concepts as 'gene', 'nuclear fission' and 'polymer'. For each of five concepts, a significant proportion of the respondents to a questionnaire expressed their understanding as having 'little sense' or 'no idea'.[22]

Roberts and Sutton have reported that the recollections of school chemistry by a small group of well-educated adults are 'relatively isolated' and do not amount to 'connected structure of chemical thought'.[23] Lucas's investigation of the understanding of selected biological topics among a representative sample of 1033 adults led to the conclusion that for most of the questions answered 'an education in science improves the knowledge of the adult population', although the effect was 'not much more than an effect of general educational level'. As he pointedly observed, the fact that 'even for the best educated only 70 per cent knew that penicillin affects bacteria, not viruses' has public health implications which 'deserve some thought'.[24]

In reflecting upon some of the above measures of scientific literacy, it is important to acknowledge that adults' understanding of science may be no worse than their understanding of other cultural activities such as history, literature or music. In the present context, however, it is more pertinent to raise the question of whether scientific literacy is being measured by reference to what the scientific community believes should be widely known and appreciated rather than to the scientific knowledge and understanding that adults themselves perceive to be of significance in addressing their everyday concerns. The potential here for mismatch is considerable. Prewitt, for example, reported in 1982 that scientists associated with a National Science Foundation survey were reluctant to probe public understanding of science in terms of such controversial issues as food additives or genetic engineering, preferring instead nitrogen fixation, black holes and plate tectonics.[25] More recently, the general point illustrated by Prewitt's example has been expressed by Ziman[26] in a reference to a 'serious mismatch between the interests of those who are already inside science, and the motives of those whom they would like to draw in'. The expression 'draw in' is, of course, significant since it hints at the root of much contemporary concern about public scientific literacy among the scientific community, namely a perceived apathy, even hostility, towards the scientific endeavour itself.

An alternative approach to estimating scientific literacy based upon the distinction between 'insiders' and 'outsiders' requires identification of the need for, and use of, scientific knowledge among adults, developed in response to particular concerns in a variety of contexts, e.g. safety at work, the siting of a nuclear plant, the care of infants. Implicit in this approach are two related notions. The first is that of a number of distinct, segmented 'publics', differentiated by interest and concern. The second is that of a multiplicity of scientific literacies which are essentially functional and directed towards specific social purposes, e.g. the civic, cultural and practical scientific literacies identified by Shen[27] as well as a wide range of more specific scientific literacies derived from occupational, domestic or recreational contexts. As far as the measurement of scientific literacy is concerned, therefore, any estimation is likely to be most useful when it relates to a particular group of citizens addressing a specific issue of common concern to the groups, e.g. the parents of children suffering from Down's syndrome, local councillors reaching decisions about the disposal or storage of toxic waste, and elderly householders on fixed incomes managing a domestic energy policy.

Although the implication of the notion of science for specific social purposes[28] for the scientific education of adults lie beyond the scope of this article, two important points should be made. Firstly, if scientific literacy is to help to empower citizens engaged with problems having a scientific dimension, then scientific knowledge will need to be structured in ways that relate to the requirements and interests of particular groups of adults. Secondly, the development of the appropriate functional scientific literacy is likely to require novel kinds of institutional provision[29] some of which are likely to be financed by resources not normally associated with formal educational systems. Together, these points make clear that the effective scientific education of adults, or to borrow Fensham's phrase[30] of 'Science for Out-of-School All', cannot be a simple extension of the scientific education provided at school and that the relationship between them, if any, is complex.

DISCUSSION

The above notions of scientific literacy and the arguments used to support them raise a number of difficulties for those with a professional interest in science education at school level. These include the following:

(1) Different advocates may well support significantly different interpretations of scientific literacy or espouse a common interpretation for different reasons. Interpretations and arguments which relate scientific literacy to economic performance, for example, may have more appeal to politicians than advocacy based upon aesthetic or broadly cultural considerations. Likewise, different social contexts impose different priorities upon the various meanings that might be given to scientific literacy. The immediate needs for scientific knowledge of the citizens of China or Bangladesh are unlikely to be the same as those of their fellow citizens of the United Kingdom or USA.

(2) Different interpretations of scientific literacy reflect different value positions. The indiscriminate use of 'scientific literacy' as an educational objective, therefore, may obscure valid and significant differences in the aims attributed to scientific education.

(3) In so far as scientific literacy involves familiarity with scientific ideas or principles, it is necessary to acknowledge that some of these ideas or principles were unknown, or not taught, to adults when they were of school age. Thus, adults over about 35 years of age in the United Kingdom are unlikely to have been taught about lasers, semi-conductors or DNA when they were pupils.

(4) Some of the arguments for greater scientific literacy rest upon, or involve, assumptions that are open to challenge. It does not follow, for example, that a greater 'understanding of science' will engender an increased degree of support for the aims, procedures or outcomes of the scientific enterprise. At best, any approval of science consequent upon greater understanding seems likely to be particular rather than general and to be strongly influenced by extra-scientific considerations. Similarly, any argument that greater scientific literacy will enable citizens in a democracy to improve the quality of policy-making about science-based issues that affect their lives

needs to accommodate the difficulties raised by the studies of the role of scientific expertise in the resolution of contentious issues. Collingridge and Reeve, for example, have concluded that 'whenever science attempts to influence policy, three necessary conditions for efficient scientific research and analysis – autonomy, disciplinarity and a low level of criticism – are immediately broken, leading to endless technical debate rather than the hoped-for consensus which can limit arguments about policy'.[31] The debate over lead in the environment, IQ, and smoking and lung cancer, illustrate the point.

(5) The various characteristics of scientific literacy outlined above 'amount to a formidable combination of qualities rarely encountered anywhere, even within the expert domains of science and science studies.'[32] The uncritical advocacy of scientific literacy as an educational objective for school science education is likely, therefore, to burden such education with responsibilities it cannot hope to meet.

Scientific literacy is an old, not a new slogan in the history of school science education.[33] If it is to inform developments in such education, other than as a slogan, the multiplicity of meanings attached to it needs to be recognized. In addition, each meaning needs to be described in terms which clarify the attendant value position. Some of these meanings seem more appropriate at some stages of education than others. Also, some relate more directly than others to expertise in the scientific disciplines and, in consequence, might be regarded as more 'internalist', less radical and perhaps even less relevant to the majority of pupils. The multidimensional nature of scientific literacy thus opens up the notion of a 'balanced' science curriculum in a way that has perhaps not received the attention it deserves.

The difficulties associated with this interpretation of balanced science are substantial. The articulation of a balanced school science curriculum with the competences required of scientifically literate adults remains problematic, not least because so little is known about the needs of students or adults for scientific knowledge, and about the ways in which such knowledge is acquired and used. It is also questionable whether a number of different aspects of scientific literacy can be accommodated satisfactorily within the same science curriculum. The values of 'objectivity', appeal to the authority of experiment, and consensus, traditionally encouraged and emphasized by school science courses may not, for example, fit comfortably within the more radical, democratic and perhaps ultimately subversive perspectives required by citizens in challenging science at the points where it impinges most directly upon their everyday concerns and beliefs. This, of course, is but one of the dilemmas associated with courses concerned with 'science, technology and society' and it raises, in an acute form, the question of 'what counts as science education.'[34]

One alternative to the above notion of balance would be the selection of a narrower, more positive and conventional range of meanings of scientific literacy as a determinant of the objectives of school science education. Collectively, such a range might emphasize the profound intellectual achievements and undoubted glories of science as a cultural activity at the expense of what is sometimes referred to as its 'social relations'. If the pedagogical difficulties of this approach are obvious, so, too, is the fact that it runs the risk of ignoring what is known about the nature of the scientific enterprise in a modern, industrialized society. Nonetheless, it is surely the case that no school science education worthy of the name can exclude an introduction to the contemporary scientific understanding of the natural world, and with a judicious selection of content and of modes of presentation, the pedagogical difficulties might not prove to be insuperable.

Finally, it is worth asking 'To what extent will the government's policy statement for science education and the proposed national curriculum derived from it help to develop a scientifically literate citizenry in the twenty-first century?' The preceding paragraphs suggest a far from encouraging answer. Indeed, by reflecting a somewhat narrow, perhaps even untenable view of science, contemporary policy for school science education might be regarded as regressive. It certainly seems unlikely to encourage an initiative such as the Chemical Education for Public Understanding Project (CEPUP) undertaken at the University of California.[35] Yet one aspect of the way forward seems clear. This is an acceptance of a point made in a lecture on 'Science for all', delivered before the Swedenborg Association as long ago as 1847, namely that '. . . the end for which knowledge was sought . . . by the learned, and the end for which it is required by the multitude, are not the same but different ends'.[36]

REFERENCES

1. Hodson, D. and D. J. Reid, 'Science for All – motives, meanings and implications', SSR, 1988, 69, 249, 653–61.
2. Thackray, A., 'Natural knowledge in cultural context: the Manchester model', The American Historical Review, 1974, 79, 672–709.
3. Heyck, T. W., The Transformation of Intellectual Life in Victorian England (Croom Helm, 1982) p. 56.
4. Huggins, Sir W., The Royal Society or, Science in the State and in the Schools (Methuen, 1906) p. 28.
5. Shapin, S. and A. Thackray, 'Prosopography as a research tool in the history of science: The British Scientific Community, 1700–1900.' History of Science, 1974, XIL, 11.
6. Shen, B. S. P. 'Scientific literacy and the public understanding of science', in Day, S. B. (ed.) The Communication of Scientific Information (Basel, Karger, 1975) p. 45.
7. SSR, 1924, 5, 131.
8. Science 5–16: A Statement of Policy (DES, Welsh Office, HMSO, 1985) para 7.
9. The Royal Society, The Public Understanding of Science (The Royal Society, 1985) p. 9.

10. Thomas, G. and J. Durant, 'Why should we promote the public understanding of science?', in Shortland, M. (ed.) *Scientific Literacy Papers* (Oxford Department for External Studies, 1987) pp. 1–14.
11. Asimov, I., *Nature*, 1984, cited in Thomas, G. and J. Durant *op. cit.* 3.
12. Rapoport, A., 'A scientific approach to ethics', *Science*, 1957, 125, 796–9.
13. Weiss, P. 'The message of science', *Bull Atomic Sci*, 1959, XV, 274–7.
14. Jenkins, E. W., *From Armstrong to Nuffield: Studies in Twentieth Century Science Education* (Murray, 1979) p. 56.
15. Sadar, M. H., 'Science and Islam: is there a conflict?' in Sardar, Z. (ed.) *The Touch of Midas: Science, Values and the Environment in Islam and the West* (Manchester University Press, 1984) pp. 23–4.
16. Arons, A. B., 'Achieving wider scientific literacy', *Daedalus*, 1983, 112, 2, 92–3.
17. Miller, J. D., 'Scientific Literacy – a conceptual and empirical review', *ibid.*, 29–48.
18. Thomas, G. and J. Durant, *op. cit.*, 12–13.
19. Hodson, D. and D. J. Reid, *op. cit.*, 658–9.
20. Miller, J. D., *op. cit.*, 41.
21. Miller, J. D., Technological Literacy, some concepts and measures. Paper delivered at the National Technological Literacy Conference, Baltimore, 14 February, 1986.
22. Shortland, M. 'Networks of Attitude and Belief: science and the adult student', in Shortland, M. (ed.), *op. cit.* 37–51.
23. Roberts, W. and C. R. Sutton, ' "Adults" recollections from school chemistry – facts, principles and meaning', *Ed Chem*, May 1984, 82–5.
24. Lucas, A., 'Public knowledge and science policy', *J Biol Ed*, 1987, 21, 1, 41.5.
25. Prewitt, K., 'The public and science policy', *Sci Tech and Human Values*, 1982, 7, 39, 5–14.
26. Ziman, J., *An Introduction to Science Studies: the Philosophical and Social Aspects of Science and Technology* (Cambridge University Press, 1984) pp. 184–5.
27. Shen, B., *op. cit.*, 44–52.
28. Layton, D., A. Davey and E. Jenkins, 'Science for specific social purposes (SSSP): perspectives on adult scientific literacy', *St Sci Ed*, 1986, 13, 27–52.
29. Examples are science shops, study circles, citizens' groups, specialist science- or technology-based clubs, societies, magazines and newletters, museums.
30. Fensham, P. J., *Science for All, a second chance for school systems and a new vision for the population outside of schools*. Paper presented at the Regional meeting on 'Science for All', Bangkok, 1983, p. 42.
31. Collingridge, D. and C. Reeve, *Science Speaks to Power: The Role of Experts in Policy Making* (Frances Pinter, 1986) p. 145.
32. Thomas G. and J. Durant, *op. cit.*, 13.

33. Roberts, D. A., *Scientific Literacy, Towards Balance in Setting Goals for School Science Programs*, (Science Council of Canada, University of Toronto, 1983) Ch. V.
34. Solomon, J. 'The dilemma of science, technology and society education' and Roberts, D. A., 'What counts as science education?', in Fensham, P. (ed.), *Development and Dilemmas in Science Education*, (Falmer, 1988), pp. 266–81 and pp. 27–54.
35. Chemical Education for Public Understanding Project, Lawrence Hall of Science, University of California at Berkeley. For a curriculum project concerned with scientific literacy, see *Project 2061, Science for All Americans*, (AAAS, 1989).
36. Wilkinson, J. J. Garth, *Science for All: a lecture delivered before the Swedenborg Association, 25 March 1847* (London) (William Newberry, 1847) p. 3.

4.3

Public understanding of science: from contents to processes

Robin Millar and Brian Wynne

INTRODUCTION

Only a small minority of the pupils who study science at school will go on to pursue science as a career, or even to follow a science-related leisure interest. For the remainder, school science is simply a part of general education. One major part of the justification for a policy of 'science for all' is in terms of the need, in an advanced technology-based democracy, for wider public knowledge and 'understanding' of science. In this article we argue that the conventional view of 'public understanding' of science – in terms of the public's level of knowledge about the *contents* of science – may be an unhelpful guide to improved science education practice. Instead, we want to suggest that it may be more useful to think in terms of public understanding of the *processes* by which scientific knowledge is obtained and validated. The correspondence or inconsistency between public experience of science in everyday life and this previous experience of science in school deserves to be more carefully examined.

Rather than argue this case in the introduction, we want to develop it through a detailed case study of the media reporting the Chernobyl nuclear reactor accident in April 1986. As much of this article is taken up with discussion of the details of the reporting of Chernobyl, it is important to emphasize again that the question we want to raise is not principally about Chernobyl, or even about nuclear power, but rather about what we might mean by 'the public understanding of science'.

A DEFICIT VIEW

A conventional approach to the 'public understanding' problem (reflected, for example, in the Royal Society's Report on *The Public Understanding of Science* (1985), and in much of the literature of risk perception) is that it is a problem of getting the public to understand the contents of science. Fremlin (1985), for example, has lamented that:

From *International Journal of Science Education* (1988), Vol. 10, no. 4, pp. 388–98.

It is an extraordinary feature of the long and healthy lives that we now enjoy, that we are worrying more about the dangers of the abundant energy supplies that have made their advantages possible, than we do about the enormously greater and potentially controllable hazards such as those arising from the ordinary things that we eat and drink and breathe. This is not due to public stupidity, but to ignorance fed with well-meant misinformation by ill-informed media avid for the frightening and the horrible.

(Preface, p. x)

Thus, if only the public was properly informed and 'understood' science better people would have a more positive view of what scientists say and do, and this would be reflected in wider popular support (and more generous public funding). Where specific technological applications of science are concerned there is a baseline of scientific knowledge, for example, of how a nuclear reactor works, or of the toxic risks of certain pesticides or food additives. The public have variable deficits of this technical knowledge and some deficits are pathologically large. The further implication of this dominant view is that if we could reduce these deficits of understanding, the public would react more 'maturely' to these things in everyday life, making government and industrial planning more stable and predictable (Wynne 1988).

Recently Lucas (1987, 1988) has explored science knowledge deficits by direct interview methods, and reports that many members of the public (at least when questioned in the street or on their doorsteps about isolated scientific facts) are unable to provide scientifically 'correct' answers to apparently simple questions. Thus he finds, for example, low levels of general understanding of the term 'radioactivity' and widespread lack of clarity about the periods of time for which radioactive wastes might continue to be hazardous. Turning specifically to the Chernobyl accident, analyses of reports in British and Dutch newspapers (Eijkelhof *et al.* 1987, Eijkelhof and Lijnse 1987, Eijkelhof and Millar 1988) have shown that the reporting of Chernobyl shows some important differences between 'lay' and 'expert' deficit terms. In particular, the different ideas of *radiation* and *radioactive material* appear to be largely undifferentiated in the lay model and this may be of some significance for science education and for public understanding of energy policy issues.

However, we want to argue here that we can learn from the reporting of Chernobyl a perhaps more important lesson about the public perception of the nature of scientific knowledge. Our main point is that public understanding of 'internal' scientific and technological processes is just as important as understanding their content; that it may be more salient to perceive public understanding of science in terms of the understanding that the general public has of what sort of knowledge science is, and what its possibilities and limitations are. Too often in real life, a specific scientific 'truth' is directly contradicted by other scientists, leaving people no means of judging between claims. We suspect that an implicit 'political model' of scientific processes comes into play, allowing evaluation according to judgements of who is paying which scientist's wages, for example. Although this may be a necessary component in lay evaluation, it is too crude and simplistic to do justice to the full complexity of the ways in which scientific observations become translated and amplified into claims of public knowledge.

In particular, we want to argue that it is unhelpful to portray scientific practice as the following of a 'method' or a set of rules of procedure. We do not want to argue this in abstract philosophical terms (of a 'proper' understanding of the processes of science and technology) but on the very pragmatic and practical grounds that it leads to unrealistic expectations and to public disorientation when any unexpected incident occurs. Our view would be that normal scientific and technological practice, that which we would consider to be competent and responsible, is less rule-bound and controlled and orderly than is usually acknowledged and that this needs to be more widely and thoroughly acknowledged and understood. Unfortunately, however, as we will see later, much of school science education tends, either implicitly or explicitly, to promote a more rule-bound view of scientific method.

With that in mind, let us turn now to specific aspects of how the Chernobyl incident was reported. We shall take our examples from the British media, as that is the source to which we have most complete access. We would suggest, however, that the general features to which we will draw attention are much more widespread, and would point to the Dutch newspaper analysis referred to above and the more general analysis of print media in Europe following the Chernobyl accident (Otway *et al.* 1987) to support this view. Similarly, if our analysis is accepted, its implications for science education are general ones.

PUBLIC QUESTIONS AND EXPERT ANSWERS

In the first week following the reactor explosion at Chernobyl [in April 1986], reports in newspapers and on television concentrated on providing details of the damage to the reactor and speculation about the effects on the local population, liberally laced with political points-scoring about the shortage of information provided by the Soviet authorities about the incident. Its practical implications for the UK were consistently portrayed as small. Under the headline 'Britain is *safe*', the *Daily Mirror* (30/4, 3) reported: 'Britain has *escaped* the radiation cloud.' 'There have been *no* increases in radioactivity in this country.' 'There was "*no* present danger".' 'There are *no* stations like it in the West' [our emphases]. Another article in the same issue (p. 6) by the Foreign Editor, presented in question-and-answer format, is similarly clearcut in its information:

Q: Will there be any effect at all in Britain?
A: None whatsoever. We are absolutely safe.

Over the weekend of 3 and 4 May, however, more than one week after the initial explosion, a change in the wind direction over Europe carried the cloud of radioactive debris across Britain. During this period, it rained heavily in some parts of the country, particularly in North Wales, Cumbria and Scotland.

Anxieties about levels of radioactivity in water, grass and milk began to grow. Reassurance continued to be couched in unequivocal terms. Having reported 'higher than normal radiation levels' at various sites in England, the *Daily Mirror* qualifies this by saying that they were described as 'very low' and pose no danger to health. Last night the National Radiological Protection Board [NRPB] said: 'People will not be placed at risk' (3/5, 1).

Front page headlines on 7 May in the *Guardian* state: 'There is no health risk'; and in *The Times*: 'No risk in Britain, Baker tells MPs.' *The Times* article went on to quote Kenneth Baker, the then Secretary of State for the Environment, as saying that there had been an increase over the weekend in the 'normal background radiation' but 'the levels found were nowhere near the levels at which there is any hazard to health'. Indeed, a general feature of the treatment of low-level radiation risks in articles throughout the period is the notion, within the lay view, of a 'safe level' of radioactive contamination below which there is no health risk. Although there was considerable dispute about actual measured levels of various isotopes and of the appropriate safety standards to compare these with, the discussion is characteristically premised on the view that below a certain safe level, determined (presumably) by experiment and endorsed by national or international regulatory bodies, there is no risk to individuals. Only above this level does action need to be taken.

By this stage in the Chernobyl aftermath, however, a clear tension had begun to emerge between public (and political) demands for clear-cut and unequivocal statements and the more qualified information that scientists could provide. On the one hand, *The Times* front page lead article on 6 May contained the following extract:

> Confusion and concern over safety was increased yesterday when people living in Scotland, north-west England and north Wales were advised not to drink fresh rainwater continuously for the next week. The warning came from the National Radiological Protection Board, which was monitoring radiation levels . . . The effect on mains, streams and well water was 'insignificant', it said. But it added that while drinking fresh rainwater over two or three days presented no significant health hazard 'it would be desirable to avoid drinking it continuously for the next week.'

Terms like 'no effect' and 'no danger' have now been replaced by 'insignificant' and 'no significant health hazard'. A *Guardian* front page report (6/5, 1) provides similarly qualified information:

> The NRPB said that . . . increases in iodine levels in milk could be expected in areas which had heavy rainfall. The danger level of iodine in milk is expressed as 2000 becquerels per litre. In some areas of the north-west of England milk samples reached 270 bq per litre and in Caithness, in Scotland, iodine had reached 200 per litre. Other radioactivity added another 50 per cent to this.

On the other hand, the *Sun* had begun its 'Nuclear Hotline', providing two telephone numbers that anxious readers could phone for advice. The questions they are reported as asking include: 'Can babies have milk? Can we eat a lettuce? Is my pet in danger?' (8/5, 4); 'Is it dangerous if your washing is drenched in the rain? Should the clothes be rewashed?' (9/5, 10). A similar set of readers' questions is answered in the *Daily Mirror* of 10 May (4). These include: 'Is it safe to drink water? Can we drink milk? Should I give my childen iodine tablets?' Demands for information at the same specific and local level are reported in a *Sunday Times* article (18/5, 9) which tells of a local Greenpeace organizer in mid-Wales reporting that:

> her phone had been jammed with calls from anxious mothers wanting to know whether the water was safe. 'I have also had calls asking if it is safe for children to play outside. One old lady inquired if she should put her cats down because they had spent three days out in the rain and another lady asked if it was safe to eat eggs laid by her chickens which had been in the rain.'

What we have then is clear evidence of a public demand and expectation for clear-cut, black and white answers from experts to direct and specific questions. Even questions about risks appear to seek straightforward yes/no, safe/unsafe answers. Scientific answers, in contrast to this, are qualified and complex, more extensive data is given, often of a quantitative kind, risks are stochastic rather than simply present or absent. In short, lay perceptions of what it is possible for experts to provide by way of answer or information differ from the experts' own view. The suggestion that it might be impossible to produce trustworthy knowledge of what is happening, and what to do (at the necessary level of resolution down to the scale of individual lives and daily practices), appears to be far from public minds.

RISK AND REASSURANCE

There can also be important differences of perception about what counts as reassurance. One expert pronouncement, intended as reassuring but couched in scientific language, reverberated through the media discussion for several days. The *Daily Mirror* (7/5, 2) reported it under the banner headline: 'A-leak "may kill some Britons". Dozens at risk, say scientist.'

> Some people in Britain may die of cancer because of the Russian nuclear disaster, an expert warned yesterday. He said the number might be 'a few tens' out of the millions expected to die from cancer in Britain during the next 50 years. The expert, John Dunster, of the National Radiological Protection Board, added that there would be no way of knowing which people developed cancer because of the Russian radiation cloud. Mr Dunster gave his warnings as the government tried to calm public fears about the health threat.

Reporting the same statement, the *Daily Telegraph* (7/5, 1) adds that Mr Dunster said: 'The extent of our knowledge is still very limited. An informed guess suggests that the eventual number of cancer deaths might be a few tens over 50 years.'

If we see this as an attempt to provide a piece of properly-qualified scientific information as reassurance, two points about the public reaction to it are worth commenting on. The first is to note that the presentation of such information cannot be entirely value-free. It is clear that there are, in this case, at least two ways of presenting the same 'scientific fact' and that these produce very different public reactions. To say that there will be 'a few tens of cancer deaths over 50 years' is, in terms of public response and impact, a very different statement from that used in the House of Commons by Kenneth Baker to paraphrase Dunster's statement. He is reported (*Daily Telegraph* 7/5, 12) as saying that 'the total exposure will result in a very small additional risk to any one person'. The second point concerns the lay view of scientific knowledge and precision. In an interview on the *Today* programme on BBC Radio 4 on 7 May 1986, Sir Hugh Rossi MP (the Chairman of the Commons Select Committee on the Environment which had just produced a report on the disposal of nuclear waste) was questioned about Dunster's statement. He replied:

> I did have a quick look at Mr. Dunster's statement and I must say, it's qualified very heavily, loaded with expression such as 'our limited knowledge' 'the best guess we can make' 'estimates of' and then he comes out with some firm figures. How he can come up with firm figures and give a number of the people likely to die of cancer . . . over a period of time is difficult to see, when he admits that he's just making the best guesses possible.

From this lay perspective, which is surely widely shared, science is, by implication, the opposite of 'limited'; data is not simply a 'best guess' or an 'estimate'; firm figures represent some kind of certainty. Yet, in fact, Dunster's projected figures, based on extrapolation from current best data, are typical of much scientific data in every field and are characteristic of almost all the available data in a field like radiation risk and radiation protection.

THE NUMBERS GAME

One feature of the brief account above of the growing public concern and the expert response to it is the way that initially qualitative accounts gradually gave way to increasingly quantitative versions. The demand for 'openness' comes to entail access to more detailed data. In a parliamentary encounter (*The Times* 7/5, 4), Dr. John Cunningham (the Labour Party's Environmental spokesman) is reported as complaining that

> the Secretary of State had not been specific about the nature and level of radioactivity involved. The public, he contended, was entitled to have these facts. Mr. Baker agreed that the public should be given explicit, frank and open information. He indicated he had asked the National Radiological Protection Board to make a full statement listing all the information available. This was very technical.

The dilemma faced by politicians and others with the task of communicating technical information to a sceptical public comes across clearly here. It is

250 CHALLENGES AND OPPORTUNITIES FOR SCIENCE EDUCATION

widely recognized that 'People simply do not believe bland statements any longer. Soothing words are no substitute for facts' (Mr. Gordon Wilson MP, quoted in *The Times*, 6/5, 1). What is needed instead are 'some publicly digestible comparisons on radioactivity before and after the Chernobyl incident' (*The Times*, 7/5, 1). Making primary numerical data available has the twin advantages of speed and of appearing to avoid any added 'interpretation'. However, one concomitant of the way such data tends to be reported in popular accounts is that it heightens the impression of scientific knowledge as precise and reliable. A *Guardian* report (7/5, 2) states that 'the readings were 225 becquerels a litre, against 220 on Monday', implying significance in the third figure cited. Another report in the same paper (9/5, 2) tells that 'concentrations of iodine 131 in milk were registered at 220 bpl (*sic*), 225 bpl and 125 bpl for May 5, 6 and 7. Goats' milk at Dounreay registered 450 bpl, 357 bpl and 224 bpl.' This is taken as evidence of a decline on the third day, but again three figure accuracy is given. In another article on the same theme, a previously reported value of 440 becquerels per litre (for iodine 131 in milk) is changed to 220, with the throw-away explanation that the earlier figure was due to 'a calibration error' (*The Times* 7/5, 1).

Whilst a figure of 3001 becq/litre (*Guardian* 14/5, 1) may be taken as a misprint, a contour map of contamination across the UK printed in the 25 July issue implies an improbably widespread and extensive set of measurements. The overall effect is to develop an already widely held lay impression that science is necessarily accurate, universal in scope, and capable of precise numerical prediction. That these apparently comprehensive data are more like hypotheses generated by a computer model is not mentioned in public, nor is it appreciated. The 'openness' issue comes to be seen primarily in terms of public *access* to data, not to the difficulties of producing authoritative knowledge in such situations. Such data, if provided, are seen as able, in principle, to inform decisions and actions, even at the local and everyday level of individuals' lives.

Within such a model of scientific knowledge and practice, disagreements between monitored data from different sources become difficult to interpret, other than in terms of bias or incompetence. Divergences between the data and interpretations of, on the one hand, pressure groups (such as Friends of the Earth and Greenpeace) and on the other, the official sources are attributed to bias; those between different official agencies, such as the Department of Agriculture, the Department of the Environment, the Scottish and Welsh Offices, the Department of Health and Social Security and the National Radiological Protection Board, to incompetence. The implication (as seen, perhaps, in *The Times* editorial of 7 May 1986 which castigates the ministers concerned for their lack of co-ordination of information, or the *Daily Telegraph*'s (7/5, 19) talk of 'the big muddle') is that data needs to be co-ordinated and harmonized to avoid confusing the public. Only in a handful of the more reflective articles in the inner pages of the 'quality' papers, in articles and letters written by scientists or science reporters, is there any suggestion that such conflicts are a product of an inherently messy and inexact measuring process and that the sorts of data that are wanted are, in principle, unobtainable. This idea does not become part of the lay discussion.

OBTAINING SCIENTIFIC DATA

The widespread belief that a personal geiger counter can somehow provide an adequate alternative to a discredited official expert system is all part of the same picture. Local authorities, environmental health officers, environmental groups and individuals bought their own geiger counters in the expectation of producing their own 'scientific' knowledge of radiation hazards. Some schools and teachers achieved media coverage (at both local and national level) for what amounted to pointing the school's geiger counter out of a window, or at a patch of grass or pool of rainwater and recording count-rates over a period of days (*Yorkshire Evening Post* 8/5, 7; *New Scientist* 12/6, 57–8). All this activity embodies the belief that generating scientific data is straightforward, and that universally transferable facts can be produced by instant observations, without the need for painstaking calibration, extensive piloting of sampling (which still remains uncertain), extrapolation and interpolation based on unverified or only partly verified assumptions and theoretical models, negotiation over relevant observations, techniques, classification and frameworks and extensive interpretative intervention in shaping the 'information' into meaningful forms for diverse audiences. In short, the conversion of measurements into data and then into useful technical knowledge is not as simple as that. Clearly, many people believe that science is rather simple, at least in the sense that the rules are clear, and that if one follows them (which of course requires competence) the automatic result is valid, universal scientific knowledge.

SCIENCE EDUCATION AND THE PUBLIC UNDERSTANDING OF SCIENCE

We outlined a case in the introduction to this article for the need to perceive the public understanding of science at least as much in terms of public perceptions of the internal processes of science and technology as of their contents. The public reaction to the Chernobyl incident illustrates, from a single case study, the barrier to public understanding that a widely shared 'naive' view of science constitutes. We argue that this neglected dimension of public education is at least as important – and, in its present form, damaging – as that to do with *contents* of scientific knowledge. If this is the case, what are its implications for science education?

Public understanding of many areas of science is an outcome of both formal and informal educational inputs. The only realistic way, however, to promote the kind of change required in the public perception of scientific knowledge and of the processes by which it is produced is through formal science education. The central point we are arguing is that there is at least as great a need for wider public understanding of the internal processes by which scientific knowledge is generated and validated as of the contents of specific areas of science. It might appear that the time is particularly opportune, in the UK at least, for making such a case. The Department of Education and Science *Statement of Policy* for science from ages 5 to 16 (DES 1985) argues that 'the major contribution of science to education is in teaching the methods of science'. The problem is that the dominant view of the 'methods of science' within the science education community, which the *Statement of Policy* both encapsulates and endorses, is entirely inimical to what we are proposing. Looked at in more detail, it emerges as a rather naive rule-bound view of an inductive science method, proceeding from observation, via classification to the identification of regularity, followed by experimental testing of hypotheses and inferences. The method of science has become an algorithm. It is a view that is at odds with all 'expert' accounts of scientific method (Millar and Driver 1987), and indeed we would argue, with regular public experience of science in policy practice.

The problems that such a framework poses for public understanding of scientific and technological issues and controversies have been noted elsewhere (Collins and Shapin 1986, Millar 1987). Our analysis of the media treatment of Chernobyl adds further weight to this. We cannot hope to promote better public understanding of science simply by tagging an STS dimension on to a mainstream syllabus that portrays scientific knowledge as 'truth' unproblematically revealed by observation and confirmed by experiment. The necessary change is more radical than that. In effect, it is to replace an image of the internal processes of science as uniform rule-following with a perspective in which doing science is seen as the practice of a craft – based on a foundation of communicable skills but also containing significant tacit elements that cannot be fully articulated or directly taught.

In general terms, this would imply a move away from a naive 'process' view of science, and from the reductionist approach to practical work and its assessment that this promotes (Woolnough 1988). As regards specific curriculum developments, historical case studies may have a role to play though their limitations also need to be recognized. It is, for example, all too easy to portray a historical controversy (or to have learners perceive its message) as steady progress towards 'truth' through the elimination of error. It is often difficult to give equal weight to the views and perspectives of people who held and propounded theories that we no longer accept. Specific strategies are needed to overcome, at least partially, this imbalance. A Dutch PLON teaching unit for pre-university level students, *Physics around 1900*, lets groups of students focus initially on the evidence either for the particle or for the wave interpretation of cathode rays, encouraging them to enter more fully into the nineteenth century controversies and to consider the role of experimental evidence in resolving them (PLON 1985). Burdett (1982) has used role-play and simulation of historical controversies in science, such as the N-rays affair, to get students more imaginatively involved in the detail of the case. Although developed using historical materials, these sorts of approaches could apply equally well to contemporary case studies of controversies involving applications of science, where the focus is on expert disagreement and the role of experimental evidence in reaching a resolution.

An alternative to case studies, whether historical or contemporary, is to look more directly at how experiment can be used in the classroom to resolve uncertainties and to make theory choices. Collins and Shapin (1986) have suggested that:

> the very *disorganisation* of the discovery method of teaching . . . has heuristic value seen from this point of view. The student can be shown why there is disagreement and disorganisation when experts are asked to comment upon matters at the limit of their expertise. Demonstrating this becomes the point of the discovery method. (p. 76)

Something of this sort may be possible but would certainly not be easy to manage. Atkinson and Delamont (1976) have shown very clearly how difficult it is for the teacher to stage-manage the 'discovery' of knowledge by students who realize that the teacher already knows the information and ideas that they are supposed to be 'discovering'. For this reason, there may be greater opportunity in topics where there is genuine current uncertainty, provided that the experimental work is technically feasible in a school. Two examples are the role of the apex (the 'tip') in the phototropic and geotropic responses of plants (see Millar 1985, 1987), and the relative rates of freezing of hot and cold water (the so-called Mpemba effect) (Mpemba and Osborne 1969, Osborne 1979). In both of these cases the points at issue can be readily grasped by school pupils, experimental work is possible in a school setting and the outcome is genuinely open. It is unlikely that school experiments could ever resolve the uncertainty around these issues, but that is just the point. The work can be used to raise and explore questions about the limitations of experiment in determining the 'facts' of the matter.

Both case study and innovative approaches to classroom experiment can be used to explore the interplay between situation-specific and universal factors that are built into scientific knowledge. Scientists can *never* be certain that they have identified the most relevant parameters and properties in designing controlled observation of nature. This insight needs to underpin and complement the more specific (and indeed esoteric) questions of precisely how they manage, in specific experiments, to exclude some variables and incorporate others. Understanding the *intrinsically* limited nature of even the most exquisitely designed scientific experiment or observation has far-reaching implications for a democratic society's mature integration of science and technology.

None of the approaches suggested above has been fully developed or evaluated, so these can be no more than pointers to possible lines of development. We would propose that more emphasis be given to educational developments of this sort. For the message for science education from the public reaction to Chernobyl is, perhaps, that the image that we present of science in the classroom is more than simply a matter of taste or of fine academic distinction about the 'method of science', but may have far-reaching implications for the real world of science policy and democratic decision-making.

REFERENCES

Atkinson, P. and Delamont, S. 1976, Mock-ups and cock-ups: the stage-management of guided discovery instruction. In P. Woods and M. Hammersley (eds.), *School Experience: Explorations in the Sociology of Education*. Croom Helm, London.

Burdett, P. 1982, *Misconceptions, mistakes and misunderstandings: learning about the tactics and strategy of science by simulation*. MA thesis, Institute of Education, University of London.

Collins, H. M. and Shapin, S. 1986, Uncovering the Nature of Science. In J. Brown, A. Cooper, T. Horton, F. Toates and D. Zeldin (eds), *Science in Schools*, Open University Press, Milton Keynes.

Department of Education and Science (DES) 1985, *Science 5–16: a Statement of Policy* HMSO, London.

Eijkelhof, H. M. C., Klaassen, K., Scholte, R. and Lijnse, P. L. 1987, Public and pupils' ideas about radiation: some lessons from Chernobyl to science educators. Paper presented at the 5th International Conference on World Trends in Science Education, Kiel, FRG, August, 1987.

Eijkelhof, M. C. and Lijnse, P. L. 1987, Denkbeelden over radioactiviteit in de berichtgeving over Tsjernobyl. *Tijdschrift voor Didaktiek der β-wetenschappen*, Vol. 5, no. 1, pp. 16–29.

Eijkelhof, H. M. C. and Millar, R. 1988, Reading about Chernobyl: the public understanding of radiation and radioactivity. *School Science Review*, Vol. 70, no. 251, pp. 35–41.

Fremlin, J. H. 1985, *Power Production: What are the Risks?* Adam Hilger, Bristol.

Lucas, A. M. 1987, Public knowledge of radiation. *Biologist*, Vol. 34, pp. 125–9.

Lucas, A. M. 1988, Public knowledge of elementary physics. *Physics Education*, Vol. 23, pp. 10–16.

Millar, R. 1985, Bending the evidence: Teachers' reaction to 'difficult' experiments. Paper presented at the British Society for the History of Science Conference, 'The Uses of Experiment', Bath, Sept. 1985.

Millar, R. 1987, Towards a role for experiment in the science teaching laboratory. *Studies in Science Education*, Vol. 14, pp. 109–118.

Millar, R. and Driver, R. 1987, Beyond processes. *Studies in Science Education*, Vol. 14, pp. 33–62.

Mpemba, E. B. and Osborne, D. G. 1969, Cool? *Physics Education*, Vol. 4, pp. 172–5 (reprinted in *Physics Education 1979*, Vol. 14, pp. 410–3).

Osborne, D. G. 1979, Mind on ice. *Physics Education*, Vol. 14, pp. 414–7.

Otway, H., Haastrup, P., Cannell, W., Gianitsopoulos, G. and Paruccini, M. 1987, *An analysis of the print media in Europe following the Chernobyl accident*. Commission of the European Communities, Report EUR 11043 EN, Luxembourg.

PLON 1985, *De Natuurkunde van Rond 1900*. Experimental teaching unit for the 5th class VWO PLON, University of Utrecht, Utrecht, in collaboration with the Universities of Amsterdam and Groningen.

The Royal Society 1985, *The Public Understanding of Science*, Royal Society, London.

Woolnough, B. E. 1988, Reductio ad Absurdum? *Physics Education*, Vol. 23, pp. 1–2.

Wynne, B. E. 1988, Unruly technology: practical rules, impractical discourses and public understanding. *Social Studies of Science*, Vol. 18, pp. 147–67.

4.4

The overselling of science education in the eighties

Bryan Chapman

J.K. Galbraith has made a distinction between 'institutional truth' and reality.[1] Institutional truth is 'what serves the needs and purposes of the large and socially pervasive institutions that increasingly dominate modern life'. As examples he cited the 'institutional truth' about Russian imperialism which (up till now!) has had to be accepted before employment with the Pentagon could be contemplated; the 'institutional truth' of the financial world that 'the pursuit of money by whatever design within the law is always benign' before a graduate could be accepted for employment on Wall Street;[2] a total belief in the curative power of bran-filled breakfast foods before joining Kellogg's, not to mention the fundamentalist fervour demanded of potential employees of the Coca-Cola Corporation. It goes without saying that, at the end of his damning indictment of 'institutional truths', he urged the graduands, against all preferment and advancement logic, to choose reality.

Of course, institutional truths do change dramatically. No one was more adept at securing such changes than the previous Secretary of State of Education. Kenneth Baker's confidence that he had got it right ensured that to succeed one had to believe, or accept, the 'institutional truth' that state education was a shambles and that teachers were incompetent; HMI reports in the late seventies and early eighties that 25% of teaching left something to be desired were cited as providing confirmation of this state of affairs.[3] By the time he left office a new 'institutional truth' was in place. The 1988–9 HMI survey of standards,[4] which actually reported much the same state of affairs, was now cited by government as providing instant evidence of the effectiveness of its educational reforms. The 'institutional truth' then became that three-quarters of schools were doing well! Clearly TVEI and GCSE have had a 'road to Damascus' impact on educational practice. Or perhaps it is the revelation of good practice provided by the SEAC and the NCC which has transformed teachers into National Curriculum Postman Pats? Other 'institutional truths'

From *School Science Review*, (1991) Vol. 72, no. 260, pp. 47–63.

that now have to be embraced by anyone seeking preferment or advancement include the value of industrial experience; the importance of education for entrepreneurship; the overriding importance of record keeping and assessment; progression; and that the educational needs of all children are identical and therefore they all have to jump through the same curriculum hoops. Woe betide those who have a different view of reality.

One 'institutional truth' embodied in the National Curriculum is that 'science' is so important that all future citizens should have it delivered to them throughout all their years of compulsory schooling. Quantitatively, education in the sciences is now twice as important as either literacy or numeracy. Whether the ability to measure windspeed; to describe how a microphone works; to name the major organs of flowering plants; to give a simple explanation of electrolysis or any other of the many 'trivial pursuits' enshrined in law, actually justifies this position of supremacy does seem open to question. Does this 'naming of parts' approach to learning science have any connection with the reality of doing science? Or is conforming to the 'institutional truth' of the National Curriculum all that now matters? The ASE, as an institution, clearly gains from embracing, indeed promulgating, this truth. It has, after all, been handed a monopoly share of the curriculum market by a government otherwise committed to the ideology of a free-market. For whose benefit is science being made compulsory, anyway? Is it the individual child who is expected to benefit from this science, or society? The logic of the labour market suggests that if the policy is only moderately successful we will have far more scientific and technologically competent young people than that market needs. Economically aware young people will be well able to draw their own career conclusions about this. Indeed, even without the National Curriculum, they already are.

Evangelical enthusiasm for science is not new. In 1854 Herbert Spanner posed the question 'What knowledge is of most worth?' His answer:

For direct self-preservation, or the maintenance of life and health, the all important knowledge is – Science. For that indirect self preservation which we call gaining a livelihood, the knowledge of greatest value is – Science, for the due discharge of parental functions, the proper guide is to be found only in – Science. For that interpretation of national life, past and present, without which the citizen cannot rightly regulate his conduct, the indispensable key is – Science. Alive for the most perfect production and present enjoyment of art in all its forms, the need for preparation is still – Science, and for the purpose of discipline – intellectual, moral, religious – the most efficient study is, once more – Science.

(*Education: Intellectual, Moral and Physical*)

Twelve years before this George Stephenson had, in his lectures to Mechanics Institutes, been warning that British Industry was in danger of falling behind its competitors. His successors are still saying more or less the same thing, ever more stridently.[5] Sir George Porter, showing his frustration one hundred and fifty years on, has asked: 'Should we not force science down the throats of those that have no taste for it? Is it not our duty to drag them into the twentieth century?' His rhetorical answer: 'I'm afraid that it is'.[6]

But is he right? It is after all the twenty-first century for which today's young people are being educated, not the twentieth century. Whether the educational priorities of what, for most young people, will be a post-industrial society really require such an emphasis on science as exists in the National Curriculum is, to put it at its mildest, debatable.

How is it that science education has become a core element of the National Curriculum? Stuart Sexton, one-time education adviser to Sir Keith Joseph and now Director of the Education Unit of the Institute of Economic Affairs, has argued that the statutory assessments associated with the 1988 Act should have been confined to 'an assessment of the child's achievement in literacy and numer-acy'.[7] He went on to affirm that it was self evident that there is more to education than these 'but that all such (other) aspects of education should be subject to constant external, statutory assessment seems to me to be nonsense'. It seems clear from this that a less prescriptive view of education would have prevailed had not Sir Keith been 'retired'.

It is arguable that the role of science education in schools has been grossly oversold over the last decade. The claims made for it have been of a proselytiz-ing nature owing more to politics than to argument. Does everyone need science education through to 16+? Will it make any difference to this country's future economic performance? Will young people be happier because, for example, they 'understand pyramids of numbers and biomass', are able to 'use bistable circuits', and 'know that things can be moved by pushing them'? Just what is it about science – or any other subject for that matter – that makes it so necessary to prescribe in such detail what should be taught and how long it should take to teach it?

THE CLAIMS FOR COMPULSORY SCIENCE EDUCATION SCRUTINIZED

That the sciences are, or can be made to be, of direct employment relevance to young people

At best this claim only applies to the small, and reducing, percentage of young people going into employment requiring scientific knowledge or skills. Such employment is extremely vulnerable to deskilling through automation. Within this group the numbers who have to use their scientific knowledge, as distinct from operating technology based on that knowledge, are minimal.[8] Can the compulsory study of any subject be justified on the grounds that a minority may eventually find some aspect of it relevant to their employment? If so, why not compulsory ballet classes?

That industry requires scientifically competent school leavers

When potential employers complain that school leavers lack employment skills, it should not be assumed that those skills are scientific or, for that matter, technological in character. Early in 1990, at yet another conference concerned with the demographic skills crisis facing British Industry the Director-General of the government's Training agency acknowledged that 75% of the growth of employment forecast for the current decade would be in management and the professions followed by construction, leisure and tourism. Unless manufacturing industry is able to compete £ for £ and perk for perk with the burgeoning financial sector for the services of able young people it will be whistling in the wind no matter what we teach in our schools.[9] In any case, surveys of employers' requirements of school leavers consistently place personal qualities and basic numeracy and literacy way above any specific subject requirements. If a science qualification is demanded it is much more likely to be for reasons of selection rather than content. If this is so, it follows that the more young people who gain such a qualification the less its selection value becomes.

That compulsory sciences will lead to increased uptake of science subjects at A-level which will, in turn, lead to an increased output of scientifically and technologically qualified graduates entering industry

This claim is unproven; SCISP [Schools Council Integrated Science Project], in all the years it operated, did not result in such an increase. Early claims for the newer double certification schemes have to be seen against a background of other changes related to the introduction of GCSE. HMI report[10] that, so far, the introduction of Balanced Science has, even in those schools where it is well-established, only led to 'a modest increase in the proportion of pupils going on to study A-level science courses'. Given the increase in uptake of 'balanced science' courses that coincided with the introduction of GCSE, the 1990 A-level results would appear to confirm this minimal influence.[11]

The 'institutional truth' about GCSE is not just that standards have been maintained but that they have actually been raised. The increase in the number of top grades awarded has been cited as evidence of this. An alternative interpretation of these figures is that 'grade inflation' has taken place and the 16+ educational currency devalued. Since the pattern of 1990 A-level results matches that of previous years, the latter interpretation is the more credible. Should changes in 16–19 science education go the same way, there is a very real prospect that, despite the rhetoric, A-level standards at the end of this decade will be roughly equivalent to those of O-level two decades earlier. Reducing standards to increase access may be necessary if the numbers entering higher education are to be increased; pretending that it is not a reduction, but just different, is not. The apologists for this new 'equal but different' institutional truth are already at work.[12]

But are A-level numbers the real problem? Young people appear far more aware of the graduate job market than previous generations ever were. Indeed, it has recently been suggested that the middle class has never been enamoured with science and technology.[13] Even if science A-levels are taken, automatic progression on to engineering/science/technology degree courses can no longer be assumed. In a competitive market, where the single most important reason for staying on in post-compulsory education has become the career prospects it delivers, degree courses in Business Studies are attracting an increasing number of students with A-level science qualifications. At graduate level the fall-out continues. A 1989 *Daily Telegraph* poll of undergraduates indicated that careers in science and engineering are not considered prestigious, even amongst those studying science and engineering. The number of engineers who, on graduating, do not take up careers in engineering would appear to put the problem of retaining teachers in teaching into the shade.[14] Forcing science and technology on all children will do nothing to change this. Conversely, if such careers were deemed prestigious, curriculum change would be irrelevant to their uptake. We may bemoan the insatiable demand for graduate accountants; but they are clearly what the free market wants and values accordingly. It is doubtful if either the curriculum or the teaching methods adopted in delivering accountancy training are significant factors in the career choices graduates eventually make. For example, how many members of today's science education establishment would have made the same career choice had they come onto the graduate labour market with ten years of free-market entrepreneurial indoctrination behind them? So successful has that indoctrination been that, according to another 1989 poll by MORI, some 40% of today's undergraduates have an active interest in setting up their own businesses when they qualify. Given the high-risk capital outlay required, few such businesses are likely to have a significant scientific or high-technology component. It will be the service sector that benefits from this indoctrination.

The continued, ever more strident, complaints of industrialists that we do not produce enough qualified engineers, scientists and technologists must also be seen in the context of rapidly changing employment patterns throughout the developed world. The 1989 OECD Employment Outlook survey noted that all its member states were experiencing a move away from manufacturing into service employment. Only in the US (11.1%) is the proportion of the workforce engaged in finance, insurance, real estate and business services higher than in the UK (10.6%) and our rate of increase is greater. Given the rewards accruing in this sector, scientists and technologists are as likely to be found there as anyone else. It may be that we do not need to train more engineers, scientists and technologists: all we have to do is to ensure that those we do train do not migrate into careers which are perceived as offering better prospects than engineering or science. If the business and financial sector pays better, offers more security, more perks, better career structures, better provision for mothers and married women returnees, than do industries employing scientists and engineers, then the remarkable thing is not that so few of our brightest young people are being attracted into [science and technology] but that so many, despite everything, continue to study them. Finding a solution to this problem, assuming it is a problem, has virtually nothing to do with education and almost everything to do with society. But even in Germany and Japan, countries in which, incidentally, a rigorous formal approach to education in the sciences has never prevented the production of creative engineers and technologists in the past, there is a growing trend for their most able graduates to opt for careers in financial and related services rather than engineering and technology. Despite all the rhetoric, the reality is that, globally as well as nationally, careers in engineering, science and technology are beginning to look like second-best options to today's career-conscious, financially aware young people.

The global nature of economic activity and the single European market suggest:

(1) that economies of scale are going to reduce significantly the overall requirement for scientific/technological manpower;
(2) that this manpower will be recruited on a pan-national basis rather than on a national one.

Not only do [these factors] make national concerns for the production of scientists and technologists irrelevant, they also suggest that the best scientists and technologists will, as they always have done, gravitate to where they perceive the opportunities and rewards to be greatest, no matter who educates them. There is nothing new in this except perhaps the focus of migration.[15] Within Europe the high-tech focus seems much more likely to be Rhône-Alpes than M4, with all the implications that will have for R & D in [the UK].

That compulsory education in the sciences will give those taking non-scientific/non-technological degrees a better perception of the science/technology and hence lead to a more favourable commercial/financial environment for scientific/technological enterprises

Two somewhat tenuous reasons advanced for the decline in [the UK's] manufacturing base are:

(1) the lack of engineers and scientists at boardroom level;
(2) boardroom – and financial institutional ignorance of the sciences, leading to an unwillingness to invest in science-based enterprises.

By ensuring that everyone has an education in the sciences to 16+, the 'institutional truth' is that this state of affairs will be changed.

Even if this anti-science/anti-technology bias does exist, it does not follow that a causal relationship exists between it and UK industry's comparative failure to invest in science-based enterprises. It is economically naive of us to believe that industry is about making products; it is about making money.[16] As Galbraith comments 'merger and acquisition mania . . . have on occasion brought to the command of our business enterprises owners who did not know what their newly acquired firms produced' – apart, that is, from returns on capital invested. If returns on investments in services are greater than returns on investments in manufacturing, why make? Japan is in the process of relocating much of its low value-added manufacturing capacity outside Japan, since by doing so, the return on Japanese investment is increased. Reinvestment of Japanese manufacturing profits in Australasian, European and US real estate, *rather than in manufacturing*, should also be noted.[17]

Arguably, it is our governments' ideological unwillingness to underwrite the development of 'near-market' technology – e.g. financing a national fibre optic network or high-speed rail links to the Channel Tunnel – that is the most serious disincentive to industrial investment in science and technology in the UK today. (According to the latest Cabinet Office review, expenditure on civil R & D, which was £4.68 in 1987–9, is set to decline, in real terms, to £4.38 by 1991–2.) France takes a very different view of such investments. Even the United States, which has a very similar ideological stance to the present UK government, has always used its defence procurement budget as a *de facto* state subsidy for commercial non-military exploitation of high-technology products.

That the sciences have a particular role to play in developing technological capability, deemed to be an essential element in the preparation of young people for life in an advanced technological society

Whether education in the sciences is important in developing the 'technological capability' of young people is only worth discussing if the premise behind the statement is accepted. In fact, technological advances reduce rather than increase the overall need for 'technological capability' within society. Washing clothes on the banks of a river required far more 'technological capability' than does the pressing of the correct sequence of buttons on a programmable washing machine. In the 1930s Keynes[18] highlighted the deskilling nature of technology and the impact this would have on employment, long before the advent of the micro-chip. In the electronics industry the need is increasingly for software rather than hardware skills. IBM's 1990 milkround recruitment target was for 200 electronics engineers with software skills but only 10 with hardware expertise. Arguably the formal logic of the classics provides a far better grounding for the disciplined logic of software engineering than does the National Curriculum in Science.

That education in the sciences develops skills which have applications in many other areas of human activities

Claims made for transferable skills are always suspect. Those made on behalf of the sciences are no more – or less – suspect than those made on behalf of many other areas of the curriculum. Furthermore if a skill has general applicability it is clearly illogical to specify an area of experience through which it must be delivered. Instead of referring to scientific skills it would be more accurate to refer to those general human skills which find applications within the sciences. This distinction is important. If the aim of education is to develop process skills – whatever they are – there is no evidence that we need a science curriculum to deliver them. Whether there is any legitimacy to thinking of the

sciences as a collection of skills, given that the nature of science is itself regarded as problematical, is another matter.

That because of the pervasiveness of science and its applications, education in the sciences is a vital element of education for a democratic society

This is the traditional liberal educationalist's claim. Of all claims made for
compulsory science education it is at one and the same time the most appealing
and the weakest. To justify it, it would be necessary to show that those already
educated in the sciences have significantly different – right? – views on societal
issues related to science and technology from their non-scientifically educated
contemporaries. Indeed, some, following Herbert Spencer, would go further
and make claims for science education which extend way beyond science. Only
if we are convinced of the first could the second be a possibility. I am unaware
of any evidence which convinces me that scientists are less likely to have car
crashes, more likely to be concerned about the environment, less prone to
catch AIDS than their non-scientifically educated peers. When a societal issue
does emerge – Chernobyl, ozone layer depletion, environmental degradation,
nuclear/fossil fuel energy production, powerline health hazards etc. – it is
clearly adult, rather than school, scientific education that matters. It is an
educational task that, up to now, public service and independent television has
served well and the majority of the press badly. What the deregulated future
holds in store is another matter; those involved appear deeply pessimistic
about their future. It needs also to be recognized that, outside their own
specialisms, few scientists are any better equipped to make judgements on
scientific matters with which they are unfamiliar than any other intelligent lay
person. Very few scientists are, or indeed aspire to be, scientific polymaths.

That compulsory education in the sciences will encourage more young women to take up careers in engineering, the sciences and technology

The issue of compulsory sciences for girls is, of course, emotionally bound up
with broader gender-related issues. Equality of opportunity should not, however, be confused with identity of opportunity.[19] Whether the 'under-
representation' of women in engineering and the physical sciences arises as a
direct result of them opting out of these subjects at school is questionable. It is,
perhaps, worth observing that career-minded young women are already attracted to the same prestigious business, legal and financially related careers as
are attracting their male contemporaries. One reason for this is that they have
been made aware that many companies in these fields have taken positive
steps, through the provision of career breaks, crèches etc. both to retain them
and provide career progression. With 1992 coming up a Combined Degree in
Business Studies and European language(s) must seem a far better career bet to
young people of both sexes, not just young women, than, say, a degree in
Chemical Engineering.

That an education in the sciences is a vital component of everyone's general education

It is difficult to argue against this one. Kenneth Baker gave as one of his reasons for making science education compulsory that 'all young people should be encouraged to see science as a vital – and enjoyable – part of their cultural heritage'.[20] Splendid sounding. But is there not an almost explicit contradiction between the terms 'encourage' and 'enjoyable' on the one hand and 'compulsion' on the other? And does it really require around 20% of the curriculum to provide this component? After all, godliness only gets 2.5%!

SCIENCE AND TECHNOLOGY: A SYSTEMS APPROACH?

Most of the utilitarian reasons advanced for compulsory science education blur the distinctions between science and technology, and hence scientific and technological education. The fact that there is a close symbiotic relationship between the sciences and many technologies should not be allowed to obscure the essential differences between them. These differences are important on both intellectual and pedagogic grounds. In brief, the sciences, ultimately, are about understanding nature; technologies are about the application of reliable knowledge, some but not all of which has been derived from science. Much traditional science that relates to technology only does so in a post-hoc sense – pulley systems may be explainable scientifically but they were in use long before this explanation existed. Even when scientific understanding does lead to application, as is increasingly the case in areas of high technology, it does not follow that understanding the science of a technology is a necessary prerequisite for applying it. A 1982 *Wireless World* editorial has posed the question 'Engineering – or Dominoes?'[21] Having first reminisced about doing 'interminable experiments on the latent heat of vapourization and the laborious plotting of magnetic fields' in his 1940s school physics course the editor continued:

> It is, it goes without saying, necessary for the modern pupil to have the use of advanced modern equipment . . .. A micro, given the correct data, will do exactly what is expected of it very efficiently . . . but where is the striving? And, without the striving, where is the learning? Is there a danger of producing a great number of people who call themselves electronic engineers but whose knowledge of electronics stops short at an ability to program and an awareness of the cheapest supplier of interfaces?
> The only answer to all these weedy, half-baked questions is that undoubtedly that is exactly what engineers will be like, and quite soon too: there is no reason why they should be any different. It has been said for years that the microprocessor is a component, to be used as any other component. There can be little advantage to a user in knowing the precise details of the internal working of a micro – it can be regarded as a machine which will do its job when asked. It is not necessary to know the finer points of oscilloscope design to use it to its fullest extent: neither is it absolutely necessary to know more than the capabilities and characteristics of a micro, or any other

i c to obtain maximum performance from it. And when the remaining parts of a circuit are also integrated, there will be no pressing need to understand the use of power transistors or passive components, either, unless one has to design the i cs. 'Systems engineering' will be supreme.

We have to recognize that most users of science and most scientists, most of the time, are systems engineers. They do not need to understand the science of which they make use. A surgeon does not have to understand the science of lasers and of fibre optic transmission in order to use them in his/her work; nuclear magnetic resonance does not have to be understood by the technician taking a brain scan; a gardener does not need to understand the chemistry of soil and the biochemistry of plants before taking advantage of the work of horticultural scientists. Sometimes the underlying science of a technology is irrelevant to the practitioner. Nigel Kennedy does not have to understand the physics of a violin in order to make it sing; Steve Davies' skills owe very little to his understanding of Newton's Laws and the Roux brothers' ability to create classic dishes hasn't been gained through studying culinary chemistry.

Perhaps the role of science education as a necessary precursor to a career in engineering and/or technology is less universally important than institutional truth commonly assumes? However, the editorial concludes:

This is not, of course, to say that all engineers will be satisfied without a detailed knowledge of exactly what happens inside the i cs. Perhaps these people will be the originators – the ones who, because they know more of the internal operation, will be able to apply i cs with a greater imagination. But do not decry the simple user of modules: he will know all he needs to know.

In this context the 'simple users of modules' are the technologists who create the deskilling artifacts of modern life. The overwhelming majority of us do not even need to know there are 'modules' in our artifacts, let alone understand them. All we need to be able to do is to read, *and make sense of*, the instruction manual! The inescapable conclusion which follows from this is that, for the vast majority of young people, neither the employment or utilitarian cases for science and technology education have much substance. But then, apart from 'basic literacy and numeracy' is this not true of the other core and foundation subject of the National Curriculum?

The case for 'technology education for all' is probably much stronger than that for science education. (Whether that applies to technology as it appears in the National Curriculum is another matter.) To make progress in the sciences an ever-increasing level of sophisticated and abstract thought is generally deemed necessary. Practical work, no matter how motivating, is of no scientific relevance if the theoretical framework in which it is embedded is not understood. By contrast technological activities are accessible at many levels. Much work can be done on and with circuits without being concerned with, or needing, any theories of electrical conduction; the physics of expansion does not have to be understood before a bimetallic strip can be deployed; an understanding of the quantum mechanics of field effect transistors is not a necessary precursor to the use of calculators stuffed full of them; and a condom worn by, or inserted in, a materials scientist is not made more effective because of his/her knowledge of the elastic properties of polymers. What technologists are concerned about is making use of reliable knowledge. It is learning how to make use of the input/output characteristics of a system that matters, not the science responsible for those characteristics.

This 'systems approach' to the use of reliable knowledge is totally in tune with the Information Technology Society which today's young people are entering. It is, in fact, the way mankind has always operated. Not 'normal science' so much as 'normal technology'. Education *aimed at providing competence in the sciences* only makes sense for those who have the potential and the curiosity to become the originators of the future. Perhaps, for the others, there are more important educational priorities.

SCIENCE EDUCATION, DEMOGRAPHY AND SOCIETY

It is very doubtful if science or, for that matter, technology would have their current high profiles in the National Curriculum if industrialists' continual ringing of alarm bells – crying wolf? – about skill shortages had not been amplified by demographic changes. But the shortfall in the number of young people coming onto the labour market will not just affect manufacturing and technological industries. Every major employer of young people faces the same problem. It is difficult to understand why science and technology education have been singled out as being of particular importance in providing manpower for a society increasingly orientated towards service industries. Even if manufacturing industry has an important wealth-creating role to play in the economy – and even that assumption needs examining – it does not follow that a large skilled workforce will be required to service it. The agricultural industry is perhaps the most dramatic example of this. With an already decimated workforce, its future profitability depends partly on further reducing labour costs through the introduction of even more automation and partly on actually diversifying out of agriculture into such high-technology leisure activities as golf and horse racing.[22] However, if the deployment of robots is taken as a measure of automation then it is clear that UK industry has a long way to go, accounting as it does for less than 7% of Europe's robots, which in turn account for only 18% of the world robot population, 65% of which may not be alive but is certainly working well in Japan.[23] One could argue that the only reason we are short of skilled manpower is that we have failed to invest in the automation that reduces the need for it. Such investment would be a far more cost-effective way of generating profit than recruiting and training young people educated in the sciences or technology, only to find they desert to the service sector later. Admittedly some skilled people will be required, but very many fewer than in a non-automated environment.

By contrast, there can be little doubt that more people will be needed to work with old people until well into the next century. If the economy prospers

– and with the life of the North Sea oil fields now predicted to last a further 25 years that seems likely – tourism and leisure services will become increasingly important employment outlets. Worldwide, tourism is set to become the major industry of our post-industrial society. Within the UK as the number of double-salaried professional familes increases, many of them having inherited, or anticipating inheriting, wealth,[24] a massive growth in domestic service is occurring as the columns of, for example, *Lady* magazine make clear weekly. Young people wishing to work abroad and be in the social swim will have increasing opportunities to become 'euronannies' to the children of the rich and/or famous. We need to face up to the paradox that the more technological our society becomes, the more we are liberated from the need to understand, or be involved in, the sciences and technologies that underpin it. The logic of a post-industrial society is the invert of the one that has led to the introduction of compulsory science during the eighties.

Why, then, has the cause of science and technology education been taken up so enthusiastically by government? Apart from rhetoric, it is certainly not reflected in the support given to science and technology where it matters. The UK contributes a grudging 7% to the European Space Agency programme compared with France's 32% and Germany's 25%. Since contracts are awarded in proportion to these contributions we are clearly going nowhere very fast in this important area of research and development. The UK involvement in the European HDTV project is minimal. Domestically we invest 0.58% of GDP in civilian research compared with 0.96% by W Germany and 0.91% by France. Despite the hype of the early 1980s our computer industry, with the exception of ICL, disappeared; we are also on the verge of ensuring the collapse of the optoelectronics industry we founded as BT halts its £200M optical cable programme.[25] By contrast the French government is actively pursuing policies designed to ensure that France becomes the focus for these key high value-added technologically-based industries of the Single European Market, post 1992. And now, with high-speed rail links due to come to an ideological terminus at the UK end of the Channel Tunnel the likelihood of even UK financiers investing in UK industrial plant must be severely reduced.

The most obvious direct consequence of this ideological parsimoniousness is the low pay and uncertain – poor – career prospects of scientists who choose to stay and work in the UK.[26] Figures produced by the Institute of Manpower Studies[27] show just how poor the rate of return on the 1980 degree qualification has been for someone becoming a scientist. Only teachers, education welfare and social workers have fared worse – but at least they had much more security of employment than scientists on research contracts. The same report also showed that, whereas between 1979 and 1988 graduate recruitment into financial services, commerce and law more than doubled, that into manufacturing rose by only 10%. About 1/10th of all graduates now enter accountancy firms and that demand is increasing.[28] A study by Cambridge Econometrics has shown that the most prosperous part of the UK, the South East, has become 'de-industrialized' with manufacturing now accounting for less than

15% of total employment.[29] Since 1982, 'little new industrial investment has occurred' in this region. Against this background one cannot help but feel the whole economic impetus for more science and technology education is an enormous confidence trick being played on the young people of this country. Is it too mischievous to suggest that what is required of maintained schools by those who control society is little more than a scientifically competent proletariat? It is pertinent to enquire whether the sons and daughters of the establishment are also responding to their parents' concern, or could it just be that they are more likely to take up careers in financial management? However, the more successful the National Curriculum is in making young people economically aware, the more realistically young people will look at what careers in engineering, science and technology offer.

The increasingly international outlook of many of our most able young people has been commented upon earlier. That they will be prepared to migrate to wherever the career and life-style grasses appear greenest appears inevitable. Ironically, having migrated, they could well be producing returns on some of the £30B of British capital invested overseas in the last decade. By the same token, if they stay, they may well be providing a return on the £7B which the Japanese have invested in UK-based industries in order to gain access to Europe. Events in Eastern Europe are bound to further affect the manufacturing investment decisions of Western European investors, particularly as there appears to be a ready-made pool of low-wage underemployed manpower in much of that region. Instead of thinking of ways of sustaining an indigenous manufacturing base we should perhaps be asking if we can afford one. (In this context, the Labour Party's plans to stimulate a revival of our manufacturing base may also be profoundly misguided.)

All of the above adds up to considerable scepticisim about the economic rationale for expanding science and technology education. But even if it had some validity at the beginning of the eighties, the events now in train in Eastern Europe have undermined it. The single most voracious consumer of scientific and technological manpower in the developed world has always been the defence industry. Whether the will exists to rationalize our defence provision simply to cover Northern Ireland and garrison Gibraltar and the Falklands seems doubtful. The caution politicians are calling for in reducing military expenditure probably has far more to do with limiting the economic, employment and social consequences of precipitate reduction than it has with any real belief that the Cold War will be resurrected. What are the consequences for the steel industries of the world once the NATO and Warsaw pact tanks become scrap iron mountains? What will happen to Westland Helicopters, Vickers Shipbuilders and Defence Systems, British Aerospace, Ferranti-GCE *et al.* when they no longer have military contracts? How will their skilled workforce be redeployed? How will the concentration of trained manpower now in the Rhine Army be redeployed? Instead of facing a skill shortage at all levels from technician upwards, we may well be faced with a skill surplus once the real implications of a breakout of peace are faced.

Is it too far-fetched to suggest that, once we are prepared to put into manufacturing automation the same level of investment which, until now, has been
poured into defence robotics, the prospect of near peopleless production of
almost everything becomes close? Voyager II's technology which in 1989 provided the 10^{-20}W from which the stunning pictures of Neptune and its moons
were assembled was, by then, already twenty years out of date. Autopilot
systems are reducing the job of airline pilots to little more than extremely
costly chief stewards. And this is outdated technology. We can only guess at
what today's technology can already do if and when it is released from the
shackles of military secrecy. The National Curriculum, designed to meet the
needs of an industrial society, is, as far as the twenty-first century is concerned,
a sabre-tooth Tiger Curriculum.[30]

SCIENCE FOR CITIZENSHIP

If employment priorities are misplaced, what of Science for Citizenship? David
Layton[31] challenged science education many years ago when he suggested that:

> Just as the classicists have questioned the extent to which a knowledge of the
> language and literature of Greece and Rome is necessary for the achievement of
> an understanding of the influence of the classical on European civilisation, so
> scientists might ask a similar question. 'How much knowledge of the procedures
> and conclusions of the various sciences is necessary in order to achieve an
> understanding of the relations of science to technology and society?'

Clearly for the majority of young people who are not going to use science, it
is this kind of understanding that matters. Whether a science education that
gives so much time and emphasis to practical 'can do' activities is the right way
to achieve this is another matter. Being able to read an analogue scale; use a
pipette; make a microscope slide are no more the stuff of democratic decision-
making than they are, for that matter, of modern scientific practice. David
Layton argues persuasively for the use of historical case studies to achieve such
an understanding. Whether understanding the role that science and technology
played in the past will help young people put them into a twenty-first century
global economic context is, to put it at its mildest, unproven. Whereas Kay's
flying shuttle, Hargreaves' spinning jenny and Crompton's mule still required
workers, mostly unskilled, to produce cotton goods, the application of the
microprocessor to production removes even that requirement unless, of course,
the cost of labour is held below the cost of investment in automation. Only in
Third World economies, or economies based on very unequal distribution of
wealth, such as the UK's, is this the case.[32]

What role will science and technology have in the kind of societies that seem
likely to exist as we enter the next century? Science and technology servicing a
global economy rooted in free-market competition and consumption would
seem to have very different priorities to those that would exist in a global
economy based on cooperation and conservation. Do we really want to

educate young people so that they can deploy their scientific and technological skills on the trivia of affluence? Developing new scents to help sell otherwise identical soap powders; four-colour striped toothpastes; elliptical teabags; production lines to convert cows into beefburgers even faster than McDonalds does at present? Or do we want to educate them for a world in which, if they do eventually become scientists and technologists, their science and technology will be directed to the somewhat more worthy end of ensuring, or rather attempting to ensure, the survival of Planet Earth? Is effective science education for world citizenship possible within the context of a world economic system which clearly depends on maintaining global inequality for its metastability?

Equity demands that a child born in China, or Ethiopia, or Bangladesh has the right to the same standard of living as one born in the US, or West Germany, or Japan. China currently consumes energy at a rate of less than 0.8 kW per person. In the US, consumption is 10 kW per person.[33] The global warming and environmental consequences of any Chinese government exploiting its fossil fuel reserves, however efficiently, so that its citizens have the same standard of living as the US are only too obvious. Yet we have an economic system which depends on ever-increasing consumption for its survival. When people buy fewer clothes the effect on the employees of Next, Laura Ashley, their suppliers *et al.* is disastrous. Clothes and cars that lasted would be an economic disaster for manufacturers and their employees alike. For the existing economic system to function we need to fill wardrobes with clothes we never wear and to have cars that fail their MoTs. Alec Guiness's White Suit[34] is a nightmare our economic system cannot afford to have come true. It really is doubtful if a science education for citizenship which called into question the twin shibboleths of growth and free-market economics (which the National Curriculum is designed to inculcate) would be permitted if it had any chance of being effective. What would a science and technology education for world citizenship look like? How would its priorities differ from one based on national self-interest? The stark contrast between the rich and the poor nations of the world is well documented. In the context of the present global economic system, better science and technology actually make it easier for the rich to exploit the poor. Satellite surveillance of crop development and the movements of locust populations in Africa is not carried out for the benefit of Africans; it is commissioned by those who operate on the world commodity markets.

Perhaps it is all too late anyhow. Irreversible damage may already have been done to the environment. Ben Elton[35] has chronicled the efforts of the unimaginably rich to escape to the moon when they realize the catastrophic consequences that their exploitation of Planet Earth has had on the environment. As Professor Durf, their scientific adviser puts it:

> I can think of no better illustration to underline the urgency of our situation than to suggest that were God to attempt to take out an insurance policy on the world, he would not be able to afford the premium.

He continues:

> Of late, certain politicians have been attempting to play the green card in their grubby scramble for public support. Believe me, such tokenism is entirely cynical. The situation can never be reversed whilst market forces remain superior to political will. The politicians have always left us alone, and they will always leave us alone, because we pay the piper, and we call the tune.
>
> . . . We all hoped, of course, that market forces would produce a solution; that ecologically responsible activity would somehow become profitable. As we know it hasn't and that is just too bad. We had a duty to progress, to make money and create wealth, that was our bounden mission. If the earth had to die in the defence of a free market economy, then it is a noble death.
>
> . . . In modern times people worship money. Money is God in that it has been deified and can clearly be said to rule our lives.[36] Hence it is fitting that you, the super-rich, those who have worshipped money with a diligence and conviction far above the faith of lesser men, that you should board the Star Arks and carry our faith to a new civilization beyond the flood, on the moon.

The survival of the planet, and the reduction of the obscene disparities of wealth both between and within nations, which characterize today's world and its economic system, are issues demanding education in economics, politics and sociology not science and technology. Perhaps that is the point of the National Curriculum. After all if 20% of curriculum time is devoted to topics which actually don't really matter at all, then that time can't be used for other more subversive purposes, can it? This issue is considered later.

WHAT NO SCIENCE?

A number of challenges have been thrown down to those who promulgate an unquestioning 'institutional truth' view of the importance of science education. The weakness of this view has been demonstrated. The question remains as to what realistic role can science education in schools play as we move into the twenty-first century?

Realistically, if the sciences are to prosper, then it is the science education of the most able that matters. For this group, is ploughing through the set of banalities which make up much of the National Curriculum from 5 through to 16 really a good use of their time and intellect? Faith in compulsion is probably misplaced anyhow. It wasn't, after all, compulsion that directed Sir George Porter's talents towards chemistry; it was a second-hand bus converted into a backyard laboratory that did this.[37] Today's middle-class parents are, of course, far more likely to give their bright offspring access to the business programs on an IBM-compatible PC than buy them chemistry sets. In any case, the lack of compulsion has never stopped young people developing their talents in music, drama, and the fine arts; compulsion has never been a guarantee young people will want to continue with mathematics. Young people and their parents who have really absorbed the economic lessons of the 1980s will want the best return on an investment of five or more years of post-16 education they can get. As long as that return seems much greater and more certain in areas like finance and law, then the sciences and engineering will continue to suffer and deserve to. But, even if this situation changes, as in a free market it must if that market really needs the scientists and engineers we are assured are required, then there is still the need to challenge and inspire a sufficient proportion of this group to continue with science beyond 16+. Perhaps we need to learn from how young people succeed in areas which the National Curriculum devalues. Standards reached in music, drama and fine art have never owed much to compulsion or, for that matter, career prospects. And no one can seriously believe that the neglect of these important areas of human experience within the National Curriculum will stop young people taking part, and continuing to excel, in them. Paradoxically, if we seriously want our more able young people to continue to be interested in pursuing careers in the sciences, it may be necessary to make the sciences more challenging to this group. In this respect the lack of emphasis on mathematical reasoning, combined, as it now is, with an over-the-top concern for practical skills, is a matter of concern. But even if all this is got right and the most able – the potential originators – are educated in science (and technology), what then? They will be joining a society which, in both civil and industrial R & D expenditure, lags behind its main competitors.[38]

What contribution has science education to make to the general education of all young people? Arguably education designed to increase awareness of global environmental problems now facing 'Planet Earth' should be a top priority. But such awareness is not dependent on understanding the science of acid rain, the greenhouse effect, desertification etc. Indeed, such education is trivial compared with education about the global economic and political changes a solution to these problems must entail. After all, no government has yet been elected that had, as part of its manifesto, a reduction in living standards.

We have reached a stage when politically neutral environmental education is a contradiction in terms. What, for example, does a 'green' science teacher do about the previous Prime Minister's view, expressed at the 1989 presentation of the Environmental Industry Award to ICI?

> I find some people thinking of the environment in an airy-fairy way, as if we could go back to a village life. Some might quite like it, but it is quite impossible . . . we have created enough wealth to enable us to consider very carefully how to reduce pollution – how to design things for the better.
> We are not going to do away with the great car economy . . .. But we are going to have to find more economical ways of using fuel and more economical engines and more economical uses of cars.

This from the first Prime Minister we have ever had who ought to have understood the limitations the Second Law of Thermodynamics imposes, even on politicans. But she was of course right. How many sixteen year-olds, no matter how idealistic they are in the classroom will forgo the gift of a provisional driving licence on their seventeenth birthday? Or for that matter the car that, in the leafy lanes of Surrey, is increasingly likely to accompany it?

A 'green' teacher may well take the view that the world economic system rooted, as it is, in competition and consumption is inherently incapable of dealing with the problems facing the world today. But is a world economic system based on cooperation and conservation a realistic possibility? The United States with 2% of the world's population consumes some 25% of the world's oil supplies. Is it realistic to think it would ever tolerate only consuming 2%? Which electorate in the world is going to help save the rain forests if it means going without hamburgers? What Dagenham family will tolerate education which might lead to reduced car production? And what will Europe do if the victims of African desertification do, as in a recent television play, take it into their heads to migrate across the Mediterranean in order to survive and claim their fair share of the world's goods? The problem for the 'green' science teacher is that her/his aims are, almost inevitably, subversive. The 'catch 22' such teachers face is that even the most liberal of governments only tolerate subversion as long as it is ineffective. Should there be any danger of 'green' science teachers being effective then the National Curriculum can quickly be amended to eliminate such subversion.

CONCLUSIONS

Education has always been a convenient whipping boy for society. Impatience with education for not delivering the economic goods is no new phenomenon, and today's National Curriculum can be traced back at least as far as James Callaghan's 1976 Ruskin College speech blaming education for the economic difficulties the Labour government was then facing. If one believes this, then it follows that one will want to have a curriculum designed to remove those difficulties. There are, however, two problems with this. First, we don't actually have any evidence that education is as directly related to economic performance as this implies. In many countries it can be shown that investment in education is a consequence rather than a cause of prosperity. Second, even if it is related, we do not actually know what the right curriculum for economic prosperity in a post-industrial, information-technology-based society should be. All one can say with some confidence is that, in the absence of certainty, a monolithic curriculum is the last thing we need. Science educators really should be well aware that diversity and adaptation to the environment go hand in hand. How much anything we do to the curriculum will matter when the North Sea oil wells eventually run dry is another matter.

Unfortunately for the 'green' science teacher, if education is impotent in the economic field it is probably even more impotent in the social field. Only if, and when, developed societies are prepared to make the necessary economic adjustments – sacrifices – will there be any hope of tackling the consequences of the environmental degradation now afflicting Planet Earth. Given that, as economic pressures in any country increase, minority ethnic groups are victimized, it is very difficult to be anything but profoundly pessimistic about a future in which each nation state continues to compete for a larger share of the world's resources than its neighbour. Does anyone really believe the government of a non-oil state would have got the same support as Kuwait did when it was invaded? Perhaps instead of worrying we should adapt Tom Lehrer's paean for a nuclear holocaust – 'We'll all go together when we go/Every Hottentot and every Eskimo/When the air becomes uraneus/We'll all go simultaneous/We'll all go together when we go' – to one for an environmental Armageddon. Perhaps the yuppies did have it right. A National Curriculum based on the principle of 'Eat, drink and be merry for tomorrow may not be' is really what today's young people need.

POSTSCRIPT

Since producing the first draft of this article, ICL, our last major computer manufacturer, has been sold to Fujitsu and British Aerospace has announced its programme of defence closures and redundancies. The expression, 'peace dividend' has been coined and the inevitability of a reduction in military expenditure is having to be faced. The UK defence manufacturing industries with an annual turnover of £11B and a million employees are in real difficulties.[39] Whatever 'the realities of the adult world' turn out to be in the 1990s, they are unlikely, despite all the rhetoric, to require the science that the 1980s have provided!

NOTES AND REFERENCES

1. *Review Guardian*, 28-8-89. Commencement address to graduates of Smith College, Massachusetts.
2. The UK government's responses to the Department of Trade and Industry's Inspector's Report on the Harrods affair and the Recruit scandal in Japan would suggest this principle has universal validity.
3. 1979 HMI report, *Aspects of Secondary Education*. A further report, *Secondary Schools – An Appraisal by HMI* covering the years 1982–6 observes that 'Nearly three-quarters of the schools inspected were performing satisfactorily in general and half had some notably good features. Fewer than one in 10 was judged poor or very poor overall but a fifth had some major areas of weakness. Standards were unacceptably low in a very small number of schools'.
4. The 1988–9 HMI report on *Standards in Education* says much the same thing. '. . . around 70%–80% of the work seen was judged to be satisfactory or better . . . But there are serious problems of low and under achievement . . . in schools some 30% of what HMI saw was judged poor or very poor.'
5. See, for example, Sir John Harvey-Jones 1986 Dimbleby Lecture, 'Does Industry Matter?'

6. Quoted in *Daily Telegraph* British Association Science Extra: September 1989.
7. Letter to *Education Guardian* during the run-up to the 1989 Education Reform Act. Reiterated in *Education 2000* article, 14-8-90.
8. Laboratory Equipment Digest is almost totally concerned with equipment which automates out of existence traditional laboratory practical and measurement skills.
9. BBC 2 Documentary *9 to 5*, 6-3-90. In this programme the representative of a major Bristol-based manufacturing company acknowledged that his firm was unable to compete with the insurance and financial companies relocating in that city for the best qualified school leavers.
10. Department of Education and Science, *A Survey of Balanced Science Courses in some Secondary Schools*, (DES, 1990).
11. Biology A-level entries from 42,138 in 1989 to 44,362 in 1990 (+5.3%); Chemistry 47,559 to 47,286 (-0.6%); Physics 44,871 to 42,564 (-5.2%).
12. 'The learning experience of A-level students too often disregards more *practical modes of learning* developed through GCSE which must be assessed in terms of different, not worse, standards of rigour.' Professor Richard Pring, *Education Guardian*, 13-2-90.
13. John Galloway, 'Working-class honours: the not so glittering prizes', *New Scientist*, 28-4-90. In this article the author points out that scientists and technologists often have working-class backgrounds and that science is not perceived as a sensible career choice by better-off middle-class parents.
14. The findings of a survey reported in the February 1990 issue of the IMechE's *Engineering News* suggest that of the 14000 students who graduate in engineering in 1989 less than 5000 are expected to follow an engineering career in industry.
15. 'If you're a student or recent graduate you've probably contemplated working abroad. In fact, 84% of you have, according to a recent survey . . . Our panel is waiting to hear what kind of recruitment plan is needed to attract top graduates to British Industry . . . You've got until 20 April to help reshape the future of British Industry . . .' Extracts from 1990 Royal Mail Enterprises Awards publicity.
16. 'British Airways has a new breed of directors. They don't know much about planes; they know everything about marketing', *Airline*, BBC2, 1990.
17. Anthony Sampson, *The Midas Touch*, pp. 87–9, (BBC Books, 1989).
18. See, for example, John Maynard Keynes, 1931 essay *Economic Possibilities for our Grandchildren*.
19. Bryan Magee, 'Women's rights and wrongs', *Weekend Guardian*, 11-11-89.
20. *Physics Education*, 1989, Vol. 24, no. 3, pp. 117–8.
21. *Wireless World*, Editorial, May 1982.
22. Source: *Farming Today*, Radio 4.
23. 1989 International Survey. British Robotics Association.

24. See, for example, 'Tomorrow's rich inheritors' in *Vision*, the Halifax Building Society quarterly (Summer 1988). Morgan Grenfell predicts that property inheritance will be worth around £25 billion per annum by 2000 AD.

25. 'The company – BT – confirmed last night that it had halted a £200M programme to provide local optical cables and was reviewing whether traditional copper would more economically meet the needs. Optical fibres offer virtually limitless capacity and costs are dropping but it had to look at what would bring maximum revenues today.' *Guardian* report, 17-2-90.

26. 'Why the brain drainers are trying to plug the leak.' *THES*, 16-2-90. Expands on the reasons why 1600 British scientists working abroad petitioned the government to increase investment in UK science.

27. 'Prospects for graduates in the 1990s', *Physics World*, January 1990.

28. See, for example, 'Life in the fast lane for those who want to get to the top', *Media Guardian*, 26-2-90.

29. 'Industry shuns South-east', *Guardian*, 15-2-90.

30. This important curriculum was developed to meet the particular survival needs of a prehistoric tribe faced with the need to protect itself from marauding saber-tooth tigers. Saber-tooth-tiger-scaring-with-fire, clubbing-woolly-horses and catching-fish-with-bare-hands formed the compulsory core of the tribal curriculum. Unfortunately, by the time the curriculum was in place climatic changes had made it not just irrelevant but dangerous. For a full account of the fate of this Tribal Curriculum see Harold Benjamin, 'The saber-tooth curriculum', in *The Curriculum: Context, Design and Development*, (Oliver & Boyd/Open University, 1971).

31. David Layton, *Science as General Education*. Paper presented to a University of Leeds Heads of Department INSET course, circa 1970.

32. 'Britain has one of the lowest labour costs in the European Community – one half of the costs of Germany and one third of the costs in France or Italy. Only Greece, Spain and Portugal are cheaper. The work-force is also skilled and flexible, since it is not limited by rigid labour laws.' Eric Forth, the Industry Minister, opening a CBI conference on Japanese investment in Britain, March 1990.

33. Dr Jeremy Leggett, 'The coals of calamity', *Environmental Guardian*, 20-1-90.

34. Ealing Comedy in which shareholders, management and unions unite to ensure that the development of an indestructible totally dirt and stain resistant white suit never sees the light of day. Even the inventor's laundry lady turns on him: 'What about my bit of washing when there's no washing to do?'

35. Ben Elton, *Stark*, (Sphere Books, 1989).

36. Anthony Sampson, *The Midas Touch*, Chapter 1, 'The world's religion', (BBC Books, 1989).

37. Sir George Porter on Desert Island Discs, Spring 1990.

38. 1990 Annual Review of government spending on R & D. Using the granting of US patents as an indicator the UK is being outperformed by all its major competitors. An OECD breakdown of research priorities in its member states paints a similar picture leading directly to 'increasing difficulty in attracting able students' into research.

39. 'MoD braces for extra £1bn cut in spending', *Guardian*, 20-6-90.

4.5

Curiosity, creativity, competence and compassion – guidelines for science education in the year 2000

Albert V. Baez

INTRODUCTION

Because I work at the Lawrence Hall of Science where people are constantly experimenting with new and exciting ways to teach and learn I could get carried away with thoughts about the future of science and education that are extrapolations of the interesting things that happen at the Hall. We think about the future of science, technology and education a lot here. And some of my colleagues are futurists who are given to reading about exotic topics like: space stations, bionic parts replacements, chemical pocket flashlights, natural disaster prediction, and corn fields that seed themselves – ideas that spring right out of science fiction. Other far-out forecasts include genetically bred scientists, and human memories replaced by computers.

Now, although it is fun to speculate this way – after all, science fiction writers since Jules Verne have done so and stirred our imaginations in the process – I will not indulge in speculative forecasting.

A more useful alternative would be to consider which projects at the Lawrence Hall might serve as prototypes for the kind of science education we would like to see in widespread use in the future. There is much to be learned at a place where thousands of children and their parents come through every year to enjoy a 'hands-on' or 'please-touch-me' approach to learning. They play scientific games, look through telescopes, handle plants and animals, see the newest science films, and hear scientists describe their explorations. No one is bored and no one is afraid of failing an examination because there aren't any.

There is plenty of self-evaluation, however, especially with computer-assisted instruction, but the main reason the children are excited about computers is that through them they can also give vent at the computer terminals to creative impulses in music, poetry, the graphic arts and science.

My own particular interest is in video-discs which promise to give us motion pictures that can be played back by the viewer at the time of his choice – this is very important – and at about one-tenth the cost of motion picture film.

From McFadden, C. (ed.) (1980) *World Trends in Science Education,* Atlantic Institute of Education, Nova Scotia.

Incidentally, Albert Einstein and Thomas Edison, to whom I shall refer repeatedly in this paper, would have loved the Hall where 'learning begins in wonder and ends in delight'.

I will forgo the temptation to write about all these exciting developments at the Hall because my task is a different one. It is to generate broad new guidelines for realistic programmes in science education applicable universally in the near future.

To do so I must first summarize what is actually going on in science education in schools right now with special emphasis on places where the needs for improvement are greatest; namely, in the less developed countries.

THE NEED FOR IMPROVEMENT IN SCIENCE EDUCATION WITH SPECIAL REFERENCE TO THE LESS DEVELOPED COUNTRIES

The real situation in science education is far from ideal. Even in California, which is comparatively affluent, a visit to science classes in schools would show that in spite of the availability of some sophisticated teaching hardware and of teaching materials of relatively high quality many of the children are bored in science classes and others miss the excitement of science because they are concentrating on memorizing without understanding – afraid of failing their science examination. Boredom and fear of failure; barriers to success and enjoyment of science education, much of it due to incompetent teachers. The preparation of teachers is woefully inadequate.

In this respect the early schooling experiences of Edison and Einstein are illuminating. Edison was taught by a clergyman. Robert Conot tells us: 'The minister, of course, taught by rote, a method from which Alva (Edison) was inclined to disassociate himself. He alternated between letting his mind travel to distant places and putting his body in perpetual motion in his seat. The Reverend Engle, finding him inattentive and unruly, swished his cane. Alva, afraid and out of place, held up a few weeks, then ran away from the school.'[1]

About Einstein, A. P. French writes: 'At the age of ten, in 1889, Einstein entered the Luitpold Gymnasium (secondary school). This seems to have been a typical school of that place and time, with a rigidly regimented system. Einstein disliked it intensely . . . the cumulative effect of the Gymnasium experience was to generate in him a loathing for conventional schooling, and no doubt helped to develop his life-long antipathy towards authority.'[2]

Returning to the present, I also know from firsthand experience, the weakness of science teaching in less developed countries – LDCs. There are, of course, great economic, cultural and educational differences among LDCs, and it would be an error to lump them all into a single category. But they have, in varying degrees, many similarities as regards science education. The following is a broad characterization which applies to many of them. And if you live in an industrialized society you might ask yourself, as you read it, whether or not it also applies to the disadvantaged areas of your own country.

In some countries many children never get beyond the elementary grades. Whatever they learn about the spirit and method of science must be learned in elementary school. Even in those LDCs where some children go to secondary school the percentage of students who actually get a university degree is very small indeed by comparison with that in the advanced countries. In some cases, health and nutrition are limiting factors. Social and economic conditions often force people to have a low sense of human potential and self-esteem. The number of pupils per teacher is excessive.

There aren't enough teachers and the existing ones are not sufficiently well trained. They just do not have adequate opportunities for training or retraining. They have to teach subjects about which they know very little. In many countries teachers have such low salaries that they have to take several jobs to make ends meet. The social status of teachers is low. It rises as one progresses from elementary to secondary to university levels, but this is, in most countries, including the advanced ones, the inverse order of importance of the teacher as a moulder of personality and character.

Facilities for science teaching are meagre. The classrooms often have inadequate seating arrangements. There is a shortage of textbooks and laboratory materials. The simplest and most universal teaching aid, the chalk-board, is in poor supply. It often consists of rough boards that chew up the chalk and generate dust. Very few schools have such luxuries as overhead and motion picture projectors. If they do have a movie projector, they find it very difficult to obtain films.

There are seldom shop facilities available where a teacher can build simple pieces of equipment for laboratory work or demonstrations.

Because space is at a premium it must be used in several shifts per day. One may begin at 8 in the morning and end at noon, another shift may begin at 1 in the afternoon and end at 5. In some schools there may be more than two shifts.

Teaching methods and approaches are often very backward. Authoritarian teaching and rote learning characterize much of what goes on. Because of the lack of laboratories and equipment, not enough is learned through actual contact with the things of science. Evaluation is still used mainly for screening pupils. It therefore becomes a threat which disturbs students psychologically. The objectives of science teaching have not been made clear to the teachers, so a great deal of the subject matter of science seems irrelevant both to the teachers and to the students. The notion that the methods, approaches and techniques of science have useful carryover value to produce leaders in non-scientific careers such as industry and management has not begun to penetrate in many LDCs.

Most of what has been said above applies mainly to primary and secondary schools because that is where the bulk of the students can be found in LDCs, but university teaching also suffers from some of the same weaknesses.

Since the participants at this symposium come from nations representing a broad spectrum of economic and social development I am sure you will all recognize that at least some of the above weaknesses in science education apply to your own country.

Keeping the above in mind, therefore, forecasting what might happen in science education in the most advanced countries would not be particularly relevant to the needs of countries in earlier stages of development. On the other hand, perhaps describing the useful human characteristics which might be implanted in students through the proper kind of science education might be relevant worldwide. I have therefore tried to find broad guidelines that would have applicability in all countries of the world. The specific way in which they may be applied will depend upon the particular circumstances in each country.

SCIENCE, TECHNOLOGY AND EDUCATION

We are presently celebrating the hundredth anniversary of the birth of Albert Einstein and the invention of electric light by Thomas Edison. This year in countless ceremonies round the world people have paused to do them honour for their contributions to science and technology, respectively. Each one illustrates in an exemplary way the characteristics of his profession. Einstein, the scientist, driven by curiosity and the desire to understand the physical universe, and Edison, the inventor, in search of technological solutions to practical problems in the real world. Their work sheds light on the difference between science and technology but also on how independent they really are.

Einstein, for example, won the Nobel prize for his brilliant contribution to our understanding of the nature of light, but Edison made it possible to turn night into day by giving the whole world electric light to brighten what had been, since time began, a night of darkness. Both men were far ahead of their times and both had dreams of a future in which science and technology would make the world a better place in which to live. At the age of 81 Edison said, 'My mind runs to the future, not to the past.'

Because we are so close to the end of a century, thinking about the future has become fashionable. To me it is fascinating not because I am capable of forecasting but because future-oriented thinking makes us aware of alternative futures. It is an empowering process reminding us that we have a role to play in deciding which future we want to work for, especially – for those of us at this symposium – in the area of science education.

Therefore, instead of trying to predict what science education will be like in the year 2000 – after all, it is not very far away – we should perhaps be more concerned with what it should be like and how to bring it about.

With regard to what *should* be, Einstein had this warning, 'That which we call science pursues one single goal: the establishment of that which exists in reality. The determination of that which *should* be is a task to a certain degree independent of the first.'[3]

To speak about what *ought* to happen demands making value judgements and choosing objectives so let me describe what I think is the long-term aim of science education. I believe that science and technology, and hence science education, should help mankind improve the quality of life on this planet. By life I mean all living things, plants and animals, and particularly people; men and women in all walks of life and in all parts of the world, developed and developing.

I mean quality of life in terms of environment, health, nourishment, shelter, resources, meaningful employment, rest and recreation, educational opportunities and cultural achievements. I have in mind also the reduction of fear and anxiety, and learning to cope with risk and decision-making.

Can science education really have an impact in all these areas? I believe it can because science and technology have already done so. They have brought about spectacular improvements in the quality of life in the past 100 years. On the average, people now live longer and healthier lives and enjoy more opportunities for self-development than did our grandparents. Unfortunately, however, the benefits of these improvements have not been distributed evenly round the world. The rich countries have benefited more than the poor ones.

Beyond a certain point, of course, science and technology have also accelerated the deterioration of the quality of life. In some countries, for example, pollution has reached intolerable limits. Industrialization requires energy and energy utilization generates pollution. The rich countries utilize – sometimes squander – energy more than the poor countries do. The less developed countries note with envy and perhaps some anger that the United States, with 6% of the world's population, uses about 40% of the earth's annual energy output. This inequity, like the feedback signal in a thermostat, is bringing into play forces that will rectify the inequalities. It may trigger into action the energy needed to move from the values of an industrial society to those of an ecological one but the price of this transition may be social and political upheaval and even violence. Even apparently beneficial effects of science such as the reduction of infant mortality and the increase in human life span, brought about by improvements in food and medicine technology, have produced an overpopulation which has increased the per-capita poverty in the poor countries. In spite of improvements in the quality and quantity of the world's wheat crop, for example, the amount of wheat available per person in a country like India is less now than it was 10 years ago. Higher population densities in cities all over the world have increased the feeling of alienation among people. Risk, fear and anxiety are mounting everywhere.

Yet, in spite of these negative impacts of science and technolgoy – and I could have given many more examples – I am led to the conclusion that *more* science and *more, not less,* technology – appropriate technology – will be needed to solve the pressing problems of society. The ills of the world will not be cured by a moratorium on technology. It has to be redirected. It cannot be a runaway technology. We must be in control. That is why we need not only a better and more universal understanding of science but new values to guide us in its use. We need science and technology with a human face. That is the challenge to science education for the year 2000.

THE FOUR Cs

What guidelines should inform science education to bring about the needed improvements? The basic theme I plan to elaborate is the following: *to enrich the quality of life education must generate four important traits in people. These are curiosity, creativity, competence and compassion.*

The first three are particularly relevant to science education. Curiosity is the motor that drives the scientist; creativity the spark that enables the engineer to design things that never existed before, and technology demands competence in putting them together and making them work. But science and technology thrive on each other and both of them demand all three Cs: curiosity, creativity and competence.

I will explain later on in what sense the fourth C – compassion – has become an important educational guideline in this era of transition from industry to ecology. It may be the key to survival on this planet. Better still, it may make life worth living on it. Let us examine these four Cs separately.

Curiosity

When Einstein was five, he was given a magnet. This stimulated his curiosity to such a degree that it planted a question in his mind which motivated him for the rest of his life to seek an explanation of magnetic, electric and gravitational forces.

Edison was given a chemistry set when he was eight. He was fascinated by the countless experiments he was able to do with it, some of which, incidentally led to minor explosions which frightened his mother.

Curiosity is the source of discoveries in sciences and technology. It seems, moreover, that all children are curious unless defects such as those brought about by malnutrition put a damper on it. Social forces also affect it. Children in poor and socially deprived homes are often apathetic and less curious than normal children.

The spark of curiosity ought to be fanned into a flame by teachers and parents. It can make learning a pleasurable experience, but it is sometimes stifled by uninspired teachers who find it easier to demand rote learning. A curt reply of 'don't bother me' from a parent who is tired of being questioned by his child may quench the divine fire of his curiosity. Thus, home and school too often turn children away from the longing to know and understand. If we want curiosity – the essential ingredient of research and the source of all new knowledge – to thrive in the year 2000 we will have to reverse this trend.

Creativity

Von Karman once said, 'The scientist explores what is, the engineer creates what has not been.' The electric light, for example, did not exist before Edison.

This statement seems to imply that creativity is more a characteristic of engineering and technology than of science. But, of course, that is not so.

Science and technology create different kinds of things. The things that are created by the scientist in search of understanding are intangible. They are often theories such as Einstein's general theory of relativity and Maxwell's electromagnetic equations. These two never existed before. Thus, creativity is exemplified by both science and technology.

But how about the creative act in music, poetry, painting and sculpture? How about psychiatry and the law? Obviously people can be creative in many areas including cooking, making love, rearing children and teaching. The world owes a lot to a relatively small number of creative people.

Creativity is probably a rarer gift than curiosity although it is claimed that dreams are creations of the human mind and, since all people dream, all have creative potential!

Creativity is probably less apt to be found in the extremely young than is curiosity. But in general children are more creative than adults. Creativity, too, can be deadened by authoritarian teachers and insensitive parents. Fear of criticism inhibits creative performance. Some people, especially musicians and artists, remain creative into old age although in mathematics and science it is often associated with youth.

Tycho Brahe made a notable contribution to astronomy by patiently collecting data on the motion of the planets – not a particularly creative act. But it does illustrate that the noble edifice of science contains some bricks that were collected and put in place by patient and steadfast people who may not have been creative. One of the heartening things about science is that you can make a noteworthy contribution to it even though you are not particularly creative yourself. In Tycho's case the creative leap was made by Kepler, who, taking Tycho's data, discovered the mathematical laws that govern the motion of the planets in their elliptical orbits.

Edison, who was more interested in practical results than in theoretical knowledge, nevertheless discovered, in the course of trying everything that he could think of, that a hot metal filament boils off electrons. He jotted this fact down in a notebook and never made use of it. He didn't realize the importance of his discovery. Electronic emission was later called the Edison effect and gave birth to the vacuum tube – the forerunner of the transistor.

What makes some people more creative than others? A recent study concludes that creative people do the following:

- challenge assumptions;
- recognize patterns;
- see in new ways;
- make connections;
- take risks;
- take advantage of chance;
- construct networks.

One thing about the future is certain. It will generate new problems demanding creativity for their solution. Even though we don't understand the origin of creativity we owe it to humanity to discover and encourage those who have this special gift and to stimulate its development in others.

Competence

This is a skill we acquire through practice. No one is born being able to walk, figure skate, drive a car, write, play the piano, design a spaceship, build a house, sing a song, bake a cake, or solve an equation.

Some skills are so important that we call them basic and build our early school curricula around them, like the three Rs: readin', 'ritin' and 'rithmetic, but in the current clamour to get 'back to the basics' we may lose sight of the fact that perhaps new activities should be added to the list of basics. New technologies make old skills obsolete. Skill in making horseshoes and fixing wagon wheels is only marginally useful today. Electronic word processors are replacing typewriters, and calculators are replacing slide rules. Perhaps physics, chemistry, biology and computer technology should be counted among the basics of tomorrow.

Plumbers, automobile mechanics and machinists possess competencies of a special kind. We would be lost without them. Scientists may understand the basic theory of the gasoline engine, but few of them could build one. A physicist can design a nuclear reactor but it takes engineers and technicians to put one together and make it work.

The future will certainly demand competent people of all kinds. One of the criticisms of present-day education is that it turns out individuals who have no particular competency. It is a sad fact that many teachers are also incompetent, and that promotion is often independent of competence.

In our daily lives the ability to plan events for a day, a week or even a year in advance demands a special competence that is closer to that of the engineer than that of the scientist. The mode of action required is more like the design mode used in engineering than the research mode used in science. For this reason, perhaps, skill in design may be more important to most people than skill in research. In other words, in the short run, for sheer survival – and that is what we may have to worry about in the year 2000 – competence in the solution of real problems may be more important than curiosity. The science education of the year 2000 may, therefore, have to infuse all pupils not only with the longing to know and questioning of all things that we associate with the discovery approach of the 60s but also with the design mode that generates the ability to solve problems in the real world.

Compassion

I got the idea of including compassion as a guideline from a statement by Weisskopf, 'There are two powerful elements in human existence, compassion and curiosity. Curiosity without compassion is inhuman; compassion without curiosity is ineffectual.'[4]

Now, curiosity leads to knowledge but it does not necessarily lead to compassion. I am using the word 'compassion' to mean 'fellow-feeling and sympathy' rather than pity.

A compassionate person seeing someone in distress wants to help. Suppose someone has been in an automobile accident and is bleeding. A compassionate bystander feels like helping, but without knowledge of first aid he is ineffectual in his attempt to help. What is needed in this case is paramedical competence. Theoretical knowledge of the circulatory system learned in a physiology course would not be enough.

If you substitute 'competence' for 'curiosity' in Weisskopf's statement, it remains true. Thus: 'Competence without compassion is inhuman; compassion without competence is ineffectual'.

Rodger Bybee says that we are in a transition stage between an industrial society and an ecological society, and he examines the values that gave each of them their motive power. He says: 'The values that have been most successful for the industrial society are now creating more problems than solutions, and ecological concepts which were given little attention 30 years ago are becoming the new patterns of social development.'[5]

He goes on: 'The dominant value system of unlimitedness has directed our social growth. Our perceptions have been of unlimited production and consumption, ideas that the environment had unlimited resources and also was an unlimited waste receptacle. The fundamental mode of existence was to have material, goods, and services satisfying our basic needs and induced wants. '. . . cultural evolution has taken us to a time when the basic struggle is between the values of *having* and the values of *being*. The being mode is based on a better quality of life and environment, personal growth and interactions based upon cooperation, and meaningful activity.'

People who became successful in the industrial society were guided by the values of *having*. In particular, having things was associated with the good life. But it is already evident in some countries that a change of values is needed to guide us in a new direction. The old values are already leading to self destruction.

We need to espouse the values of cooperation, equality, harmony, quality and being if we are to bring about an ecological society – one that can survive without plundering and polluting the earth. In particular, Bybee emphasizes *being* rather than *having* as a dominant value. He concludes: 'There is an Ecological Society emerging and science education must contribute to the evolution.'

All of this links nicely with the idea of compassion as a guide for education in general and for science education in particular. Science and technology have given man unprecedented power. Compassion can lead to a proper application of this power. It is the basis of social responsibility which to me does not mean collective responsibility but the responsibility of the individual to society.

Unlike curiosity and creativity, which seem to be in-born, compassion has to be learned. In this respect it resembles competence, and like all the other Cs it can serve us throughout our entire lives.

Pure science in its search for knowledge and understanding may be ethically neutral, but scientists and engineers, and for that matter the general public, had better be endowed with a fellow-feeling or the monstrosities generated by technology will multiply. Ecological and environmental sanity depend on affection and respect for mankind.

CONCLUSION

I have now indicated what human traits – the four Cs – I think the science education of the future should stimulate and develop in people if we are to survive and enjoy life in the 21st century. But I haven't specified just how this should be done. This task itself will demand creativity, competence, devotion and hard work. There is no magic formula applicable worldwide that can guide us in infusing education with the four Cs. Our educational systems differ, and we start the task at different levels of advancement.

But we can begin by looking critically at the job of science teaching we are doing right now and asking, at every turn: Does my present way of teaching promote the four Cs?

Looking back at Einstein and Edison, our prototoypes of creative scientist and technologist respectively, we find that their early schooling failed them miserably, and we should rectify the errors committed by their teachers. They succeeded in spite of everything because they were self-motivated, daring individuals who were willing to break open their own trails.

Although they had some traits in common like tremendous perseverance – the remark that genius is 1% inspiration and 99% perspiration is attributed to Edison – they were also very different from one another in other ways.

Einstein could not rest if he didn't understand the basic cause of things. His own method of study was to read deeply into the original literature of physics. He carried some problems around unresolved in his mind for years.

Edison, on the other hand, did not even understand Ohm's law and once said that he didn't want to understand it because it might stop him from experimenting. His curosity was satisfied if he could make something work.

About Edison it has been said that 'No other man has had such influence on the lives of so many people.' Whoever said that probably had the electric light, the phonograph, the microphone, the mimeograph machine, the sewing machine, the motion picture kinetoscope, and countless other inventions in mind.

But surely the world of space travel, lasers, fibre optics, nuclear power, semiconductors and computers would never have come into being without the fundamental knowledge that sprang from Einstein's theoretical creations even though these devices were not his goal. In fact, his theories have helped us understand some of the deepest mysteries of the cosmos.

In some ways Edison exemplifies the Horatio Alger success of the industrial era. He was no stranger to competition, and he was not above proclaiming his discoveries in self-serving ways. But he was not a ruthless businessman and made much less money than the Wall Street manipulators who got rich on his inventions.

Einstein, on the other hand, exemplifies the values that I think should characterize the forthcoming ecological society. He was deeply interested in education and concerned about its effect on the welfare of mankind. He lamented the 'crippling of the social consciousness of individuals'.

Arturo Loria quotes Einstein: 'This crippling of individuals I consider the worst evil of capitalism. Our whole educational system suffers from this evil. An exaggerated competitive attitude is inculcated into the student, who is trained to worship acquisitive success as a preparation for his future career.'[6]

Surely Einstein was more interested in *being* than *having*. He supported causes that exemplified the values of co-operation, equality and harmony – especially among nations. He was an advocate of peace and world government. He once said: 'The ideals which have lighted my way, and time after time have given me new courage to face life cheerfully have been kindness, beauty and truth.'

A trend seems to be developing in which science education will play a role in promoting a greater awareness of the role of science in society. For example, John Lewis has noted that many of the course content improvement projects of the '60s stressed the discovery approach and that during the '70s much emphasis was placed on integrated science. Due primarily to the efforts of UNESCO the integrated approach to science teaching was experimented with perhaps even more widely in some developing countries than in the industrialized ones. For the '80s, Lewis advocates science for society as an approach whose time has come and has launched his own Science in Society Project.[7]

UNESCO is starting a new project whose provisional title is: *Adapting Science and Technology Education to a Changing Society and to the Diversity of Needs of Member States.* The United Nations is holding an International Conference on Science and Technology for Development in Geneva almost concurrently with our Symposium. ICSU (International Council of Scientific Unions) has many activities including those of CTS (Committee on the Teaching of Science) devoted to international collaboration in science and technology for the benefit of mankind.

Science educators like Thomas B. Evans are writing articles urging their colleagues to become active in determining the future of science teaching so that it helps to bring about the needed transformation from the values of the industrialized past to those of the ecological future.[8]

All of these are straws in the wind which indicate that there is a growing worldwide concern for the human use of science and technology and a need for a corresponding science education.

In conclusion, I leave you with the difficult task of introducing the four Cs into the curricula and syllabi of science education and into non-formal science education activities of the 21st century.

REFERENCES

1. Conot, R. (1979) *A Streak of Luck*, p. 6, New York, Seaview Books.
2. French, A. P. (1979) Einstein – a condensed biography, in French, A. P.

(ed.) *Einstein: A Centenary Volume*, p. 53, London, Heinemann.
3. Kuznetsov, B. (1979) Einstein, science and culture, in French, A. P. (ed.) *Einstein: A Centenary Volume*, p. 167, London, Heinemann.
4. Weisskopf, V. F. (1972) The significance of science, *Science,* Vol. 176, 14 April, p. 138.
5. Bybee, R. W. (1979) Science education and the emerging ecological society, *Science Education* (New York), Vol. 63, January, pp. 95–109.
6. Loria, A. (1979) Einstein and education, in French, A. P. (ed.) *Einstein: A Centenary Volume*, p. 222, London, Heinemann.
7. Lewis, J. L. (1978) Science in society, *Physics Education* (London), Vol. 13, pp. 340–3.
8. Evans, T. P. (1977) Deciding the future of our discipline, *The Science Teacher* (Washington, D.C.), Vol. 44, no. 9, December, pp. 28–30.

Author index

Subject index